# AUTHENTIC

**Paul Van Doren**

# AUTHENTIC

## A MEMOIR BY THE FOUNDER OF

Paul Van Doren

with Louise MacLellan

**AUTHENTIC**

Copyright © 2021 by Paul Van Doren

Cover design by Nicole Caputo
Cover photo by Jason Ulep

For information, contact Vertel Publishing at
www.thebookauthentic.com
2837 Rivers Avenue
Charleston, South Carolina 29405

First edition

Manufactured in the United States of America
1 3 5 7 9 10 8 6 4 2

Hardcover ISBN: 978-1-64112-024-1
eBook ISBN: 978-1-64112-025-8

Library of Congress Cataloging-in-Publication Data has been applied for

*To family, who always come first*

# Contents

**Foreword**   by Doug Palladini, Global Brand President, Vans · · · · · · · ·ix

**Preface**   by Paul Van Doren · · · · · · · · · · · · · · · · · · · · · · · · · ·xiii

**Chapter 1:**   Be Authentic · · · · · · · · · · · · · · · · · · · · · · · · · · · · ·1

**Chapter 2:**   The Education of an Entrepreneur · · · · · · · · · · · · · ·7

**Chapter 3:**   Organize a System · · · · · · · · · · · · · · · · · · · · · · · · 27

**Chapter 4:**   Respect the Workers · · · · · · · · · · · · · · · · · · · · · · · 47

**Chapter 5:**   Take the Reins · · · · · · · · · · · · · · · · · · · · · · · · · · · 63

**Chapter 6:**   Never Waste an Opportunity · · · · · · · · · · · · · · · · · 89

**Chapter 7:**   Listen to Your Customers · · · · · · · · · · · · · · · · · · · 109

**Chapter 8:**   Sell What You Believe In· · · · · · · · · · · · · · · · · · · · 123

**Chapter 9:**   Go Off the Wall · · · · · · · · · · · · · · · · · · · · · · · · · 145

**Chapter 10:**   Get Out While You Still Have Your Sanity · · · · · · · · · · · 167

**Chapter 11:**   Shit Happens: Get On with It · · · · · · · · · · · · · · · · · 185

**Chapter 12:**   Embrace Change · · · · · · · · · · · · · · · · · · · · · · · · 213

**Chapter 13:**   Get Back to Core Culture · · · · · · · · · · · · · · · · · · · 237

**Chapter 14:**   Surf the Waves · · · · · · · · · · · · · · · · · · · · · · · · 257

**Afterword**   Dress in Overalls · · · · · · · · · · · · · · · · · · · · · · · 273

**Acknowledgments** · · · · · · · · · · · · · · · · · · · · · · · · · · · · · 277

**Photo Credits** · · · · · · · · · · · · · · · · · · · · · · · · · · · · · · · 281

# Foreword

My eyes fought to adjust to the dimly lit, Boston-area pizzeria—vinyl dinettes and a vintage cash register, frozen in time. "Lynwood—Since 1949," I read from the logo on a sticky menu. I watched as a short, stocky man with a ruddy complexion and silver hair came into the space, screen door banging closed behind him. I had yet to meet Paul Van Doren, Vans' founder, despite having worked for the brand he started for much of a decade at that point, and I honestly wasn't sure what to expect.

As it turned out, Paul, or "PVD" as we often call him, wasn't really sure what to expect, either. Living in Kentucky, with his horses, Paul and Vans had quite frankly grown apart and lost touch. Paul missing from our conversations had been a gap I was intent on closing—as Vans' global marketing leader and big fan of legacy and its role in brand storytelling—which is why our entire global marketing leadership team was crammed into Lynwood on this particular evening. This was the Randolph, Massachusetts, pizza joint where Paul would take his family on Friday nights, after a long week of work overseeing shoe manufacturing at the nearby Randolph Rubber Company plant. Meeting here was part of my master plan to lure him back into the Vans' fold.

Paul shuffled quietly up to a table and sat down next to his son Steve, our global brand ambassador and public face of the brand. Father and son were an interesting contrast in styles: Paul seemed to be understated and reserved. Steve was boisterous and gregarious. Paul didn't come with any prepared remarks, so Steve waded in, carefully prompting and coaxing his father's memories. Paul's voice and energy rose viscerally with each response and, as his reticence fell away, so did his timidity. Several hours later, having held us rapt in his remembrances throughout the meal, our team had been taken on a truly remarkable journey of the American Dream, and Paul Van Doren was back.

Since that cathartic evening, Paul's presence, both literally and figuratively, has returned full strength to Vans. And our brand is better for it. With the American Dream on the ropes in our current caustic culture, Paul remains as resolute in his tenth decade as he was in any of the first nine: hard work, honesty, and caring for people are what yield success. The beauty lies in simplicity, so don't overcomplicate things. Instead, focus on blocking and tackling, consistently, one day at a time. I found Paul's old-school mindset almost revolutionary in its utter lack of pretense, one of those "so old it's almost new again" ways of thinking about business. "The boss can grab a broom and sweep up just like the rest of 'em" is the traditional, blue-collar kind of ethic that remains steadfast in Vans' culture today.

Years later, as Paul and I moved cautiously through crowded shopping mall corridors and into a Vans store, his pace slowed to a stop, and I watched his face turn to a look of wonder as he took in his surroundings. Paul took hold of a display case, seeming to steady himself as he soaked in what his small family shoe brand had become. A small rack with a few shoeboxes leaning carefully against it had been replaced with hundreds of footwear styles, patterns, and colors on every wall. Apparel and accessories flowed through the space where none had existed before. And intelligently designed shelving, lighting, signage, and the like augmented the space and the products where once five-and-dime tchotchkes covered the bare walls.

"How many of these did you say there were now?" Paul asked.

"A couple thousand, globally," I replied.

Paul shook his head as if trying to make sense of the "from" he created in 1966, the "to" we were living in now, and all of the space in between. He sold maybe a dozen pairs that first week, six decades prior. Now we were selling more than two million pairs a week. I tried to give Paul some space and let him wander on his own. I watched as he stepped gingerly around tables of flannels and chinos, past racks of socks and belts and shoelaces. But it wasn't long before he found himself in front of the footwear wall, an imposing array of rubber, canvas, leather, and foam. He picked up shoe after shoe, running his deeply rutted fingers along the waffle patterns pressed into the rubber soles.

Eventually, Paul waved me over to where he was examining the white "foxing tape" sidewall of a Classic Slip-On not dissimilar to those he had first built decades before. "What do you see here?" Paul thrust the shoe at me as if to further emphasize the question.

"Right here." He pointed to where the tape overlapped at the back of the heel. I took the shoe and ran my finger over the rubber step. "The tape overlap is a sign of this shoe being handmade. There isn't a machine that can do what a good shoe builder can."

Of course, Paul was right. Somewhere in the space between 1966 and 2016, between his one factory in Anaheim and our dozens of factories across Asia, between 12 pairs and 120 million, our manufacturing base had shifted from California to Asia, but the pride in hand-assembling every pair remained. Maybe the scale, the complexity of what Vans had become, was impossible to fully comprehend. But Paul could still pick up any pair of Vans sneakers, any day, anywhere, and see just how it was made a little better than the others. It wasn't about that specific pair of shoes as much as it was about the approach, the attitude, the commitment to excellence. It was a classic Paul Van Doren teaching moment.

And one that I'll never forget . . .

*Doug Palladini*
Global Brand President, Vans

# Preface

My entire life, I never had one big idea. I like to think I woke up one day and figured out how to make the world's best canvas-and-rubber, waffle-soled deck shoes, how to distribute said shoes, and thus create the first vertically integrated tennis shoe company in the world; but the fact of it is, I could have been growing potatoes.

Actually, shoes have nothing to do with my success. What I've accomplished comes down to one thing: my knack for identifying and then solving problems. What I do better than anything else is cut out distractions. If a system isn't working efficiently, I can see where it's jammed, eliminate the problem, and find a way to keep everything moving forward.

Everyone has something they naturally do better than anyone else—this happens to be mine, and I was lucky enough to have the opportunity to leverage it.

Then there's everything I learned by doing. Much of Vans' early success was the happy result of hard work and creative troubleshooting. It helps that, at Vans, we used vulcanized rubber on the soles of our shoes. It helps that we identified retail spaces. It helps that we dialed in production like Lee Iacocca on his best day at Ford or Chrysler. It helps that we knew our customers, especially the skaters and the surfers and the moms. It helps that we cared about making a really good quality shoe at an affordable price, and to give exceptional customer service—always. It helps that I handed over the reins in 1980, when I got burned out, and was able to return in 1984 per an order from Judge Peter M. Elliott of the bankruptcy court in Santa Ana, California.

It also helps that we listened to trendsetters. My son, Stevie, perfectly articulates what we learned about expanding our business by working with kids on skateboards and surfboards: Listen to your customers, who will tell you what they want. If it's a checkerboard, if it's bright pinks and yellows, or if it happens to be dinosaurs or a skull and crossbones, listen to their two cents' worth about colors and designs and what they think a graphic should look like on a shoe or a shirt. Pay attention to the people using your product—or even better, work with them to create something completely new.

It also helps that we were tenacious. I've learned that what makes a successful entrepreneur is the same thing that makes a good skateboarder or good surfer: you need grit and determination to get back up every time you're knocked off the board.

In the world of successful entrepreneurs, I'm not Phil Knight. I'm not Yvon Chouinard. It never occurred to me to disappear for a month here and there to pursue other interests. I'm not Bill Gates or Jeff Bezos or Mark Zuckerberg or Elon Musk. My guess is, I'm unlike any other founding CEO. I'm just a small business owner who did well and found the right partners. I'm the guy who held tight to the kitchen faucet until he could hand over the valve.

When I was approached to write a business memoir, I wondered how I could explain my life as a series of tidy lessons learned. Eventually, I realized that what I would offer to other businessmen and women is less formula and more whatever the opposite of formula is—let's call it fluidity. I don't know where to draw the line between the business me and the personal me. It's something I failed to teach my children. The lines have always been so damned blurred.

The way I've run my business is the way I've lived my life. The one thing that has always been sacred to me—and this goes for life as much as business—is just this: always try to do what's right.

I learned early on that what's right is right and what's wrong is wrong. If you put thought into something and do what's right every single time, you won't be far off from doing the best you can—the best any of us can.

Many of my guiding principles are equally simple, and they've served me equally well. Don't sit still or rest on your laurels. Do the work—don't just look on as others do it. My famous credo: get your hands dirty. If a young entrepreneur came to me today and asked how to start a company, I would say right off the bat: know what goes into making what you're selling. If you sell from a place of total confidence in the quality down to the details, you will succeed.

I also say find honorable people to be your partners, work with creative people, and be fair. Be kind. Give a shit about how you treat people and be aware of how your actions might disturb or distress them. In other words, don't be a jerk. Stand up for others. Until our last breath, we can do something good for someone else.

The fact is, no one gets anywhere alone; and in the end, what a person makes isn't as important as how and with whom he or she makes it. I always said that Vans is a people company that makes shoes—not the other way around.

I've had one hell of a ride, and in telling my story, I tell Vans'; but that isn't the whole of it. Without my kids, Vans wouldn't exist. They, alongside their mother, Dolly, and me, got their hands dirty and worked for tacos; my in-laws dropped everything to help us launch. Bob Cohen listened to me when I was a sixteen-year-old supply boy at the Randolph Rubber Company. Serge D'Elia handed me a parachute when Bob left me no options but to jump, and Gordon Lee and my brother Jimmy took that flying leap alongside me. My debt to each is as obvious as the words on this page.

I've experienced a lot of joy; I am also all of what I've lost. While my kids, their kids, and their kids' kids are healthy, I outlived my wife Drena and a number of peers. I've lost brothers, business partners, colleagues, and friends. Everyone I knew from my shoemaking days is gone.

Suffice it to say, no one is around to fact-check most of what I offer herein. You'll have to take my word for it, and as you read, keep in mind I wrote from memory, recreating situations from the near and far past as best I could.

Five decades after I started the Van Doren Rubber Company, our brand is associated with "expressive creators," the artists, musicians, skaters, and surfers—the trendsetters, the ones who go their own way.

I could not be prouder, because that's how I always did things, too.

*Paul Van Doren*

# AUTHENTIC

# CHAPTER ONE

# Be Authentic

All I needed to know about making canvas shoes I learned at the Randolph Rubber Company in Randolph, Massachusetts. My mother got me my first job at Randy's, as we called it, as a service boy (a kind of runner or material handler) when I was sixteen. I went on to spend the first twenty years of my career learning the trade.

Soon after I had been promoted to a supervisory position at Randy's, my boss Bob Cohen invited me to attend the industry's semiannual trade show. The Boston Shoe Travelers Association show was the place where retailers scout lines and preorder shoes for the following season. In the shoe manufacturing world, this was the big time.

I was still very low in the pecking order, so the invite was contingent on the fact that while the "suits" wined, dined, and entertained each other, I would do the grunt labor of setting up, arranging, organizing, and breaking down the display booth. I didn't mind skipping

1

the cocktail events and industry dinner, not a bit; I was just excited to witness deals being made. Besides, my boss, whose father owned Randy's, had a Buick convertible. Traveling together meant I would have a chance to drive it.

That first industry trip turned out to be the most instructive in my twenty years at Randy's. I learned a few things about the business, of course, but more important, I had one of the defining experiences of my career—and it didn't have anything to do with shoes.

■ ■ ■

At the time, Randy's wasn't exactly the darling on the shoe block, but given the company's longstanding relationship with Keds, they were a minor player. Back then, Keds and Converse were the heaviest hitters, and we were far from being a Keds or a Converse.

The first day went about as I expected, with buyers from different department stores and retail outlets perusing our wares, along with aisle after aisle of our competitors'. Bob chatted up folks while I tidied things.

One of the people Bob made a point of talking to was a major buyer named Harry, who worked for a big retailer that represented more than 50 percent of Randy's business. He and Bob left at some point in the afternoon, and when they returned much later, when it was time for Bob to collect me and drive home, Harry was sideways. Bob was tipsy toasted, but Harry was smashed.

If Bob wanted to call it a day and hit the road, he didn't show it, and Harry certainly didn't seem as if he was ready to part ways, either. He stumbled around a while, then he got right up in Bob's face and slurred, "Bob, I want you to go out to Boston Common and catch me a pigeon."

Bob might have been baffled, but he replied good-naturedly, "Come on, Harry, let's do something else, something more fun."

Harry was not having it; there was no convincing him otherwise. "Damn it, son," Harry insisted. "I want you to catch me a pigeon."

I was stumped. These men were roundabout the same age. In present company, no one was anybody's son. Besides, surely Harry was joking. Surely, he'd come to his senses or, barring that, Bob would knock some sense into him.

And yet the next thing I knew, I was leaning on a lamppost on Tremont Street, watching a man I admired nearly as much as my father falling over himself trying to catch a pigeon.

My reaction was visceral. I was disgusted. Maybe Randy's would have lost half their profits that year if Bob had told Harry to take a flying leap; we'll never know. Clearly, Bob wasn't about to jeopardize the account. He was intimidated.

Try as I might, I could not put myself in Bob's position. I could not imagine letting some jerk humiliate me. It wouldn't have mattered to me that Harry bought more than half the shoes Randy's made. He could have bought every last one. I would never let one person have that sort of control over me.

In fact, damn it, there had to be a better way. Why were we depending on a handful of buyers, anyway? Someday, someway, somehow, I would figure out a way to get rid of the middlemen. Because no amount of business would ever be worth my integrity.

I will never forget that hour in Boston Common watching Bob Cohen chase pigeons. Not only did it help me figure out what sort of folks I wanted to work with, but it crystallized for me what I would be willing to work my ass off to avoid. I would never work with jerks.

I also credit that experience with giving me the courage, many years later, to start my own company. By then I had worked my way up to run Randy's most successful factory. I had learned the essentials of shoe manufacturing and a thing or two about business.

One day, in an effort to appease management, Bob—still my boss, many years later—decided to promote to top positions a bunch of guys who had just driven an entire manufacturing operation into the ground. As far as I was concerned, asking my team to report to people who didn't know how to run a business—who, in fact, had proven only that they knew how to ruin one—sounded a lot like a request to go catch a pigeon. That was my last day at Randy's.

A few fortuitous turns of fate later, I found myself establishing my own shoe company.

The Van Doren Rubber Company, as it was first known, wasn't perfect, but for me that's what it felt like. Thanks to backer Serge D'Elia and my other partners, I suddenly had the luxury of being 100 percent myself, free to do things exactly as I saw fit, and with abandon. For once I didn't need to check with "corporate," or ask the owner, or listen to some Harvard graduate who was timing production workers with a stopwatch about what was efficient.

As Vans grew, I might make concessions, but I would never let other factors besides my own convictions influence decisions. Mine would be a business that felt authentic—not just in making a quality product, but by operating in a way that was true to who I was. I can say with conviction that building the company that became Vans was a personal expression all the way.

My idea was to make the best shoe, with the best materials and workmanship. Making shoes is an art. I never wanted to make second-rate anything, and when it came to shoes, vulcanized rubber was synonymous with quality. By then, Charles Goodyear had figured out how to vulcanize rubber (by mixing in sulfur, then heating the rubber to ensure its durability and elasticity), and Keds had innovated the bonding of a canvas upper with a rubber sole. Add to that my twenty years working every section of the production line, and I knew everything I needed to know about the art and chemistry of making a quality pair of canvas sneakers.

After we opened the Vans factory, I took every opportunity to show anyone interested how the shoes were made. I loved the science and art behind it and got a kick when anyone else did, too. That was another way we found to compete, and to establish a difficult-to-imitate position: our pride in how we made our shoes was at the core of our identity in a crowded marketplace.

Had I never learned how to manufacture shoes, I could never have designed them. But when I got the chance to call the shots, I decided to create a shoe that would be as innovative as it was familiar. The key feature of my design was a diamond-patterned cupsole, twice as thick as any other sneaker on the market, so the shoes would be more durable and wear longer.

From Day One, I knew my success would depend on the team I assembled to make the best quality shoes with a common purpose. I needed people around me who would share my conviction that nothing in life or business is impossible. It might be expensive, or it might take more time than someone wants to put into it, but I can assure you, barring those obstacles, nothing is impossible. Anyone who tells you otherwise is full of it.

What I considered most important about people was their attitude, their integrity, and their desire to do things the right way. Without knowing it at the time, I was initiating what would eventually become the Vans empire by molding the inclusive, people-centric family vibe that became our signature Vans culture. I was building it person by person, not brick by brick.

The night I watched Bob chase pigeons was a foundational experience. Money is the best reward for effort, but it ain't got nothing on respect.

At Randy's, I learned more than how to make sneakers. I learned that fulfillment, efficiency, waste, profits, and liability—everything that happens in a company—comes down to being able to understand, respect, and appreciate one thing: good people. People who would never ask their coworkers to humiliate themselves.

One of my credos, which still stands at Vans decades later, is that we weren't a shoe company, but a people company that made shoes. That distinction may sound like nothing, but believe me, it was everything.

# CHAPTER TWO

# The Education of an Entrepreneur

E ver since I was a boy, I've loved going to the races. When I was no more than six and my brothers nine and four, our dad took us to Narragansett Park in Rhode Island, Rockingham Park in New Hampshire, and Suffolk Downs in Massachusetts, where I was born and raised. Back when we were too young to be allowed at the track, we would wait for Dad in the car, a 1931 Model A Ford he'd bought brand-new the year after I was born.

We should have had a lousy time, waiting two hours in the midsummer, but somehow anticipation outweighed discomfort. Inevitably, Dad would spring for ice cream either along the way there or the way back. Besides, each of us recalled the time in 1938 when he hit the daily double on a horse named Lady Carat. The grand he made off that single $2 bet was half an entire year's salary for him. Dad wasn't the sort of man who would leave anything, however promising, to chance. But a friend at the track would throw him a tip every now and then. On those occasions, he drove to the track, placed his bet, then immediately headed home so he wasn't tempted to gamble his winnings.

So much of who I am, what I believe in, and what I know how to do I learned from my parents. I'm as much a product of my family, both then and now, as I am a self-made man.

My father, John Bert Van Doren, may have liked to place bets, but he was the kind of gambler who more often bet on himself, taking calculated risks that required skill and smarts. A lifelong entrepreneur, he invented and built things for a living: wooden things, things that popped and exploded, things like toys and fireworks. He invented a new kind of sparkler in 1898 when he was sixteen.

Over the years and throughout his life, he devised all sorts of gadgets. He also happened to be a checkers champion and a hell of a card player. He could engineer anything, build anything, fix anything, and outsmart just about anybody about anything. His projects were endless, and he loved doing them. Dad was a very wise, gifted, and creative man.

The only time my father worked for someone other than himself during my lifetime was from 1942 to 1945, when he was employed by the National Fireworks Corporation. Dad had worked there as a teen during World War I. For years, Dad made sparklers by hand and sold batches of them to National Fireworks in advance of Independence Day. He also made caps. When the plant once again took to manufacturing munitions to support World War II, Dad returned to spearhead the effort. His area of expertise was making tracer bullets.

But like most successful creators, he was never satisfied with the status quo. While he was making tracer bullets, my father devised a new formula for making sparklers, rendering them safer and longer lasting. He went on to an illustrious, if exclusive, career in sparklers for two decades, which just goes to prove if you do something no one else can do, or do something better than most, the odds are in your favor for success.

■ ■ ■

Another formative influence—or accident of fate—was the timing of my birth. Born in 1930, I'm one of a generation whose childhood was bracketed by the Great Depression and World War II. I was born into a world in flux, where the only constant was hardship and hard work.

The year I was born, the Dow Jones Industrial Average wasn't 10,000 or 1,000; it was 40. An average income was $1,300 per year, and spring lamb cost 17 cents per pound, twice as much as a gallon of gas. Unemployment was 25 percent. A minimum wage of 25 cents an hour wasn't set until 1938.

There is so much I've failed to commit to memory, but I don't remember any talk of the American Dream when I was a kid. We talked about droughts and sandstorms and the Dust Bowl. The only housing growth I knew about was expanding shantytowns. I knew that success wasn't always guaranteed and that failure wasn't always deserved. Founding fathers John Hancock and John Adams—both of whom hailed from my hometown of Braintree, Massachusetts, southeast of Boston—couldn't have foreseen the kind of economic disaster we accepted as everyday life.

Only later, maybe when my kids were taught about it in school, did I understand what the Great Depression meant, and that it lasted the entire first decade of my life.

And yet, for an ordinary, working-class kid, I enjoyed an extraordinary childhood. Yes, I shared an outhouse with seven people, and no, we didn't have hot water on tap. We bathed in a basin with a cup and a half of water we would heat on the stove; it was a pain in the rear. I knew no one had much of anything, but we had what we needed. We had electricity. We had a furnace in the basement that burned coal and we had running water. I don't think we ever went hungry or went without, but then I wouldn't have known any different.

My family lived on fifteen acres in the Italian part of South Braintree, Massachusetts, which is to say we were better off, at least financially, than the majority of our neighbors, most of whom still farmed with horse and plow. More than our home and barn, which were both modest, we had a compound. The property's crowning glory was Dad's workshop.

Actually, his shop was a series of buildings: there was a utility room, a boiler room, a woodworking shop, a packing room, a printing room, and a saw room. There were also four separate storage units. My father put all of us to work. By age five or six I knew I could do things to help support our family, even if it was to sweep up after my father in his workshop.

■ ■ ■

Back then, as now, family was everything.

Dad was forty-five when he married Rena Rita Van Doren. Years later I learned Mom had been married before Dad, and Mom was Dad's third wife. Growing up, as far as any of us kids knew, our parents only had each other, and all of us only had one another.

Little did I know then how profoundly this reliance on family would affect my life in business, mostly for good, but also in ways I never anticipated.

Johnny was the oldest, always the most charming and sly. Robert, three years my junior, was more serious and so much like Dad that I don't know if in the whole of childhood, I ever saw him without a screwdriver clutched in the palm of his hand. Our sister Bernice was born disagreeable and indiscriminately quarrelsome. She was the queen of the family and thought she had the right to boss us boys around.

When Jimmy came along, when I was almost ten, there was no shutting that kid up. Jimmy had a little of all of us. He was smart in ways I wasn't and gifted in all the ways that mattered. Like Dad, Jimmy could build anything he didn't already have. Like Johnny, he was charismatic and popular. Unlike Johnny, who was more of a one-man show, he could prove himself on a team. Like Robert, he was good at mechanical things. Unlike Robert, who didn't care about sports or whether he won or lost unless it was against me, Jimmy was a fierce competitor. I quickly took Jimmy under my wing, and by the time he was six, wherever I went, whenever I went, Jimmy went, too.

That's not to say we always got along. My siblings and I were a competitive bunch, and rivalry colored everything we did. Whether it was Hearts or Rummy or stickball, each sibling sought to best the other. Johnny and Robert were shorter sighted. They wanted only to beat each other and me, whereas I wanted to best everyone every day, my brothers included. Whether it was a foot race, or who could hit a ball the farthest, I wanted to be the best. Everyone was fair game.

One of my clearest memories is returning home from my first day of kindergarten to announce that I was smarter than elder statesman Johnny. I have no idea now why I'd made this appraisal, only that I wanted to make it clear to Mom that, after me, Johnny was the second smartest.

The thing that really brought us kids together was athletics. These were dog days through the Depression, and all the kids we knew dreamed of playing shortstop or pitcher or being middle or welterweight boxing champions. We played a lot of stickball, which amounted to us pitching a tennis ball as hard as we could to try to strike out our opponents.

Jimmy was better than me with a broomstick, but I was a good enough pitcher and had a certain way to pitch so I could beat him. I taught Jimmy to play baseball, and he grew into a really fine player. In the end, I didn't mind being second to Jimmy, not one bit.

But oh, how we fought over that game. Johnny and I were die-hard Red Sox fans. Dad and Robert were Yankees fans. We harassed one another constantly, childishly. I'd go to the mat arguing that the Red Sox were better than the Yankees, but the truth was that I could take or leave most of it. At least until 1939, when the world and I met the greatest hitter of all time.

Of all the baseball stars of that era, the one that truly captured my imagination was Ted Williams. He was my hero. I admired his honor and tenacity. He studied his pitchers and committed to memory everything any of them ever threw him. He led the American League in home runs four times. To this day, his career on-base percentage is the all-time best, his career slugging percentage second only to Babe Ruth's.

And think about this: he did all of that despite missing five seasons while he flew fighter planes during World War II. Ted Williams was a lot like my old man in that he played his own game. He didn't tip his hat for anybody. Hell, to me, he *was* John Wayne, but more John Wayne than John Wayne could ever hope to be.

No one can say that 1941 wasn't one of the finest years in baseball, what with Joe DiMaggio's fifty-six-game hitting streak and Williams batting .406, making him the first player to break .400 in a decade. Folks commented on how Joe was regal and Ted was real, but what I recall with utter clarity is that Ted Williams could have sat out the last three games of the season instead of risking his record-breaking average.

Ted didn't have to step up to the plate. He had a .39955 hitting average on the year; a statistician would have rounded that score up to .400. But Ted Williams refused to take the bench. If he was going to break a record, he wanted to earn it. The *Philadelphia Bulletin* headline declared, "Williams Risks Batting Mark," but as Ted himself avowed, "I want to have more than my toenails on the line."

I liked that. I recognized the thrill of potential failure.

Williams went six for eight that day, a doubleheader at Philadelphia's Shibe Park, and raised his batting average to .406. What did Ted say to that? "You know, I'm a pretty good hitter."

Not only was he the best, he was also humble. What an inspiration.

■ ■ ■

Like all families, my family had a certain way of doing things. Our rhythm, split personality that it had, paced itself on mad habit. The

Dutch half, my father's, insisted on order and discipline. He was duty bound that everything had its place. My mother's Italian side was more intimate, refusing any regard for personal space. The day-to-day family dynamic left an imprint. Sometimes I can't say why I do something a certain way, except it's how my mother or father did it. And how they loved us, and how their love, unrelenting, demanded that all of us be the best versions of ourselves.

My parents taught me so much, more than I ever learned in school. Most of the positive attributes I still carry with me were taught by their good example. My parents taught me long ago that people were the most important thing in your life—more important than money or prestige or possessions. My father believed that family always came first. So do I—that's how I've conducted my own life and run my business.

Dad had a strong moral compass and was always pretty clear about what we kids should and should not do. My father never preached; he practiced. He often quoted the Golden Rule of "Do unto others" and he always insisted on doing the right thing. He was the one who taught me that no opportunity is worth more than your integrity. His motto was "Right is right and wrong is wrong."

There was no in-between with my dad. If you were wrong, you had to say you were wrong. You had to own your decisions and their repercussions. My mother had an in-between. If you pretended to be sick because you wanted to skip school, my mother would give you a note and say you were sick. She might say, "You son of a bitch," or swat you on the head with a broom, but she would give you a note. My dad would never give you a note.

My parents taught me the principle of working hard by example. They both put in long hours, on the job and at home. My mother worked in a factory, and Dad labored in his workshop every single day. He was the most hardworking man I have ever known.

There was never a question that the kids wouldn't work equally hard. It's curious now, perhaps, what was expected of me then, and what I later came to expect from my children. When I was growing up, kids worked. I knew kids as young as five who worked on their family's farm. Now some might call it slave labor, indentured servitude, or some form of abuse. Even back then there were child labor laws, but none of us—parents or children—ever questioned the expectation that we would contribute to the group. Neither of my parents offered validation or gratitude in exchange, and I didn't need it. We all participated in the family business, and there was dignity in being of service—dignity and pride in a job well done.

■ ■ ■

Traditionally, spring was sparkler-making season in the Van Doren household. As a general rule, Mom never did things the way Dad told her to, but she always got the job done. Since Mom didn't listen to Dad anyway, he let her do things however she wanted, which, when it came to making sparklers, was just fine. She happened to be an expert dipper. The frames would really fly when she was on the job.

To make sparklers, we dipped large frames of wire wicks into vats of liquid fireworks formula. It's a lot like making candles. Sparklers are just skinnier, so you could do a whole lot more of them at one time. When you think about it, not many kids receive such an intimate introduction to chemistry. When I was thirteen, fourteen, or maybe fifteen, I shook frames, starting at 6:00 a.m. I would do a hundred frames at 10 cents a frame and be through at 10:00 a.m., ready to go to the races.

There is nothing like aluminum, strontium nitrate with boric acid, steel, and dextrin to spark a boy's imagination. Sparklers were fun to make, but within a year or two, I was moved off the pyrotechnics line and tasked with making clothespins.

At some point during World War II, clothespin-making manufacturers stopped churning out product. Even if clothespins weren't rationed, they weren't easy to find. Looking back, I guess the company that earned its bread and butter making clothespins started making something the army or navy or air force needed more. Or it could have simply been that the wire spring at the center of the common clothespin wasn't available anymore.

At any rate, my dad decided he would make a better clothespin, one that didn't require metal to clasp. His design was a simple dowel about the width and length of a grown man's pointer finger that was able to slide up and down a clothesline.

I was twelve when Dad taught me how to make them. Making clothespins didn't have as much appeal as making sparklers, but dang, I made a lot of them.

I don't think Dad made a single one; he was the mastermind, and I was the workforce. In order to make a clothespin, you need two saws and a block of wood with a hole in it. Dad would set up the equipment: he positioned a delta blade atop a jigsaw with a small hole in it. The second saw put in its wedge. This allowed for a six-inch stick to be pushed down until it hit the bottom to make a slot. The slot is what allowed it to slide over a clothesline. I would push it all the way down and back so there was a slot with a bevel at the end. There was another saw on the axle, but it was only a little one, so when you pushed the slot in, you didn't hit it till you were a quarter of an inch from the end. That's what cuts a bevel. It's one push up, then down, then up again.

The downside to his technique was that burrs needed to be filed. For that, we used an eight-sided tumbler. Dad had rigged it so that the motor, which might be running at 2,000 rpm, could slowly shift from a big pulley to a small pulley, then back to a big pulley, then back to a small pulley. Afterward, we used pebbles, ones that were smaller than sweet peas, to tumble about and polish the clothespins.

We made a bushel at a time and sold eight dozen for a dollar. Since Dad was busy with bullets, I ran clothespin detail. When Mom joined Dad's workforce, she became my first coworker. She took the orders, and I filled them. We tag-teamed packing and shipping. Dad ran advertisements in the *Pennysaver* magazine.

Early on, I learned that teamwork and a smart division of duties are what make any kind of operation effective.

■ ■ ■

Even as a kid, when it came to work, I was always about putting in that extra effort. One year I worked on a dirt farm picking weeds—one day at that was enough for the rest of your life. Then I went to work on a dairy farm. After other people mowed, you had to turn the grass over so it could be raked and placed in rows. After the grass dried, you would end up with rows of hay. Then you had to bring in a truck and pitch the hay on it before you could take the truck back to the farm. This was in the summertime; in the wintertime, we shoveled cow shit.

I remember one day there were four of us kids out pitching hay for 10 cents an hour, three of them on one side of the truck, me on the other. I was the smallest one. They were messing around all the time I was working, but I didn't care. I pitched all the hay on there by myself.

Whether I was honoring the work ethic of my family or just trying to show up the bigger kids, I always tried my hardest, even when the stakes were low.

■ ■ ■

Another lesson I learned young: it's important to know and speak your mind, and sometimes, in order to be heard, that means you have to be . . . loud.

The Van Dorens were a raucous, loudmouthed bunch. My people communicate in decibels, and when we fight, man, do we fight. Whoever bellowed loudest won. An Italian mother is one thing, a Dutch father is something else altogether, and the two of them in tandem was mayhem.

If the Van Dorens had a coat of arms, it would feature a lasagna and a bullhorn. Family came first, but food was a close second, and it was a big part of our lives. My mother was an extraordinary cook. Bowls of Bolognese, chicken Parmesan, veal cutlets: Mom served big suppers midday, but more so after the war. War might have changed a lot of things, but not everything.

In the war years, my biggest problem was eating. I couldn't get enough. Every dollar I earned for anything went for food. My father was the only person who would eat a normal meal. Not one of us had enough, so we were always hoping he would sell us something. He'd sell us a pork chop or a piece of pie. He used to cut the pie in seven pieces. Six is pretty easy, so is four. But seven? We would all look to see if one piece was bigger than the others because everybody wanted that bigger piece.

■ ■ ■

Our bickering—a Van Doren tradition—is what held us together and at bay. One could say we had lively debates, ones that woke the entire neighborhood.

Though Mom bested Dad in volume, Dad was the conductor. He orchestrated sibling squabbles, endless tiffs. Dad made it so we didn't ever agree on anything. As far as he was concerned, there wasn't any point of having two people in one room if they agreed.

My father made it his job to instigate and fuel discourse and did so, I think, to get our dander up, to get us to take a position. All my childhood, there was always an argument about something. We were always looking at something two different ways. Is this bigger than that? Is this better than that? Other kids didn't argue with their parents like I argued with mine, at least no kid I knew.

Almost everything is a matter of opinion, but whether something was good or bad didn't matter as much as the ability to state and defend any given point. Such strife caused endless heartache and unnecessary turmoil, but I didn't begrudge Dad for it. He always pushed me to come up with the why, and I've always had a knack for figuring out the how. Those two skills have served me well my entire life.

Whether we were working or playing, Dad always made sure I was on my toes. I remember one day he sat down at the table and fanned a deck of cards in front of me. With a tone meant to imitate a carnie, but decidedly more like a drill sergeant, he commanded, "Pick a card, any card."

I chose the king of diamonds. Then, following his direction, I returned it to the deck. Behind his back, he shuffled the cards, then asked if I wanted to shuffle. I snatched the pack and further sorted them in hopes of guaranteeing there was no possible way he'd trace my card. When I handed the deck back, he began one by one to place cards face side up before me on the table in our playroom.

He would shake each card and touch it to his temple or in the air a few inches from his forehead. With each card, he would say, "No, that's not it," or, "Hmmm, no, no, that's not it," as if he'd been touched by a sixth sense.

"Whoa," he would say, as if the cards were calling out to direct him. I made a mental note when he passed the king of diamonds and did my best to keep my round face stonelike.

The poor guy hadn't a clue and continued in this fashion another dozen or so cards until he damn near bristled with epiphany. With the surety you might claim the sun rises before the dawn, he proclaimed, "Paul, the next card I turn over will be yours."

Look at this guy, what a putz! That clown missed my card. Hell, he'd passed my card many cards ago, and since he had, I made the first wager I'd ever make: "Listen, Dad, I'll make you a bet. If I win, you pay my allowance for the rest of my life. If I lose, as of today, I forfeit my allowance."

I had never been so certain of anything in my whole entire life. I knew I couldn't lose.

He nodded. "Paul, are you sure you want to place that bet?"

Earnestly, cheekily—I mean, I hated to take advantage of him—I countered, "Absolutely."

Dad returned to the cards and, without ceremony, from the spent pile plucked out the king of diamonds.

"You can't do that!" I cried out.

"I said the next card I'd turn over would be yours. Son, that's what I did."

He had just taught me a painful lesson: don't bet the ranch if you don't have all the details. I would argue that's another lesson best learned early.

In a span of five, six seconds tops, I went from being the king of diamonds to a schmuck. I'd gambled the fate of my entire fortune—I mean, Dad gave me a nickel a week in allowance; you do the math—and I'd done this, bet the farm, the whole of it, and lost, because I had failed to analyze all the variables.

The next time around, I vowed I would be more disciplined. I would pay attention. That afternoon, Dad also taught me a lesson in strategy: when someone affords you a chance to rethink a hasty decision, consider accepting that act of mercy with grace.

■ ■ ■

My parents might have expected us to work and play smart, but otherwise we were feral mutts given autonomy to make decisions, bad or good, as we saw fit.

Dad didn't tell you to do this or that. About smoking, he said, "I smoke. If you want to be dumb enough to do what I'm doing, do it." We didn't smoke.

The extraordinary thing about being kids was that we were allowed to stretch out in any direction that pleased us. We were allowed to explore our whims on any given day, to have goals by noon we hadn't considered over breakfast, to spend the day adventuring and come home dirty. No one questioned how we planned to spend our day. No one micromanaged our time. No one set boundaries or perimeters or directed us on how to entertain one another. The expectation was that we would figure it out, and that nature, through patterns or connection or wonderment, would be our teacher.

That kind of freedom proved instructive in ways I couldn't have anticipated.

In 1939, right around the time my mother gave birth to my youngest brother, Jimmy, Johnny ran away. Johnny was twelve, the oldest of us, and second smartest. I was about to turn ten. Robert had just turned seven. Bernice was four or thereabouts. I never knew for certain, but I had long suspected that Johnny, the firstborn, was Mom's favorite—at least until Bernice had come along. Even then, I surmised, if she was favored, it was only because she was a girl. Needless to say, whether or not he was Mom's favorite, Johnny's departure left her a wreck.

Dad tracked Johnny down in New York City and brought him back to Braintree. I cannot recall the right-before he'd gone or the just-after he came back. What I remember is that, a few months later, Johnny ran away a second time.

I guess Johnny's first escape failed to prepare Mom for his second. Her desperation was palpable. Frantically, adamantly, she pleaded with Dad, "We have to get Johnny." I remember thinking, *Yes, he's one of ours. Of course, we'll find him and bring him home,* but Dad shook his head. "Mother, he's just going to run away again. This is what he wants. Let's see what happens."

I was gobsmacked. My parents had given us all a good bit of autonomy. In our family, we were required to be upstanding citizens, but other than that, I cannot recall a single instance when our parents made serious demands on us. Hell, I cannot recall my parents ever making any demands on us other than helping in the work-shop, which I loved to do.

We may have been used to making our own decisions, but when Johnny ran away, I could barely wrap my head around this level of independence, self-determination, or uncertainty. You mean to tell me we get to choose how we live, even where? You mean to tell me Johnny is ready to make his way all on his own? Sure, the kid had grit, and wow, could he sing, but dang, was letting him go an act of love or just loss?

Johnny always wanted to be in show business. Later, we learned Jackie Gleason had taken Johnny under his wing and helped him get an occasional acting gig; but for two decades, my brother was mostly gone. At best, we might receive the occasional birthday card from him. There was no rhyme or reason as to why Johnny remembered our birthdates in any given year, but it was always something special when he did.

The fact is, Johnny was a con man. He could con the cons—that was his real talent.

When he did come home, he always had nice clothes, like people in show business. Always a nicer jacket, a nicer shirt: jewelry, rings, watches. Every now and then, when he'd come home and left, he'd leave something behind. If he forgot a ring, I would pick it up and wear it for a while.

Looking back, what strikes me now with clarity is that in allowing Johnny to go his own way, my parents—as our captains, our family's governing body, our champions in how to live—provided a solid lesson. Holding on can do more harm than letting go. Yes, it was painful for my folks to let Johnny go and live life on his terms, but it would have been more painful to force him to stay.

When we hold onto someone too tightly, at best we're saying, "I don't trust you," and at worst, "You're not capable." Nowadays you could argue that Johnny was too young to make his way on his own. Nowadays things are different. But no matter how badly any of us might want it otherwise, we cannot force someone to be anyone other than who they are—and we shouldn't try.

In running off to join the circus, or so it seemed, Johnny did the boldest, most courageous thing I had ever known a boy could do. He'd made no excuses or apologies, and to their credit, my parents said, "You've got this. Go. Enjoy. We trust you. Don't be afraid. Your adventure is waiting."

■ ■ ■

The first time I went out to embrace my own life's adventure, I was about fifteen, and I went out to meet it in a fury of righteous indignation.

By that time, I'd made so many clothespins during the war, and sparklers after the war, that I had saved enough to be thinking about the sort of car I wanted to drive when I turned sixteen. Then somehow, I found out Dad had been paying some Italian guy he occasionally employed to make sparklers for 30 cents a frame—three times what he paid me. I was furious. Ain't that some shit? Here I'd been shaking frames at 10 cents a frame for years.

It was the first time, but not the last, that I was furious about getting less than what I felt I deserved.

I was out of there. I hit the road with two friends who were both a year older than me. Willie First and a guy named Pete were both sixteen and had convinced me we should be merchant marines. Their declaration was compelling enough that the three of us thumbed a ride to New York City. I wasn't convinced I should be a merchant marine, but I'd heard somewhere that if a fellow decided he wasn't cut out for it, he could quit without any hassle, so I figured I'd be no worse for wear in spreading my wings. Hell, Johnny was pals with Jackie Gleason; surely something equally remarkable awaited me in the Big Apple.

Maybe there was more in store for me than life in Braintree, making sparklers. There was only one way to find out.

Our first night on the lam was the worst night of my life, before or since. We didn't have much money, so we decided just to ride the subway all night. We rode from Sheepshead Bay and back all night, all the way out, then all the way back again. Let me tell you, there's nothing worse. Who could sleep?

The following night we got a room no matter what it cost. We pooled our resources for a hotel room on Coney Island, which we ended up trashing. The next morning, we went to the recruiting station. As it turned out, I was underage for the military, and Pete and Willie were scared.

Whether it was to drown our sorrows or take the piss out of a few locals on the pool tables, we found ourselves at the bar nearest the recruiting station. Pete and Willie further weighed the idea of being soldiers over draft beer while I drank a Coke and checked which horses were running where. I noticed a horse named Ghost Bound was running back home at Rockingham Park. The name struck a chord with me. I knew every horse, and I knew this horse loved the mud and was good in the mud and on the outside post.

The only New York bookie I was able to track down in the city told me to take a hike, so I took the money I'd stuffed in my sock and purchased a train ticket home to South Boston. Then I took another train that dropped me a block from my usual pool hall and a mile from my home in Braintree. With two minutes to spare in the twenty-minute deadline for placing a bet, I put $20 on Ghost Bound. The odds were twenty to one. I could win $400.

Back then, an announcer named Ralph "Babe" Rubenstein called races. It was said Babe never miscalled a single race; and while at first there wasn't a mention of Ghost Bound, I knew the horse would come from behind. And since a horse coming from behind always does so on the outside, my heart quickened when Babe shouted, "Here comes Ghost Bound on the outside, coming on strong—and it's a photo finish!"

And by photo finish, I mean to say that Ghost Bound came in second.

What can I say? Shit happens. Suddenly I was done with this adventure. I was exhausted. I may have bet on the wrong horse, but at least Ghost Bound had brought me home.

I walked the mile back to our house, and my father met me at the door. When he asked me why I had left, I told him I needed to be fairly compensated for my effort, same as anyone else for the same work, especially when I was better and had been there longer.

I was stunned when he simply looked at me and said, "Son, you're right. I'm sorry."

In hindsight, I was foolish to run off so half-cocked. I guess I was trying to prove I was an adult, but I did so by acting like a child. I'd had my ass handed to me in the big city; I'd lost $20; but at the end of my adventure was this small but profound victory: my father admitted I was right. In my little world and our family home, that was a milestone moment. At that point, I think we both knew I wasn't a kid anymore.

# CHAPTER THREE

# Organize a System

've always had an innate sense for numbers. I'm just naturally able to see the whole, eliminate variables, subtract any sum of aspects, and limit factors in order to compare or strategize or problem-solve. Finding patterns in the data has always been second nature to me.

The truth is that almost everything in life hangs in the balance of likelihoods or odds. That sounds ominous, but it should be of some comfort that odds are driven by basic arithmetic anyone can understand. In other words, math.

Think about what it means to roll a single, six-sided die. You've got a one-in-six chance to roll any given number. Let's say you want to roll a five. There is one chance to roll a five, and five chances you won't. You have five-to-one odds, or five losses to one win. I learned early on that the better you are at calculating odds, the better you are at finding ways to tip them in your favor. All you need is a system.

■ ■ ■

In school, they called me Dutch the Clutch. I'd like to think I earned the nickname because I was the sort of ballplayer who made outstanding saves or home runs at critical points in big games—but the fact is *clutch* rhymes with *Dutch*, and I was half Dutch.

It's true that I've always liked the adrenaline of a do-or-die play. As my hero Ted Williams said to *Time* magazine in 1941, "I'd like to have the bases loaded every time I come up." To me, the more critical the situation, the better I'll perform. I don't create clutch situations just to feel the rush—I'd prefer to eliminate risk than encourage it—but I for one have always found defeat intoxicating, especially when it's someone else's. And when it's mine, I can't say it's ever done anything but make me think smarter and behave differently, even courageously.

Hell, it's only after I lost something or when something didn't go my way that I was afforded the opportunity to shine. That might be what I love about horse racing.

Win or lose, nothing beats a day at the races, where every thirty minutes legends are determined, and in two minutes, some champ and his or her wee jockey escape defeat. There's satisfaction in choosing a winner, but someone almost always has better information than you. In almost every race, there are many unknowns and even more variables. And in almost every race, it's just as important to figure out who isn't going to win as who is.

My dad had introduced me to horse racing at an early age, and I enjoyed betting the odds, even if there usually wasn't any real money involved. I liked the challenge of figuring out which horse would win based on snippets of overheard conversations, how the horses behaved, and other clues.

Dad had taught me to watch and listen carefully to what was being said around me. His lessons in situational listening taught me the wonders of keeping my mouth shut. I'd listen to the owners, jockeys, and oddsmakers and then distill what I'd overheard.

For me, the trick to it wasn't just in keeping my mouth shut: it was in learning how and when to lower the volume in my head, so that once I made up my mind, I wouldn't rethink or unthink a well-considered decision my gut had already signed off on.

I had plenty of opportunity to sharpen my betting skills. My best friend, Murph Damiano, and I had been sneaking into the track for years. Murph's mother had a ton of brothers, almost as many as his dad, and before we had cars of our own, his uncles were our lifeline to and from the track. Mind you, for years we jumped the fence, but it was getting to the track that was the hassle. If there were two races any given afternoon, Murph's legion of uncles would bet fifty cents on our behalf. Fifty cents on a $200 daily double meant we'd win $50, which was an unimaginable amount when you're thirteen—at least when I was thirteen.

Now, Murph was a hell of a gambler. His longshots won. His favorites won. My gambling ability may never have matched his, but I was a dedicated student of probability and the nature of chance. On any given day, the two of us were always betting on something.

Murph was a year older than me, but he repeated the third grade, so we ended up in fourth grade together. The kid was built like a tank. When I was fifteen, I looked ten, and when Murph was ten, he looked twenty. This often came in handy. Anyway, I don't know if I chose him or he chose me, but I'll be damned, he's been my best friend for over eighty years.

Murph was an amazing athlete. Gifted with a nearly inhuman natural ability, with almost no effort he could do anything better than anyone else. In high school, he played first-string varsity football, basketball, and baseball. His best skill was pitching. He had a special three-finger pitch that really sailed and broke downward at the last minute. When you get a pitch like that, wow, it's really hard to hit or catch. And Murph never bragged about what he could do. He just played.

One day, to settle a dispute, I suggested an older kid at school run a mile against Murph. I made a wager he couldn't refuse: if he could beat Murph in a one-mile race, I'd give the guy $2. The older kid happened to be the best runner in Massachusetts at the time. Murph had never run track, not in his life; but I knew Murph and I'd choose those odds any day.

The first clue this runner kid was about to lose $2 came halfway round the third lap, when Murph called out, "Hey, Dutch! Tell me when you want me to go fast." On the next lap, I shouted, "Okay, Murph! Let it rip!" By then we had our track coach's attention, who stood dumbstruck as Murph zoomed past his star runner.

Murph beating the best miler by half a lap illustrates one key fact: if you know and believe in your gut in what you are doing, taking a risk isn't risky.

■ ■ ■

Having spent the majority of my formative years calculating odds, I eventually came up with a foolproof system to beat them.

I didn't have access to racing forms in my younger years, but I got the newspaper. Back then *The Globe* listed the races, riders, trainers, and handicaps. I kept a log and spent a good amount of effort tracking which horses ran when and how. My system grouped horses and jockeys by percentages, but I was paying special attention to how the handicapper had handicapped each race.

Handicapping has nothing to do with gambling. Handicapping is looking at the big picture and eliminating variables based on chance.

In handicapping horses, you assess them based on their running history. When horses run eyeball to eyeball, the idea is that the better horse wins. As much as any of us might hope otherwise, the fastest horse doesn't always win.

Some people think handicapping is a science. It's not. Everyone handicaps differently. There's class and ability and form and breeding. There are also race conditions to factor in, such as mud. Horses feel good one day and don't the next. A horse can run fast against good horses but not run fast against bad ones. Some horses run faster than other horses at different times of the day. Some horses are fast out of the gate while some are slow. There is always a horse in the race that wants to run longer and one that wants to run shorter.

To be clear, after three runs or a win, horses are given a rating, which determines their handicap. Then moving forward, their rating, or handicap, is adjusted in line with their performance. A horse's rating determines which races it may enter. When horses run better, they move up in class. When a horse drops down, it means he's not doing so well, but the system I'd devised didn't rest on the horse's performance or even the jockey's.

My system rested on the handicapper. Back then, Dave Wilson was Boston's top handicapper. I'd come to realize that Dave picked the first race and last race better than any other race on any given week, and he never went three days without winning. In simplest terms, my system was to hedge the handicapper, who I had to assume spent more time than me assessing any given horse's running history.

I was convinced that I'd come up with a failproof system to beat the bookie. I told my dad all I needed was for him to place the bets. He would need to quit work in order to focus his efforts. That was a no-brainer, but even my more conservative estimates suggested that we would easily bring in $25,000 a year.

Dad scoffed, then softened. "It isn't that easy, son."

I knew in my heart of hearts he was wrong. The old fool: I'd never looked up to anyone like I looked up to my father. But it was within my power to make us rich beyond our wildest dreams, at least in my mind. I mean, didn't he want indoor plumbing? Didn't he want hot water and our very own commode somewhere in the house?

Our folks supported us well enough, but I thought about how much easier life would be, and Mom—dear, beautiful, broom-swatting Mom—I imagined how much better things would be for her.

Besides, how could I lose?

My father valued the fact that I saw things in wholes. He told me there was something to be said in figuring out a system, in considering the big picture. He was proud of how I had dissected a process from it; but the devil was in the details, and no one, but no one, was ever fully able to take the flimsiness of chance into account.

Besides, he said, I cared too much.

A true gambler, one who can make a living from it, can't be happy when he wins or sad when he loses. A true gambler has to have the same feeling no matter what happens. That's just not me. Take poker: I'm pretty good at poker, but there's no way I'm hiding a bad hand and there's no way I'm hiding a good one. I know I'm supposed to be expressionless, but anyone can see if I'm happy. I can't imagine anything worse than not caring if I win or lose.

I care. I'm emotional. Hell, I have too much emotion. To be a gambler you can't have emotion. I spent the whole of childhood wanting to gamble, but I wasn't a good bettor and never would be. I could win seven races in a row, but if I lost the eighth race, I was down in the dumps, inconsolable. Winning seven out of eight races would never be good enough. I'm not wired that way; I'm really bad at losing. For that reason alone, it was probably a good thing I never got the chance to test my system.

■ ■ ■

If my earliest memories are parables in weighing the odds, my later memories—my favorite ones, at least—are in defying them.

After ninth grade, I dropped out of school. I was sixteen. I had decent enough grades and was top in my class in math and science, but I just didn't see the point. School didn't challenge me and hadn't ever since I could remember. I would rather figure the odds on a horse than crack a book on subjects that seemed wholly irrelevant.

The idea of being a high school dropout—the idea that I would rather work—never bothered me, and it certainly didn't bother my parents. Half the kids I ever knew dropped out. Back then, there wasn't a stigma to it. Back then, being strong and able and eager was enough to assure someone opportunity.

Physical capital was to last century what technological capital is to this century. Economically, life after World War II was a lot more stable than during the war, and a hell of a lot better than the decade before the war, but you could hardly argue that things were particularly rosy for the working class. And make no mistake, when a kid drops out of high school after his first year, undoubtedly, he is working class.

A friend of mine asked me recently if I was a rebel. The summer after I dropped out of school, I would say I had been more of a delinquent. If I wasn't at the racetrack, I was at the pool hall. Really, no one ran a table like me. I was so good, the house bookie fronted me the $10 I needed to challenge the other players, and there were plenty of gadders to take. Whenever I had an extra buck or two, I would place small bets with the same bookie, who had become a one-stop shop. Without breaking a sweat, I could tap two very different revenue streams.

It was 1946, and the country was full of ex-GIs who had returned home from the war. More than seven million soldiers were discharged from the military in 1945 alone. Add to this the fact that millions of union members had worked in the war industries during the war and had put off making any major demands about salary or working conditions for the sake of national unity.

Once Japan surrendered, these demands resurfaced and led to the largest series of labor actions in American history. First it was the oil workers, then the auto workers. Strikes mushroomed to the point of national crisis. Striking meat-packers, teamsters, steelworkers, and mine workers were followed closely by railway employees.

All this to say, like many other young men around my age, I found myself with a lot of time on my hands.

My mother did not approve.

There came a day when I had to give up working the pool hall and start working a production line. Reluctantly, I applied my natural talent for numbers and systems to a more respectable purpose.

During the war, Mom had gone to work for Randolph Manufacturing Company. She figured she could get me a job and went so far as to set up an interview. I wasn't keen to give up my side hustles, which were lucrative enough to sustain my lifestyle, which I liked to split evenly between the bar and the track. So I sent a friend of a friend in my place. That worked out as well as you can imagine.

Mom wasn't what anyone would describe as patient. Her broom-over-the-head, do-what-I-say-now tactics guaranteed that I would personally attend a second interview a week later. If for no other reason than to quiet her complaints about my behavior, I went.

The first time I ever worked for someone other than my father, it was for a man named Herbie, who'd been with Randy's since its inception. I didn't know then what a good guy Herbie was, only that he'd called in sick. As a newly designated service boy, I was on my own. My sole responsibility was to deliver pieces of fabric, thread, and other whatnot from a storage room to dozens and dozens of workstations, where typically women like my mother sat at sewing machines stitching shoe uppers in eight-hour shifts.

To be clear, Randy's did one thing: they sewed the canvas part of tennis shoes for Keds. That was it. It was a big factory with more than a hundred employees, and my new mission was to keep the sewing room moving efficiently. It was a vast space crammed full of sewing stations. Here thread and needles flew in a constant clatter. The *chucka chucka thumping* was in concert a deafening buzz, but it was the smell—canvas mingled with rubber with a hint of diesel and human sweat—that was wholly novel.

In Herbie's absence, the women directed me on the process. They explained how the assembly line—they called it "the conveyor"—worked and showed me where to find the various components I'd need to supply them with.

There's a surprising amount of material and effort that goes into making a shoe's upper. A bunch of smallish fabric parts are sewn together, using the correct color and size for a specific pair of shoes. There are two fabric sides, the toe piece, the tongue, the back panel above the heel, and two narrow strips onto which metal eyelets for shoelaces are fastened.

All of these various fabric pieces were bundled together in sets—for a left shoe and a right shoe—by color lot and size. These bundles were put into baskets of twenty-four, which were then sent to the first sewing station. Randy's made thousands of uppers per day, so there were hundreds of bundle-filled baskets barreling down the conveyor at any given time.

Each bundle contained all the needed parts to build one pair of uppers, and for tracking purposes, each was given a unique number. As each bundle proceeded down the assembly line, various parts were sewn together in a specific order. Each individual seamstress was in charge of sewing one set of parts together, such as sewing tongues to sides. Then she would pass the basket of twenty-four bundles to the next seamstress, and so on, until each pair of uppers in the basket was complete. Some seams were difficult to sew and some were easier, so each seamstress was assigned a spot along the line depending on her skill.

Randy's didn't make a lot of different colors, just the basics. As anyone who has ever painted a room using more than one gallon of paint knows, there is a subtle color difference in different dye lots. So each of the various tennis shoe parts needed to be cut from fabric of the same dye lot to ensure that the color was consistent throughout the entire upper. Once a basket containing shoe parts for twenty-four pairs was complete, the sewing-room workers relied on those parts having a matching dye lot.

As far as I could tell, the bottleneck hinged with the stays, the long, narrow strips of fabric that hold the metal eyelets for the laces. One edge had to be bound, as it would show on the top of the shoe. The strip was separated and sent as one long, continuous ribbon to a binding machine in a different part of the factory, after which it was cut into individual pieces containing four or five eyelets each, depending on the size of shoe. Before the entire upper could be completed, the eyelet stays—again, for twenty-four pairs of shoes— would need to make their way back into the original basket with the matching tracking number.

Inevitably, there were massive delays as the service boy ran around trying to reunite a set of stays with its correct basket. Until that basket was reunited with its stays, the group of uppers couldn't be completed. Baskets would be set aside until the service boy could find the matching eyelet stays. Every. Single. Basket.

I thought there had to be a better way.

While making clothespins and sparklers, I had learned the importance of logical progression in setting up manufacturing systems. It did not take a rocket scientist to figure out that Randy's routines, methods, and procedures did not make sense.

This realization was strange and exhilarating. Clearly the problem started at the bundling stage, and as my first afternoon muddled along in stops and starts, I started to consider ways to make things run smoother. By closing time, the solution was obvious, or at least it seemed obvious to me. So, I stuck around after the 4:15 p.m. quitting bell rang.

Those eyelet stays measured half an inch across by two inches long, or thereabouts. In other words, they were really small. I had perfect vision, and it was all but impossible to see the color difference between that one teeny piece and any other. The rest of the shoe upper had to be from the same dye lot, that was clear, but those pieces were never separated from their original group. It was only the pesky eyelet stays that were sent off, and trust me, if they didn't make it back to their original basket, no one was ever going to notice a color difference.

The answer, in my four-hours' worth of experience, was to cut stays according to basic color and size and put them with any matching basket. We did not need to bother finding the exact tracking numbers. That was a waste of time, and it literally brought production to a grinding halt.

I didn't ask permission. It never occurred to me to ask. It never occurred to me that I might be breaking a rule. In my mind, there wasn't time for rules or decorum. I was busy getting things done, rearranging the baskets and storage areas, and moving around the binding and cutting machines to determine the most efficient way to reorganize the eyelet stay production.

The factory was a five-story building. I was way up on the top story and didn't see another soul until nearly midnight on June 17, 1946, when a guy younger than my father but older than me showed up. He didn't introduce himself. He didn't have to. I knew this guy was a soldier fresh home from Europe, and that he drove a Buick. I knew the Buick was a convertible.

When your mother is Italian, after she asks whether or not you've eaten, she tells you everything there is to know about everyone she knows. As a result, I knew that the man towering before me was Bob Cohen, the owner's son.

"What the hell are you doing here?" he barked.

He seemed a little drunk. Not menacingly drunk, but drunk enough that he wobbled a bit as I explained, "This system is stupid. I'm trying to straighten it out."

I hadn't intended to be a jerk, much less sound like one, but I also didn't fully realize my own audacity.

The guy was asking a valid question. I didn't have permission to be there. I certainly hadn't run my idea by my immediate supervisor. I hadn't even met my boss yet.

All I knew was that when something isn't right, you fix it. That's what I'd done.

It hadn't once occurred to me that identifying inefficiencies wouldn't necessarily dictate an immediate remedy, even on my first day on the job, even if I wasn't being paid for the extra hours. I can't say why I hadn't considered the possibility that my plan might ruffle a lot of feathers. Maybe I was cocky. Maybe I knew better. If I'm being honest, I knew that I knew better.

Two things about this moment stay with me: first, rather than react, Bob listened. To have the boss, or the boss's son—which, in my limited experience, meant the same thing—listen to me, a sixteen-year-old on his first day on the job, was striking. I believe that in that split second, I began to take my work, and my future, seriously.

Then, equally instructive, instead of walking away and letting me finish, Bob rolled up his sleeves to help.

The next morning, with the new system in place, things moved along seamlessly. Nobody congratulated me. Nobody said a thing. It was as if the system I'd devised had been the system all along.

That first day established new procedures at Randy's, and also was the foundation of my rapport with Bob. Our fellow workers treated Bob with deference but didn't get too chummy. I welcomed his friendship. He liked to pick my brain and he was good company. One afternoon, we grabbed a pint after work and were kicking around ways to improve the factory. I asked, "Why does Randy's only make the uppers? Why not make the whole shoe?"

He stared blankly, as if I'd just told him Jacob's Tavern had run out of beer and we'd have to give ours back. Then he said, "Hell, I have no idea."

To the day a month later, Randy's announced they would stop stitching uppers for Keds in order to manufacture whole shoes for themselves. We would also change our name to the Randolph Rubber Company, which made sense, seeing that the new venture was a completely different gig and a hell of a bold gamble.

In material, it cost twice as much to make a whole shoe. Add to this, we'd need a lot of money and a completely new infrastructure: huge, heavy cylinders for rolling out the rubber, different machines to mix different rubber formulas for the different parts of the shoe, and giant vulcanizers to heat cure the rubber.

When Bob and I were speaking freely about the possibilities, I was all in. Of course, it wasn't costing me a dollar on my birthday; I wouldn't be missing out on anything. My mom and all the other women in the sewing room, on the other hand, would be laid off for the months it'd take to redesign the production line; source, purchase, and receive everything; and put the redesigned plant back together.

Everyone was promised they could return to their jobs when Randy's reopened, but it would be a long six months for a lot of families.

During the transition, I did my ever-loving best to be useful to the new hires who were experts in various areas of production. I was too young to be intimidated, but if the seamstresses were kind to me out of pity, the newly hired experts proved to be suckers for my enthusiasm. It felt really good to feel as if I were indispensable, almost as good as the $2.25 extra I was making.

Three months in, two huge crates of secondhand shoe lasts arrived. A *last* is a piece of metal formed in the shape of a foot that fabricators use to build a shoe around. It's basically a mannequin of a foot. Randy's had bought three thousand pairs of used lasts, or six thousand individual ones, and every blessed one of them was corroded. Clearly, they had been a lot cheaper than brand-new ones, but now Randy's had an expensive problem.

If you've never made shoes, you wouldn't know this, but you can't make a canvas shoe on a corroded last. The fabric would snag on the protrusions, and the rubber would be pitted on the finished shoe.

Bob had assigned a guy to use a wire polishing wheel to grind away the corrosion and shine the lasts. A single last took him about half an hour to shine, which meant it took about an hour to polish a pair. At that rate, even with a team of guys, we were looking at months of work. We were screwed.

Without a vague notion other than absolute confidence in my dad, I told Bob I needed two weeks and $600. I was familiar enough with tumblers, at least with the one I used to smooth the wire springs of clothespins. Couldn't we polish lasts the same way? Having pretty much no other option, Bob gave me the job, and to my relief, my Dad was up for the challenge. Using metal munitions boxes Dad had left over from his wartime job, he and my younger brother Robert built a bunch of tumblers in no time—just like our clothespin tumblers, only bigger. Two motorized axles rotated each tumbler, so they wouldn't jolt and jerk. We added a scoop of pea gravel to serve as grist. It worked liked a charm.

Bob was impressed. I sort of assumed Old Man Cohen would be, too, so when I went to collect the $600, I was in for a hell of a shock when he handed me a hat instead. A hat. Seriously? I didn't want a stupid hat.

The longer the old blowhard talked, the more exasperated I got, until finally I blurted out, "Forget it. I quit," and stomped out.

Bob caught up with me just as I got to the door and talked me into coming back. I got my $600. If Bob reiterated his lesson about listening, his father taught me never to accept less than I was promised or less than I deserved.

■ ■ ■

Early on, whenever I saw a better way to do things, I started taking matters into my own hands. It came naturally to me.

Manufacturing shoes takes a surprising amount of chemistry. Of all the new hires at Randy's, my favorite was the chemist, whose job it was to figure out the best formulas for tennis shoes' various rubber components. There are the soles, the edge band that binds the fabric upper to the sole, and the little labels for the heels. Having only recently retired from sparklers, I knew a bit about chemistry and found myself asking him a lot of questions and making myself useful whenever he experimented.

I was endlessly fascinated by his connections and how he could order bulk chemicals cheaply. It blew my mind further that his orders were shipped quickly, and within weeks, delivered right to the factory's door.

I knew well enough the ingredients needed to make sparklers, and I knew roughly what Dad paid. Using my newfound knowledge to help our family business, with the chemist's help, I figured out how much we needed to make a million fire-cracking light sticks. I'd done the math twice and had no doubt we could sell them all, so out of hubris or folly or some combination of both, I placed the order for $600 worth, including the wire that served as the sparkler's backbone. I didn't have $600, but I had bought the material anyway on credit. With $600 in materials, there would be $10,000 in profit.

Ten thousand dollars was a fortune. When I'd placed the order, it had seemed like a really good idea, but $600 was a lot, too. It would take me six months to earn that much—in fact, more than six months.

After a week, I thought maybe it had been a dream. Maybe I hadn't ordered hundreds of dollars' worth of chemicals. Maybe Dad wouldn't kill me. Another week passed. I still hadn't given Dad a heads-up that enough explosives to light India were en route to us.

The truck pulled into the driveway while the entire family was eating lunch. Without thinking, or possibly out of terror, I jumped up from the table, ran out the door, and hopped into the truck. It occurred to me I should try to make a run for it, but instead of telling the driver to hightail it and fast, I directed him to Dad's workshop and calmly helped him unload his delivery.

When Dad had finished his sandwich and was turning the corner from the house, I felt him before I saw him. The delivery truck drove away too quickly. If I'd had any sense, I would have stalled him. Hell, I would have done almost anything to put off whatever Dad had coming my way.

With the bill of lading in his fist, Dad marched toward me, a dead ringer for Popeye, except the imaginary steam didn't rise from a corn pipe but from the general vicinity of Dad's ears. He sputtered and shook his head, but he didn't actually say anything. He seemed to be assessing the mess of drums and boxes. When he fell silent, I did the only thing I could, which was to say I was sorry and launch into my grand plan.

I told him that the amount of supplies we'd received was enough to make one million sparklers for the upcoming Independence Day season. I had calculated that between Dad, my younger brother Robert, and myself, we could accomplish our goal from February through July third.

In the same way that I had first imagined, Dad could see that what I had sourced was cheaper and better than what he'd been ordering. He nodded, then nodded again.

"That's really good wire you have there," he said. Then, as if it were an afterthought, he added, "Son, if this is going to work, you're going to have to quit that job of yours in the shoe factory. You need to be here helping me full time."

I agreed. It was a good time to quit. Randy's was still in the midst of its transition, and the factory was in chaos. They had plenty of experts on hand, so Bob wouldn't need any of my piddly advice. I promised to come back after the Fourth of July if he wanted me to. He was okay with that.

Now, a sparkler is a product with a narrow, immovable market window. No one, but no one, buys sparklers on the fifth of July.

So for the next few months, my family got to it.

This was the first time Dad would be making sparklers on spec rather than to fill an existing order. The driver had delivered supplies with a bill to follow. If we didn't sell all these sparklers, we'd be up the creek.

I put my head down and threw myself into the work, knowing my latest money-making scheme was brilliant except for one small flaw: I had rolled the dice and made a commitment that would affect my entire family, and we're not just talking about the money, but the time it would take to make a million of anything. That was a real failure of judgment. Being blindsided is bad enough, but when our actions blindside someone important to us, someone we love and respect, that's a serious miscalculation.

Months later, on the fifth of July, after we had made a million sparklers and sold every blessed one of them, I had my own Independence Day. Dad was visibly proud to count six crisp hundred-dollar bills out to me, six crisp hundred-dollar bills out to my brother Robert, and smaller amounts to Jimmy and Bernice.

I remember being so proud that I'd figured out a way to leverage what I'd learned at the factory to help the family. I had found a better, cheaper, more efficient way to make the product my father had spent his entire adult life making. If I had overstepped, certainly it was to good ends.

Turns out, my sparkler-making venture wouldn't be the last time I'd come up with a way to do things differently and earn a windfall for my family. But it also wasn't the first time, nor the last, that my family would bail me out when I got in over my head.

# CHAPTER FOUR

# Respect the Workers

My belief is that you can always teach people how to do things. What you cannot teach people is how to understand other people. If someone does not understand people, that person might as well just go in another direction because they are never going to get it right.

I'll say this: working with such a diverse group of people in my earlier days, most of them women, actually gave me insight into something far more important than how to make sneakers. I built a level of trust with all the production people I supervised. I knew their names and their spouses' names and their kids' names, and I made a point to ask their opinions about things going on with production. I respected them, and in return, I think they trusted and respected me—a teenager.

I never evaluated people based on their gender, race, religion, or any other bias. What I learned was most important about people was their attitude and their integrity.

■ ■ ■

Two days before Thanksgiving, each department at Randy's had a drawing for a turkey. Everyone put their name on a ticket and dropped it in a hat. Since I was still the new kid, Herbie pulled me up front to draw the winning ticket. When I pulled out the winner, I looked down to see my name.

I didn't know what to do. Surely people would think I'd peeked or somehow cheated, and in a rush, I told Mr. Cohen, who was standing beside Herbie, "I don't want the turkey."

He smiled and announced, "Paul picked his own name, so he wants to pick again. What a nice kid!"

This time I chose Annie Simense.

Now, refusing a turkey was an easy thing for me to do. I was still under my parents' roof and they still supplied the Thanksgiving turkey, but the women I worked alongside were often the breadwinners for their families. They supported homes and kids and sometimes even their parents. All of my basic needs were met—not to mention that we had made a killing on sparklers that summer.

The turkey drawing shouldn't have been anything more than an anecdote, and I never wanted to make it more than it was, but after that day, Annie would do anything for me at the factory—anytime, any task, no matter what. Somehow—and this was obviously something to be chalked up to a quirk of fate—I had won her loyalty.

Looking back, Annie's devotion might have been less about turkey and more about solidarity. There's just something about working long hours in a factory alongside people who have rolled their sleeves up next to you—it's a special bond.

During all my time at Randy's, seeing Mr. Cohen on the factory floor was a novelty. He was the sort of boss who came around to pass out a few turkeys. I suspected that's how it was with other titans of manufacturing, which is the arena I'd put him in even before he tried to pay me with a hat. Like Henry Ford, who'd died that spring, his mission was less about fostering a positive work environment and more about keeping production lines moving at full tilt. Why not give away a few turkeys and make the workers feel grateful?

He might not have been hated or even feared, but the way he ran his factory drew a clear and unadulterated line between the haves and the have-nots.

Everything we accomplished in the factory was a group effort. Any of our job descriptions might have been fluid enough, and we helped one another when and however we could. I'd gone from being a service boy to a supervisor in only months, but beyond that, I didn't ever once receive a new job title. What I learned at Randy's about how people should treat one another came down to turkey. If you give without the expectation of gain, you receive much more in return. There's just no better test of the quality of someone's character than how they receive, and also how they give.

■ ■ ■

After the factory had been retooled and workers returned, a few things were different from how they had been before, but much was the same. The transition from sewing uppers to producing the whole shoe failed to fix whatever was broken, and after six months it was clear that the company was still in trouble. The Randy's owners were good people, and they had money. The suppliers were competent. The problem was that Randy's was an undisciplined organization.

Maybe they figured that in the first years after the change-over, they'd operate at a loss. That wasn't how I would run things. Production remained sluggish. The new routines we had adopted were messy and inefficient. We were able to process nine hundred pairs of shoes per day. I happened to know that Keds' standard was twenty-four hundred pairs per day.

You can't make any money when you're producing nine hundred pairs per day, but your accountants have costed things out at twenty-four hundred pairs per day. That would have meant that each pair of shoes costed nearly three times the amount budgeted for, which wasn't sustainable, yet no one in management seemed worried about the lack of profits.

They'd had the right idea when they put a second conveyor into the factory. The actual conveyor, what they called the assembly line, was a mechanized belt or chain that moved the shoes through the factory, carrying them up and down the five stories to each floor where one part of the process would be completed. There were twenty-four workers along the conveyor, doing the various jobs to build the finished pair of shoes.

When I came back to Randy's, the first best thing Bob did was put me in the making room on the second conveyor, working as a "laster." My job was to cement the different parts of the shoe onto the foot-shaped metal last. The lasts were hung on a bar, five pairs at a time. There were two bars on each carrier attached to the conveyor; therefore, each carrier held ten pairs.

After I finished cementing the shoes onto the lasts, they were sent along to be dipped in latex, and then the bars were transferred onto big racks and wheeled into the vulcanizer (basically a big oven) to heat cure, which took a few hours.

There were two colors of latex: white for white shoes, and natural for everything else. If you used the wrong color latex for dipping, the finished shoes would turn out looking either old and yellow or dingy and dull. You had to switch the dipping tank every time you wanted to do white shoes, which took five to ten minutes or so to accomplish. We changed tanks back and forth three or four times a day, depending on the orders.

Changing tanks all the time made no sense to me. I told Bob it made more sense to make all the white on one day and all the colored shoes on another day. The packing and shipping guys didn't like that idea. Alternating production days meant they would have to hold an order until all the shoes had been made to fill it.

In other words, they'd have to get organized—so naturally, they protested. Bob overruled them. He thought the idea was worth trying. Sure enough, making that one change saved enough time to noticeably edge up production. Bob was pleased, and I got a promotion. I was put in charge of conveyor no. 2.

■ ■ ■

I learned early on that while the machines we used every day were essential to our work, they were useless without the right people operating them.

In factory work, there is a lot of absenteeism. As a supervisor, I noticed whenever someone was absent on conveyor no. 1, the supervisor borrowed people from conveyor no. 2 to fill the spots, which stands to reason that it threw off my crew on a pretty regular basis.

To solve this, what amounted to a bigger problem, I suggested that Bob hire a couple of utility people who would substitute whenever someone was out. Production increased, of course, because all the positions along both production lines were always filled.

In short order, I made conveyor no. 2 as efficient as humanly possible. I gave pep talks and encouraged my people. I got to know them personally and tried to help if they had a problem. As a result, we started working together as a team, and conveyor no. 2 hit the goal of making twenty-four-hundred pairs per day. At that point, I was promoted to supervising both conveyors.

One of the best things about serving as a supervisor for conveyor no. 2 was working with Gordon Lee. We had stitched uppers together before the shutdown. After the reopening, he ran the machine that wiped in the toe and the heel, what we called the bed laster. The side laster jobs were the next toughest. You had to be a real beast to run that machine. Gordy was ridiculously strong—so strong, in fact, that he came off as dumb—but he wasn't.

Since I had spent February to July making sparklers with my family, his company was especially welcome; but then, everyone liked him. He was the sort of guy who, if you asked him to move a hill, that hill would come down. He was a natural leader and just a hard worker. I thought he'd make a good supervisor, but before there was any hope of that, Gordy left Randy's to take another job.

I was making progress not only as a supervisor, but also on the personal front. Dolly MacLellan worked at Randy's as a clipper. The first time I saw her, she was a vision in yellow, with beautiful brunette hair and a winning smile. One minute I was going about my business and then *bam*, everything crystallized to a watershed in my life. I was eighteen, and the contours of my future were becoming clearer.

It took me a whole year to get up the courage to ask her out. When I did, she said yes. Turned out she was not the least bit shy. She was strong and independent and knew exactly who she was and what she wanted out of life, and she was a high school graduate.

It took me another whole year to save up for a ring, and even longer to talk her into marrying me. In those days, most kids got married right out of high school, so I was way behind in the program. No matter that Dolly's idea of spaghetti sauce was to pour a can of Campbell's tomato soup over pasta; I was determined to marry her. One day in January 1950, we walked down the aisle. I'd never seen a more beautiful bride, and I was sure I was the luckiest man in the world.

My in-laws were a little less sanguine. Dolly's mom, Margaret, was a sweet woman. Luckily, she had taken a liking to me right away. Winning over Dolly's dad took a bit longer. Angus MacLellan was the town blacksmith, a strong, muscular man no one in his right mind would mess with.

Our first year of marriage wasn't easy. Dolly and I were living paycheck to paycheck. One day her dad happened to mention he was going to hire someone to paint his house and pay $500—a fortune—so naturally, Dolly volunteered me. The money would be a huge help.

Angus was still unsure I was good enough for his little girl, and I was equally determined to make a good impression. I started painting at the break of dawn, and when Angus got up that day, I had already finished prepping. He invited me into the house to have a bit of breakfast, but I declined. When Angus came home for his lunch break, I was still painting. He offered me lunch, but again I said no and kept painting.

He seemed surprised I was still painting when he got home at the end of the workday. By then, the only thing left to paint was the very peak of the house gable. Angus insisted on doing that himself because it was at a dangerous height and angle to reach. I guess he didn't want to be responsible for killing his daughter's husband.

When he finished, we stood back and admired the house. I couldn't help but be proud of the job I'd done. The house looked brand-new.

Painting the house had gone a long way in helping us understand each other. From then on, Angus proudly acknowledged that I was a hard worker. That's when I knew I had finally won him over.

My work ethic was always my calling card, in business and in life.

Our first daughter, Kathleen, whom we called Taffy, was born in 1951. Two years later Paul Jr. arrived, and then Steven in 1955. I needed to look to our future as a family.

■ ■ ■

One day at Randy's, Bob confessed, "Paul, we're not going to make it. I cannot get this factory to the point where it's profitable. I honestly don't know what to do."

When I told him that I knew what to do, he rolled his eyes.

"Really. I know what to do."

He admonished me with a chuckle, then shook his head and asked, "Okay, what's that?"

"Let me run the making room," I said.

Bob snorted.

"Don't give me a title," I said. "I'm not asking for a raise. Just let me run it."

He must have been desperate, because by some miracle he told me to go ahead and run the making room, which is where the shoes are finally put together. This was the most important part of the whole process.

Randy's system was to make shoes according to the orders that came in. If the order was five hundred white shoes, two hundred red shoes, and one thousand blue shoes, then that's what they made. When the next order came in, they would start all over again.

This was complicated and time-consuming and required that we change the entire conveyor from one color to another. This entailed hours and hours of downtime and production loss. Workers sat idle while a few people made the changeover. It made no sense.

Orders came in every day. There was enough history to at the very least approximate the average demand for each color and size over a given period of time. Without much guesswork, you could stockpile inventory in advance.

The first best thing I did after taking over the making room was to change how the production schedule was organized. I called the finished production schedule the "ticket." The job of organizing the ticket had been assigned to a nice guy with the wrong skillset. Whoever was in charge of it needed to understand the whole system, what had to be done in which order, and the most efficient time for changing colors and styles. This poor guy, who'd been promoted for no other reason than his seniority, just didn't get it.

Bob wasn't willing to fire the guy or even move him to a different position, so on the sly I started taking the ticket home whenever I could to rewrite it. Eventually, Bob realized what I was doing and gave me the job. What this meant was that instead of changing colors three or more times a day, for one or two full days we'd make white shoes, then the next day or two we'd make blue shoes, and so on. I would adjust the number of days per color until the number of shoes in the warehouse reflected the orders coming in. From there I tackled child sizes, which also demanded that equipment be changed.

When we really got going, we were vulcanizing twice a day. This, too, solved a lot of the factory issues. That said, it didn't solve any of the warehouse issues. Heck, until Bob mentioned it, I wasn't even aware the warehouse had issues. When I took over production, dealing with the big picture sometimes kept my attention away from what was happening on the factory floor, much less the warehouse. This occasionally bit me in the butt.

That's what happened when Dan, a former classmate who ran Randy's fitting room, decided to go rogue. Without prompting or permission, Dan eliminated the arch from all the shoes we were making. He did this for about six months without anyone noticing, and to make things worse, we learned of this indiscretion when Harry, a lead buyer who purchased most of Randy's shoes (we met him in chapter 1), came storming in.

I couldn't blame him. I was horrified when I learned what had been going on, and for how long. I couldn't believe this had happened on my watch. How was it that Dan never mentioned it? Worse, why hadn't I noticed?

When Bob called me into his office and told me I was going to have to fire Dan, I took a deep breath and said if he fired Dan, he would have to fire me, too.

"What are you talking about?"

I couldn't tell if Bob was annoyed or confused. "It's my responsibility to oversee his work. Dan didn't mold the shoes or make the cement for the shoes or pass them through quality control, so everyone else down the line also took part in this disaster. But I was in charge. If Dan goes, I go, too."

Bob was not about to let me go, and Dan kept his job, but now the executives, who never liked me very much, disliked me even more. I wasn't bothered by that—well, not much, anyway. I had the support of the workers on the floor, every single one of them, and that mattered most to me.

Around this time, I happened to hear that Gordy had been fixing his car when it fell on him. He had been injured, and the injuries were severe enough that, in order to recover, he'd had to quit his job. To be clear, I'd rather have one Gordy instead of a whole roomful of Dans. I had really missed Gordy, so when he was well enough, I hired him back to Randy's. I put him in charge of the stitching room, making sure things were being done in the correct order, which had been a problem. Once he started back, those issues disappeared, as I had known they would.

We were doing really great in the making room, but the other departments weren't keeping up. I ended up going from department to department to ensure everything was consistent, so that in every step of the process, each department had a goal of the same number of shoes every single day. We had to ensure that everything was set and ready to begin all over again the following morning.

For things to work, we needed a continuous chain of events. To make that happen, I decided I needed a person from each department to be my liaison. We met every day for fifteen or twenty minutes each morning; this way, every liaison knew what the other departments were doing. I told them not to listen to anyone else—not to Bob or anyone else in management—and to always defer to whatever we'd discussed in that morning's meeting. This way, we got all the production departments on the same team and working together.

If you don't work as a team, you're nowhere. The problem with most people is they don't listen. Sometimes I had to tell people things ten times until they got it right. And when that happened, I could tell immediately I just had the wrong person in the job. By that point in my career as a supervisor at Randy's, though, I rarely picked wrong, because I had developed good instincts about the people I needed on our team. And that's always how I viewed our staff—we were a team.

It had always seemed to me that when someone made it to top management, or to any position with added responsibility, they never hired anyone smarter than themselves. This would expose their incompetence. Too many people holding critical positions in the business and manufacturing worlds are in over their heads.

Case in point: one day the head of the sales department came to a management meeting and announced that, according to the feedback they were receiving, we had an ongoing problem with quality control.

I agreed. We always had too many shoes set aside as seconds, which our inspection and grading routine had deemed subpar. I'd seen those shoes and had my suspicions about the grades, but the top executives handled quality inspections and graded the shoes, not me.

I told Bob I wanted to conduct a test with the executives in charge of the inspections. He obliged, and I took twenty-five shoes and displayed them for the group of execs to inspect and grade. The categories were (1) Reject, (2) Poor, (3) Acceptable, and (4)

Excellent. I gave each person a piece of paper, then we passed the shoes around, one shoe at a time, to be graded. Naturally, I threw in a ringer: one perfectly made shoe.

I passed around the ringer twice. No one noticed the repeat. The vice president of sales first graded that shoe as Poor, and the next time it went around, he graded it Excellent. Even Bob gave that shoe a different grade each time. My experiment proved that we did indeed have a serious quality control problem: the people in charge of quality control had no idea what they were looking at.

If those Randy's execs had started out as workers on the floor, they would have been able to grade those shoes correctly with ease. They would have known exactly what flaws to look for. As it was, they didn't have a clue.

The average factory worker often dislikes top executives because they are almost never willing to get their hands dirty. Most haven't worked their way up in a company, so they aren't familiar with the actual work being done and aren't interested in learning. They prefer to stay in the comfort of their ivory tower.

Back then in Boston, ethnicity mattered to a lot of people. As a Dutch Italian-Catholic dropout, I was discriminated against in my youth. I hate discrimination.

Everyone who didn't belong to the elite consortium of business owners who ran the garment industry was discriminated against. Hard work only got a person so far. Seriously, I can't think of a single instance when someone from the factory was promoted to an executive position.

There was a constant tug-of-war as company policies and politics pitted working men and women against the establishment, which was almost 100 percent male-dominated. It was us against them, and in other industries, you might as well add the dynamic that some workers were union and others weren't.

You might have thought that the short order improvements I had made might have pleased Randy's management and their consortium of suppliers, but that wasn't the case. On the contrary, whenever something I'd suggested panned out, they seemed to dislike me even more. They resented the hell out of an upstart kid who thought he knew better than they did how to run their business.

The thing was, I did know better. Every single time I made a change, profits went up in equal proportion to the executives' annoyance.

Bob was my only ally. He knew I was the main reason for the steady increase in production. As the son of the owner, he hadn't started at the bottom and worked his way up, but he listened. I'm sure he caught a lot of flak for supporting me and defending the systems I proposed, but he liked me and he knew that when I said I would do something, he could let me do it.

He also respected my work ethic. At one point after Dolly and I had several kids, I was feeling as if I had more than I could handle. I had a second job at night on Saturdays. I'd bring my family and we would wash windows and floors in the supermarket. The regular staff used to go in and wash the floor in the market in two and a half hours. We did it in 56 minutes. Why would somebody who'd washed floors all their life not want to do it more efficiently?

I did it that fast by organizing the family force: all of us, including the kids, pitched in. Who's on the water? Who's on the scrub? We found the most efficient way to wash floors. Then Bob found out about it and he gave me a raise, so I wouldn't have to wash floors anymore.

I think the executives were afraid I wanted to wrest control from them and take over the whole factory. I had never intended to run anything myself, never had any ambition to be some big shot, or to open any kind of factory of my own. Despite their steady opposition, Bob boosted me another step up the ladder, and then another. Any promotion I might have earned in the future was an annual 3 percent raise for time served.

I'm not saying I was a maverick or an innovator, and yet absolutely everything that went in the right direction in my years at Randy's was something I had pointed out. I held my own in strengthening Randy's manufacturing efforts.

Not one of my ideas in questioning Randy's processes and standard operating procedures failed, and yet despite our mutual respect, I never got the sense Bob was grooming me for an executive position. Sure, he listened to my ideas, and sure, he took my ideas. I sort of had the run of the place. I followed the rules, and I definitely had management's ears from the get-go, and I really enjoyed the sense of being somewhat untouchable.

But did I want to be in management at Randy's? After the notorious pigeon-chasing encounter with Harry the buyer on the Boston Common, I had to wonder. And there was only so much I could do as a factory supervisor.

Despite our successes, Randy's continued to have problems, and often the problems could not easily be solved by someone at my level of authority. Since I wasn't part of management, I didn't have the power to fire anyone, and that was one area where Bob didn't listen to me. Ever. It seemed as if he was caught between acceding to executive orders or doling out unpleasantries in the name of company efficiency. I respected his loyalty to people who had worked for the company, sometimes for years, but having seniority did not necessarily mean these folks were good at their jobs.

Take the guy who'd been writing the ticket before I took over, or the guy in the costing department who was figuring out the costs wrong. I had to do all the production calculations myself, again on the sly, and act on my own numbers.

People in the purchasing department weren't doing their job correctly, either. They would order the wrong things or the wrong amounts of materials for the number of shoes we were producing that week or month. For some reason, they found it impossible to do simple math.

This caused huge problems. We would regularly run out of something, and production would grind to a halt. I tried over and over to explain to them how to do the calculations, but they just didn't get it. I pulled my hair out. It was an issue that could not be solved because the people involved could not understand the problem.

Unfortunately, that happened all too often, and the result was that management was either forced into the uncomfortable position of letting that person go, or else transferring them to another department where their skills were more suitable. That is, on the rare occasions management was willing to do either of those things.

For the most part, they simply chose to ignore the problems.

That would never be my way.

# CHAPTER FIVE

# Take the Reins

I have always been aware of my own shortcomings and have never had a problem admitting them or taking the advice of experts. I believe honest self-evaluation and the ability to listen to others has been one of my greatest strengths, one that has served me well over the years. If someone had a better idea than mine, of course I would adopt that. I really didn't care if I didn't get credit. I didn't need credit; I needed success.

■ ■ ■

By 1963, I had been at Randy's for more than fifteen years.

Apparently one of Randy's most vexing problems was an ongoing issue with the warehouse and shipping. I'd never worked in either of those divisions. I was always in production, so this was news to me when the situation was brought up in a management meeting I was sitting in on.

It seemed the company was missing a huge number of shoes. Like, almost a million. No one could find them, and it was a total mystery as to where they were. Unbelievable!

An endless discussion ensued as to what was causing the disappearance. Theft had been ruled out because the random quantities of shoes and the timing of their disappearance didn't make sense in that context. Accidentally thrown away, maybe? Perhaps shipped out and invoiced incorrectly? Had green men from outer space—or, more likely, the Russians—swooped down and pirated the shoes away?

Seriously?

I finally said to Bob, "Do you want me to go to the warehouse and straighten this out?"

He said, "Paul, you don't know anything about warehousing."

I shrugged. "Right, but do you want me to go and straighten this out?"

No response. Just a wave of dismissal.

Whatever.

So, of course I went to the warehouse. A smart guy named Skip who had been at school with me ran the operation. I asked him what the heck was going on.

He shook his head and said, "Take a look around. What do you see?"

Clearly no one in management had taken a look around.

When we sold shoes, we shipped them out in cases of twenty-four pairs of the same style and color, but in different sizes, according to what the client had ordered. That was also how they were packed coming off the conveyors. Each case contained the same style and color, but different sizes, depending on what had been produced that day.

When I looked around the warehouse, I saw cases and cases and more cases of shoes, floor to ceiling, neatly arranged by style and color. Cases filled every square inch of every single shelf in the entire warehouse. In fact, there was no empty space left in the warehouse—none at all.

I immediately grasped the issue. "It's full. No place for storage."

What wasn't so obvious was that the actual problem was worse than that.

"Right," Skip said. "But we could deal with that part. We do have just enough space for everyday operations."

"Then what's the problem?" I asked.

"Returns," Skip said.

He went on to explain that whenever a customer returned shoes for whatever reason—maybe a size they'd received didn't match their order, or there was a defect in one of the pairs of shoes—the warehouse staff would grab a replacement pair out of one of the full cases and ship it out to the customer. But then the label on that case would be wrong, and the case wouldn't be full.

To avoid confusion and shipping errors, the broken case had to be set aside, because it was no longer complete and couldn't be used for future shipments. Because there was no set routine in place for dealing with those broken cases, they kept accumulating until there was no space left for anything else.

How had the warehouse crew gone about solving the problem? I asked Skip.

With a grimace, Skip explained that since one of the warehouse workers was active in his church, he had offered to store a bunch of the excess cases in the church basement. When the church ran out of space, someone suggested asking a local hardware store where he knew the owner. When the hardware store's storage room was full, thanks to a worker who was also a volunteer fireman, a load of cases was stored over at the firehouse. After that, still more cases were put in the back room of the local movie theater.

Holy shit! I couldn't believe it. Our shoes were being stored all over the damn town! I suppose you had to give Skip credit for creativity, but why hadn't someone gone to management with the issue in the first place? Maybe they had.

In practice, with the broken cases being stored off-site, it was impossible for the shipping staff to use them when a client had a return that needed a replacement pair. Skip had no choice but to break a new case, thus not only perpetuating the problem, but making it exponentially worse.

My head was starting to ache. I asked Skip, "How do we put this thing right?"

He said, "Easy. You have to 'solid' the warehouse."

I'd actually heard of that. It meant arranging all the shoes in the whole warehouse first by style and color—as we were already doing—but then separating them by size, as well. That meant unpacking the incomplete cases and then repacking them—this was called "double handling"—at least until we could reorganize how they were packed coming off the conveyor.

The idea made perfect sense to me. If we could solid the warehouse and then restructure how cases were packed, the broken cases would slowly disappear—problem solved. Ideally, I thought, we should also get a bigger warehouse.

I called Bob over to the warehouse and had Skip repeat the saga.

When I told Bob we needed to solid the warehouse, he shook his head vehemently. "No way in hell. Are you telling me you want us to unpack and repack every damn pair of shoes we make, every damn day? Is that what you're saying?"

"Yes, Bob, that's exactly what I'm saying."

He said, "You're out of your ever-loving mind. There is no way I'm willing to do that. Do not solid the warehouse, Paul, or I'll fire your ass."

I wasn't happy with his edict. I offered to straighten out the warehouse anyway, on the condition that Bob would leave me alone so I could do it my own way.

We came to an agreement. Bob promised to stay out of my hair for three months, as long as I didn't solid the damn warehouse.

After Bob left the meeting, I turned and said to Skip, "Okay. Now we are going to solid the warehouse."

Skip looked vaguely alarmed. "Bob said not to."

I replied, "I don't care what he said. We have three months to do it." I knew I could lose my job, but it was the right thing to do.

I had told Bob I was going to reorganize the warehouse on a Wednesday. On Thursday, I went out looking for a new location big enough to hold a million pairs of shoes. I found a building on the road from Randolph to Brockton, Massachusetts, so we wouldn't have to switch roads in order to move stock. The building had belonged to Hathaway Baking Company, which had gone out of business.

We emptied out five stories in a building with no elevators. Then we carried up cases of shoes, twenty-four pairs to a pack. You had to be pretty strong to pick up a case and throw it around, but you had to be *really* strong to take it up three, four, or five flights of stairs.

By Thursday night I found some trailer trucks and we loaded them up in Randolph. Then we picked up the shoes at the drugstore and the movie theater and every other place known to man in Randolph that had our shoes.

I was moving trucks fast; I could load a trailer truck in 1.8 minutes. Who could do it fastest? My men were competing: one hundred guys going up and coming down five flights with the cases of shoes. We worked Thursday, Friday, Saturday, and Sunday. I never left. Skip had to go home and sleep, but he was the one who would have to tell us where to put the shoes in the new building. Everybody had to get their sleep except me. I never stopped. I helped unload. I helped carry up shoes. And on Monday morning it was done.

We spent the next three months getting the warehouse in order. Yes, it was a lot: We started with individual pairs of shoes, until we had all the sizes, then a case or two or three or four, with each case containing twenty-four pairs. Once we had eighty-four cases, we could stack them up five high.

Why do I tell this story? The boss was telling me, "Don't do it." I said he was wrong and then I proved it. Most people won't do that—which is why things don't get done.

Three months later, Bob came in, and I offered to walk him around.

He said, "No, I'll go myself." He came back about half an hour later, sat down in the chair, and cried. I had never seen a grown man do this.

He cried. It was all so right.

Bob didn't fire me. Instead, he asked me to run the relatively new Randolph Rubber Company West in Garden Grove, in Southern California. By 1964, Randy's had become the third-largest manufacturer of shoes in the United States. Even though the company had installed new management at the West Coast location, Randy's West was still losing a lot of money.

I would be taking over a plant that had been in business for a few years and had never made a profit. In fact, it lost $5 million in two years, the equivalent of $50 to $100 million today. I was to take charge of the entire production side and right the ship. The move came with a big raise and the title of Vice President.

Still, it wasn't an easy decision to leave the place where I'd spent my whole life. I would have to leave behind my mother and everything familiar to me, including all my lifelong friends in Massachusetts. My friends were like family, and to me, family was everything.

Bob understood, so he offered to fly out with me to take a look at the plant to assess what I was getting myself into. Arriving at the factory, which was still running, it took no more than five minutes to see what was wrong—pretty much everything. Nothing was being done right. For one thing, the various departments didn't communicate with one another. People were running around like chickens with their heads cut off, trying to figure out what to do next.

No wonder the company had lost money!

I told Bob if I accepted the job, it would be on the condition that I got to take at least five people from Randy's East with me, people I had personally trained. It was impossible for me to be everywhere at once in the factory. In order to cover all the bases, I would need people I could trust to oversee the making room, the stitching room, the mill room, and so on.

Bob agreed to my conditions. When I eventually left for California, I was accompanied by my brother Jimmy, my friend Gordy, and three other guys who were outstanding supervisors.

When I announced our move, in hindsight, I know I should have discussed it with Dolly and the kids first. By then, Taffy, Paul Jr., and Stevie had been joined by Janie in 1958, and our youngest, Cheryl, in 1960.

In those days, it was just expected that families followed the dad's job, wherever it would take them. Truthfully, it did not occur to me that my wife and kids might object. I know—totally selfish and Neanderthal. What can I say? Back then, I was pretty clueless in a lot of ways. I learned later that Dolly really struggled with the decision.

The plan was for me to fly out first to get started with the hard work of setting up the factory before the family arrived. I would be there for six months before they joined me. I figured, given that amount of time, if things didn't work out, I could always quit and come back to Massachusetts before uprooting them.

With a crew of five, I worked nonstop to reset the factory. I had so much to learn in this new role. I knew nothing about administrative things like accounting; and even if that wasn't my responsibility, I wanted to understand more for my own peace of mind.

When I moved out to California in advance of the family, I purchased a house in Costa Mesa on a peaceful cul-de-sac fairly close to the Randy's West factory. It was a typical California-style rambler, the first one-story house any of us had ever lived in. The neighbors were great, and the street was full of other kids, so I knew mine would make many friends. They were starting to build a brand-new high school close by, and I calculated that Taffy would be part of its very first graduating class.

At the time, I couldn't have known our family would end up living in that house for almost forty years.

Since my kids deserved something really special for having to pull up roots and move three thousand miles from home, friends, and beloved grandparents, I decided to have an in-ground swimming pool installed in the backyard of the house. It was big and beautiful, with shiny tile. I couldn't wait to see the looks on the kids' faces the first time they saw it.

Then one day I looked at the calendar and got a real shock. I had been so busy working to put the factory to rights that I had totally lost track of time. The six months was up. I'd neglected to set up the house for the family.

On top of that, the moving truck with all of the furniture from Massachusetts was due to arrive the next day, just one day before the family was flying in. I looked around the house and saw nothing but unpacked boxes. Tomorrow would be even worse, with many boxes and rooms of furniture being delivered.

I really had to hustle to get everything in place. The next day, the moving truck arrived. For most of that night, I set up furniture and unpacked every single box. When I was finally done in the wee hours of the morning, I thought the house looked like a model home.

As I eagerly awaited the family's arrival in the morning, the last thing I did before leaving to pick them up at the airport was to shut the blinds in the living room, blocking out the view of the newly installed pool. I wanted it to be the biggest, most fantastic surprise of the kids' lives.

I suspected that the kids were still unsure about the move. I really wanted them to be happy here. To make an extra-good first impression, on the way home from the airport, I stopped at a big toy store and told them they could get anything they wanted.

Their eyes got big, and smiles broke out all around. With a whoop, Paul Jr. went right to the model cars and planes, and Stevie headed straight for the section with army men and trucks. I couldn't help grinning when I saw the girls had taken a wagon and were going up and down the aisles filling it with all sorts of toys and games.

Dolly and I just rolled our eyes and laughed.

When we got to the house, the kids sprinted in every direction, calling out all the new things they discovered in each room. To my horror, the first thing Stevie did was run into the living room, shouting, "What's out back?"

He flung open the blinds, exposing a panoramic view of the gorgeous new pool. Then he shouted, "Guys! We live in a mansion!"

There went my carefully guarded surprise.

Of course, it turned out just fine because the kids were all totally shocked, excited, and overjoyed. Seeing their reactions to having an honest-to-goodness in-ground pool in their very own backyard told me they were going to love living the California life.

No surprise, they did. What was not to love? This was California in the sixties, the land of endless sun, snazzy convertibles, and the Beach Boys. As I'd hoped, the transition from the East Coast to West Coast turned out to be an easy one for all of us.

Steve remembers vividly not only his first sight of the pool, but also a trip we took to Disneyland. It put family trips to Paragon Park in Nantasket, south of Boston, in perspective. As he put it, "To see [Paragon Park] compared to Disneyland, was like putting a strawberry up against the biggest watermelon you'd ever seen in your life."

We may have had fun, but like my father before me, I made sure my kids knew how to work.

Back in Massachusetts, I had gotten into the habit of washing my car at least once a week. As the kids got old enough, they would come out and help. I would hose and they would wipe.

Since the weather in California was nice virtually all year round, I expanded the family tradition. Every day when I got home from work, I would call out, "Hey, kids! Dad's home!" and everyone would troop out to the driveway with buckets and hoses.

I taught them how to go over both the exterior and the interior of the car and clean off every speck of dirt and grime. Janie and Cheryl were still pretty young, but I arranged them by height, assigning them tasks they could easily reach. Cheryl was smallest, so she got hub cap duty. That was her job for the first few years.

It might sound like I was a slave driver, but we had a lot of fun splashing and sudsing and catching up with what everyone had done that day.

Once the kids got the hang of cleaning the car thoroughly, I had them do it by themselves while I watched. If it wasn't done right the first time, I would wet the car again and we would wash it all over again. If necessary, we'd do it yet again until it was done right.

After we finished washing the car, often I would take them out for ice cream, which of course they loved. We followed this same routine most every day for years. It didn't take too long before the car was sparkling clean the first time around, and it also established our beloved Van Doren tradition of having dessert first, and then eating dinner afterward, which we are all still fond of doing to this day.

They learned to do things right the first time, something I'd learned from my own father. My daughter Cheryl says, "It taught us responsibility, and that there was no value in not doing things the right way."

To this day, my kids' cars are always clean—most of them, anyway.

Little did we know that in just one short year of our California dream, our fate would take a drastic, unexpected turn, and our orderly lives would be upended.

■ ■ ■

One of the first things I had to do at Randy's West was raise the quality of our materials. A lot of the stuff they had been using to make their shoes was pure crap.

We had been importing materials from Serge D'Elia, a wealthy Belgian entrepreneur living in Japan. He had inherited an import-export business there from his late father. The former management at Randy's West had contracted him to supply our canvas tennis shoe uppers. One of his Japanese subcontractors was stitching them for him at a cost of 35 cents a pair. They were made less expensively than we could stitch them in California, but they were the worst quality I'd ever seen. The uppers rattled like pieces of paper crinkling.

I estimated that in the past at Randy's East, it had cost us about 80 cents for the material and labor to completely stitch a pair of uppers. Serge was selling uppers from Japan for 35 cents! Incredible, but unfortunately, his uppers were completely useless.

If Serge's company was going to make the uppers for Randy's West, I wanted it done right. I devised a simple sample kit that would instruct anyone on how to stitch a tennis shoe upper correctly.

First, I took all the parts of an upper, such as quarters, tongues, eyelet stays, and the heel, and I put them in an envelope marked no. 1. My next step was to stitch two quarters together and put them in an envelope marked no. 2. I continued along each step until the upper was completed correctly so that even a kid could make a tennis shoe upper properly.

Then I contacted Serge D'Elia for a meeting. He asked to meet on the following Sunday. I tried not to work on Sundays so I could be with my family, but he was coming all the way from Japan, so I agreed. When we sat down together, Serge started babbling on and on about how he could do anything, get me anything I needed.

I was getting steamed just listening to him. Clearly, he couldn't do everything well or the uppers he was sending us would be made a whole lot better.

Finally, I interrupted: "Mr. D'Elia, I have a whole warehouse of uppers I have to throw away. They are the worst crap I have ever seen."

I started to give him my sample.

He stopped me cold when he shrugged and said, "That's what they asked for."

How could I blame Serge if he'd made what they asked for? I eased up on him and we wound up talking things over amicably.

We agreed to start working together. I gave him my samples and the right formulas for the shoe paste, and then I showed him what to do so that everything would turn out perfectly.

After that, Randy's West got all our uppers from Serge. He was still charging us just 35 cents a pair, even for the new and improved version. That meant a 45-cent gain for us compared with Randy's East. That was when we finally started to get over the hump to profitability.

There were still so many other problems to fix at Randy's West. I was talking to one of our supervisors, George Felix, and mentioned that there were whole nights when I couldn't sleep from worry.

George looked at me, pursed his lips, and said, "Have you been doing the best that you can, Paul?"

I nodded. "Sure. Of course I have."

He raised a brow and asked, "Are you still doing the best you can?"

Surprised he even had to ask, I assured him, "Yes, I am."

"Okay," George replied. "So then, what the hell are you so all-fired worried about?"

That was a simple statement, but his words finally penetrated my thick head. They made a lot of sense. All I could do was my very best. Anything else was beyond my control and not worth losing sleep over.

After that, I stopped worrying and I never lost sleep again.

That's not to say I wasn't still pulling out my hair in frustration over ongoing problems, like the damn labor union. At Randy's East, we hadn't had a union. Here, the California plant had the rubber labor union, and when I took over, they had 250 grievances lodged with Randy's management. In no way am I saying that any number of the complaints weren't justified, but in my opinion, a union wasn't necessary when management and workers did the right thing and treated each other with respect.

I understand that unions are there to protect workers from owners who take advantage of the people working for them, who don't pay them time and a half for overtime. If you've got a bad owner, you probably need a union. But if you've got a good owner, you don't need a union.

Personally, I don't like unions. I don't like somebody telling me what I can and can't do with my own company—that goes against my grain. Even when I was a kid and heard union people saying an owner could hire this one or couldn't hire this one, it rubbed me the wrong way. Hiring was the owner's responsibility, not the union's.

I took over a plant that had been in business a few years and never made a profit. I was focused on trying to keep Randy's afloat—to find a more efficient way to save a few pennies. The management there hadn't been controlling all the important ingredients: costs and the warehouse. If you don't control your warehouse, you're going to go out of business. Worst of all, from my point of view, they weren't controlling their production line, either.

When I'd first walked into the place with Bob Cohen, I could see the problem immediately: the teams weren't working together. Every department was independent and had nothing to do with the next one. All those departments produce things that help you make the shoe. And you can't make the shoe if you're missing an arch, for example. Each department has to work in concert with the other. At Randy's West, none of the departments were finishing their work because other departments hadn't finished theirs. The current situation was ridiculous, and if it continued, we'd all be out of our jobs.

I knew what to do. When I ran the production at Randy's East, I never hid out in an office. I was out on the floor getting my hands dirty. Now in California, my Randy's team and I had been trying to tell the employees how we had to do things the right way if we wanted to improve production. I realized that talking about the right way to do things just isn't enough—I was going to have to show them.

So I hired some guys I trusted, and we stayed in the factory all night tackling unfinished work, going from the packing room to the fitting room to the mail room until we caught everybody up.

By around 7:00 a.m. the next day, every department had finished a ticket, which meant the maker rooms had everything they needed to complete a whole day's work.

When workers arrived that morning, I told everybody, "Look around. You didn't finish your job, so we stayed here and did it for you..This is how we're going to work together from now on. You've got to get your job done so everyone down the line can do theirs."

People listened to me because I wasn't just telling them to do the work. I'd gone in and done it with them.

The plant electrician, who happened to be the head union guy, was not happy. We understood he was already against us when he said, "You cannot change these systems. You're making production go more than three miles an hour."

Whatever the hell that meant. Apparently, there was some kind of union limit on how fast things could move on an assembly line. Who could possibly tell what three miles an hour was? It made no practical sense. We weren't sure what to do.

The six of us went into the administrative office and talked about it for five minutes. Then I said, "Screw it. This factory is my responsibility now, and I'm going to damn well do whatever needs to be done to make it work."

When we went back out, the union guy was up on his ladder. He almost fell off it when I told him loudly, "We will do exactly what we have to do, and sorry, your union has no say over us."

He didn't like that, but he kept his mouth shut for the rest of the day. However, he watched us like a hawk from then on, trying to find issues to complain about.

One of the things I happened to agree with the union guy about was the need to get rid of the three industrial efficiency experts the former management had hired. Their job was to use stopwatches to time all the workers to see how fast they were working. Maybe they knew what three miles an hour meant.

There is nothing in the world worse than someone putting a timer on some poor schmuck who is just doing his job on the assembly line. He's just not going to perform as well as he could or should. He knows damn well that if he goes too fast, you're going to make the daily quota way too tough for him. If you're watching and timing him, he's just going to dog it, and work at 75 percent instead of 100 percent.

Pretty soon you have everyone else along the line just dogging it, too. Not good.

I didn't want anyone using a stopwatch on my people. I went onto the floor and saw one of the experts timing the workers as usual. I told him I did not want any stopwatches in my plant. He looked at me blankly.

I came back an hour later and he was still time-studying with the damn watch. I took it out of his hand, dropped it on the floor, and smashed it with my heel.

Astonished, he asked me, "How are you going to figure out the rates and the quotas?"

I shook my head and waved my arm toward the staring workers. "You just ask them."

After that, the efficiency experts all quit.

I knew how fast my people worked because I was always on the floor with them. One of the workers I had gotten to know was a cutter named Joe. I knew he did ten cuts a minute, so he wasn't going to tell me eight. If he did, I would say, "Come on, Joe, I know your rate. I'm going to pay you right, and I know it's really ten."

Even if he could actually do fourteen cuts, he was only telling me ten. That was okay, because I implemented a piecework system whereby the faster the people worked and the more they produced, the more we paid them.

They did the calculations, just like Joe, and were thrilled when they realized they could now work six hours and get paid for what took eight hours under the old system. It was a great incentive to keep at it and strive to increase their speed even more. I was able to adjust the daily quotas to reflect what the workers could truly do at a reasonable pace.

The workers were happy to be making more money, and I was happy with the increased production, but the union wasn't so happy. They were losing their grip on the factory because no one was complaining about management anymore. They kept making trouble, trying to stir up the workers against us.

At one point one of the advisors at the plant said to me, "Honestly, I don't know how you are ever going to defeat the union."

I knew I wouldn't have to; the workers themselves would do it when they realized I was on their side, which I was.

I told the advisor, "Not a problem. I plan to organize this plant my way, same as back East, and everything will work out fine."

I decided to create an incentive plan for the benefit of the workers. Essentially, if they could complete eight hours of work in six hours, they would be free to go home.

This was a system I'd started several years ago at Randy's East. When I had initially brought the idea to Bob Cohen, he'd said it was the stupidest thing I had ever thought of. "Don't you realize that if you let the workers go home early, they are just going to want more work so they can make more money?" he exclaimed.

Wrong.

I convinced Bob to give it a try for three months, to see what would happen. He reluctantly agreed, but he said that as soon as the people started asking for more work, he was shutting it down, pronto.

"Deal," I said. I knew my people, and I knew that was never going to happen.

Sure enough, not one soul in all those years, not a single one, ever asked for more work. Hell no. After getting out early, they were all sitting in the pub or at home with their spouse, drinking beer and celebrating the fact we were paying them for eight full hours while they were only putting in six.

The reason I had developed the idea of incentives in the first place was because I'd had a problem with production quotas versus quality. When I focused on production numbers, quality went down. When I worked on quality, production went down. It was frustrating.

Finally, I convinced the workers that if they produced the quota for eight hours of work and made whatever parts they were assigned to produce at top quality, but did it in fewer hours, they were free to go home early that day.

At first the workers were all skeptical. I mean, what factory did stuff like that? It took a few days before one of the ladies gave it a try. Sheila Wilson completed her work in six hours, then waved me over to inspect her production. Every eye in the house was on us by this time. Thankfully, the shoe parts she made that day were all top quality.

I smiled broadly and said, "Thank you, Sheila. You are free to go for the day."

Eyes popped wide all around the production floor. They couldn't believe I'd meant what I promised.

It didn't take more than another week before everyone else had gotten on board and finished their work in six hours, all while keeping quality up to the highest standard.

I was triumphant.

We eventually reached the point where we agreed that if the workers accumulated enough hours, we'd allow them to take Friday off. The goal was to make in four days what used to take five days. This meant they worked a four-day week but were paid for five days. As long as they maintained their production quotas and quality, everyone was a winner.

I put the same plan in motion in California. Again, it didn't take very long for the workers to realize I would deliver what I'd promised. They embraced the new system, and when they were given the opportunity to vote on whether or not to be controlled by the union, the result was unanimous. They voted the union out.

From that point on, I could do no wrong in the eyes of the plant advisor or the workers.

Everyone at Randy's West was finally on the same team. This was a major change: the workers were now winners, and so was management. The new system cut down their hours at work while putting more money in their paychecks, and for us in management, production—and profitability—was steadily going up.

Pretty soon Randy's West was killing it. In eight short months, we had turned the place completely around, and our fledgling factory was doing even better than Randy's East.

When Bob told me that bit of news, you can bet I was proud as hell. Take that, you pompous management assholes! I could hear that Bob was extremely happy, too. I'm sure he'd had to wade through buckets of crap from them when he'd made me a VP.

Being in charge was really teaching me a lot. In addition to the factory and admin skills I was picking up, day by day I was also increasing my skills at dealing with people.

After working hand in hand with the factory employees to improve conditions while increasing productivity, I had learned to read many of them just by looking at the expressions on their faces. If I asked, "What's wrong?" and someone replied, "Oh, it's nothing," I would say, "I can see on your face that it's not nothing. It's something," and eventually we had built enough trust that they would share their thoughts with me.

For example, my friend Joe had worked an hour overtime, and he was down because he didn't get that extra hour's credit on his paycheck. I learned about it only because he had "that look" on his face and wasn't his usual cheerful self. I asked what was wrong, he told me, and I took care of it immediately. Just as quickly, he was back to his old self.

When people know you truly care, everyone comes out ahead.

We were still working through the many problems at the factory, of course. One of them was with the delivery system. I discovered to my astonishment that when a client ordered one hundred pairs of shoes, we were only shipping that dealer around sixty-five pairs. What was up with that?

Yep. We were back to warehouse problems.

When the guys in shipping couldn't find the right styles or sizes in the warehouse—which was apparently every time they filled an order, because the place was so damned disorganized—they shipped the order out anyway.

Having learned the hard way how to reorganize a warehouse, I corrected that situation right away.

Soon afterward, things in shipping started to run smoothly and efficiently, and finally the correct number of shoes in the orders would go out, but doing so had a few unexpected consequences.

For one thing, because we were now shipping every dealer the number of pairs they had actually ordered, instead of just the 65 percent, our accounting books immediately picked up another 35 percent in sales. That was a good thing.

However, our efficiency created a new problem for the dealers. They were accustomed to receiving only a portion of their order, so they had always compensated by ordering a lot more than they actually needed. Now when they received the full order, they suddenly had way too many shoes in stock, and nowhere to store them. It took a while for them to recalibrate and get in the habit of ordering the correct number of shoes.

Once things settled down and clients got used to our new shipping process, they were much more satisfied customers. No more guesswork.

■ ■ ■

I was learning that the California shoe market was a lot different from back East. Because of the amazing weather, people wore tennis shoes year-round, and not just for playing tennis. I steered Randy's into doing more colors to cater to the SoCal market. I had also put out a specialized skateboarding shoe called the Randy's 720. Unfortunately, it didn't sell very well because management in the East insisted it only be sold in specialty sports stores. The shoes were largely unavailable to the kids who might have actually used them.

In the summer of 1964, I tried to increase awareness of our coolest styles by setting up a Randy's booth at the US Open of Surfing held in Huntington Beach. The legendary Hawaiian surfer and father of the sport, Duke Kahanamoku, was there.

An expert swimmer, Duke won his first gold medal and broke the world record for the hundred-meter freestyle at the 1912 Olympics. One of the first American athletes to challenge the color barrier, he went on to win five Olympic swimming medals. In 1925, he saw a fishing vessel capsize off the coast of Corona del Mar in California. With an act of heroism that garnered national headlines, he paddled out on his surfboard and rescued eight people.

That day at the US Open of Surfing, Duke Kahanamoku was there along with Fred Hemmings, a world champion surfer who went on to become a Hawaii state senator later in life, as well as Butch Van Artsdalen, Corky Carroll, and Paul Strauch. They were all wearing matching blue Hawaiian shirts.

When Duke Kahanamoku came by our booth to check out the shoes, I introduced myself. Looking at those shirts, I was suddenly struck by an idea.

"Say, I could make you a pair of sneakers that match your shirt, if you'd like," I told Duke cheerfully. "It would only take me a couple hours." The factory was just a few miles up the street, after all.

The Duke's eyes widened in pleasure. "Paul, that's great!" he said, then motioned to Fred Hemmings and told him, "Come here and give Paul your shirt."

For the rest of the day, poor Fred ran around without a shirt, not that the ladies objected, I'm sure. Duke got his shoes, and we got some good exposure with the surfer community.

All in all, I felt I'd been doing a great job, along with the team I'd brought with me from Randy's East. We had every reason to believe that Bob, now the owner, and the other stakeholders back East were pleased with the excellent progress we were making.

Apparently, some things never changed.

One day in February 1965, out of the clear blue, Bob called and told me that he had decided to promote two of the Randy's West management staff and would be making them assistant vice presidents.

Those guys had been a big part of the reason the former company had been failing.

After I got over the shock, I said, "Bob, you can't do that. You have loyal employees who have worked at Randy's for a dozen years and more." Men like Jimmy and Gordy, or any one of the other guys I'd brought out with me, or even many people working at the Massachusetts plant. "How can you promote these two guys we had to show how to do everything right, and who were never successful at their previous jobs? They lost millions of dollars!"

Bob replied simply, "It's my company. My decision."

God knows why he made this stupid decision. He may have been under pressure from the old coalition back East who still hated me and everything I did, or possibly there was some other circumstance I wasn't aware of.

The reason didn't matter. Bob was making a giant mistake on many levels. A mistake I just couldn't live with.

I told Bob, "This is wrong. I can't let you do it."

His response was, "I'm sorry you feel that way, Paul, but it's my company, and I'm going to do it." This from a guy who went to work in the morning and was home before noon.

"All right, Bob," I said. "In that case, I quit."

If I had expected Bob to change his mind or somehow talk me out of leaving, as he'd always done before, I was destined to be sorely disappointed.

He didn't say a word other than, "Okay, Paul. If that's what you have to do."

That was the end of my career at Randy's, and the start of the biggest adventure of my life.

# CHAPTER SIX

# Never Waste an Opportunity

I have always found that there are basically two kinds of people. The first kind will tell you all the reasons why a certain thing cannot be done, and the second kind will start formulating ways to accomplish that very same thing. Usually within two minutes of meeting a person, I can tell which category he or she falls into.

From Day One, anyone I hired had to think positively. I never wanted to work with people who told me why something couldn't be done—even if they were right. If someone told me they couldn't get into the backyard, I would say, "Jump over the fence." I didn't want to just hear "I can't," because complaining that a task was impossible was a waste of analytical time. If you don't believe you can succeed, you surely won't. It's as simple as that.

Really, I have found the only reason things don't get done is because someone doesn't want to do them. Mark my words: where there's a will, there's always going to be a way—at least eventually.

That's not to say that everything always works out, that you win every single challenge. There's always the chance for failure. Each and every day that we live, we roll the dice.

But what in life isn't a gamble? And if it's worth a risk, isn't it worth some effort?

■ ■ ■

I'd taken a big gamble in quitting my job at Randy's. I had no idea what other job I could possibly do. All I had ever done was make canvas shoes. Could I really start my career completely over at the age of thirty-five? It was a daunting prospect.

As I drove home, reality hit me hard. I had slammed shut a very big door, and there was no going back. Ever. I thought to myself, what in the world was I going to do now? I dreaded telling Dolly and the kids.

Thankfully, my mom had drilled good money management skills into me when I was a kid, so I had built up a healthy savings account in California. Financially, we would be okay until I found other employment.

When I got home, I sat Dolly down in her favorite chair, lined up the kids to sit on the fireplace hearth, and broke the news to them that Daddy was now unemployed.

To her immense credit, Dolly didn't panic. She had taken a chance on a Dutch boy when her father wasn't so sure about me, and she wasn't going to bail now.

She just took a deep breath and said, "Okay. I guess it's baked beans for dinner for a while."

The kids, of course, didn't really understand what was going on, or about how serious things might get. They took their cues from Dolly and me. By unspoken agreement, we both acted as if this was just a little bump in the road.

I told my family I had some ideas. I also stressed there wouldn't be any "Can I"s: "Can I have this?" or "Can I have that?" Everybody got the point that they weren't to ask for anything then, because we all had to hunker down and get through.

I knew with certainty I had done the right thing by quitting, but I won't lie—I was more than a little scared. The future was one immense black hole of the unknown.

Fate turned out to be firmly on my side, thank God.

As it happened, Serge D'Elia, now a good friend, called me from Japan two hours later, that very same night. Total coincidence? Maybe. But after hanging up, I found myself starting to believe in miracles.

Serge listened to my tale of woe, let me vent my anger at the injustice, and reassured me that everything would be okay. Talking with him was some sort of grace—a reprieve to catch my breath, to think clearly, to strategize. Serge was a smart guy and a shrewd businessman. He could cut to the heart of a matter and suggest courses of action better than almost anyone I knew. I figured that if anyone could help me figure out what to do with myself now, it was Serge.

After we talked for a while, he asked if I would like to get together to discuss possible plans for the future. I had wrongly assumed he would drop in for a visit on his next trip to the States. Instead, he said he was going to send me an airline ticket to fly to Japan next week and would book an open ticket for my return. On him.

I was a bit shocked. It sounded great. I'd never been abroad before but I knew it was a long flight to Japan, which would give me ample time to think about my situation. I was extremely grateful for his generosity. A few days later, the tickets arrived with a letter.

*From the desk of Serge M. D'Elia*
*Kobe, Japan, February 3, 1966*

*Dear Paul,*

*As promised, I enclose herewith a return ticket Los Angeles—Kobe—Los Angeles and look forward to having you here as my guest as long as our discussions take.*

*As you already know, there is practically unlimited potential for trade between Japan and the US, and with a good man on either end of the line, there is no reason why part of its potential could not be turned to our mutual advantage.*

*Your coming over in no way engages you nor does it constitute a commitment on my part. I just happen to feel that for two people who seem to understand each other and work together as smoothly as we do, there are definitely many interesting possibilities to be explored. I will be extremely happy if you will accept my invitation and come over at the earliest possible time so that we may explore them together.*

*The enclosed ticket is open. You can make your own reservations when ready by calling any Japan Airlines booking agent in or around Los Angeles and asking for space on one of their flights to Tokyo via Hawaii, by telling them that you hold open ticket No. 1314-1384359. Although it is a slightly longer flight via Hawaii than it would have been via San Francisco, I felt you would prefer it this way as it will give you a chance to drop off in Honolulu for a few days on the way home, if you feel like it.*

*As soon as you have your reservations, call me collect or cable, giving me date, flight number, and time of arrival in Tokyo, and I'll meet you at the airport there.*

*I remain,*
*Sincerely,*
*Serge*

When I landed, Serge met me and drove us to his home in Kobe. For five days we tossed around ideas, the most obvious being about sneakers. Making canvas shoes was what I knew best. Hell, making canvas shoes was the only thing I knew. After twenty years, I had learned every aspect of the sneaker business. I could make them in my sleep and suggested starting a small sneaker factory in Southern California.

Most of Randy's business was still back East, so the new venture should be kept small, and very much local. Given free rein to hire my own people, to build my factory from the ground up, and to run things as I saw fit—and no chasing after pigeons—I was confident the business would be a success. Serge was wealthy and looking for a good, profitable investment. We had known each other for more than a decade, and he trusted me. It could work.

After thoroughly discussing our views on business, ethics, and principles, Serge and I were confident we had much in common. He trusted my abilities. Most important, he believed in me. I was somewhat astounded by all that was happening. And flattered—not to mention more than a little terrified at the thought of starting my own business.

But I knew I would be completely insane not to seize this opportunity with both hands and run with it—before he changed his mind. Serge agreed to invest the $250,000 I'd need to start up the business. We shook on it, and the Van Doren Rubber Company was born.

The outbound flight was as long as the inbound flight. I had more time to think. If I was being honest, I had to admit that I'd never dreamed of opening my own shoe business and competing with Randy's, not to mention Keds and Adidas, companies that had been around forever. I never had that kind of lofty ambition. More to the point, even if I'd wanted it, I would never have had the financial means to start my own company.

Now I did.

From our first discussion of the business, Serge and I settled on making whole shoes and making them right. In the beginning, our manufacturing and fulfillment process was simple: our employees would make the shoes in the factory, and we would sell them straight out of the attached factory store.

Other than informing Dolly and the kids, I didn't have anyone else to tell. I definitely didn't want word to get back to Bob about the new competition in town. I needed to keep my plans a secret as long as possible. Jimmy and Gordy were still working for Randy's. After filing all the paperwork, I needed to put together the actual factory where we would make the shoes. There were no existing factories available for sale, so I'd be starting completely from scratch.

Before long, I found a good location on East Broadway in Anaheim. I leased a sprawling, one-story warehouse. I would need to contend with a bunch of flimsy interior structures, but the building itself had tall, solid bones and an arched roof that was somehow supported with no columns or posts in the middle. The best part was that there were no stairs to climb. The warehouse was pug-ugly and rundown, but with a little spit and a little shine, it would fix up nicely.

As usual, the new venture was a family affair. Dolly's parents and her brother flew to California to help. Angus and our daughter Taffy were in charge of clearing out the debris. My brothers Jimmy and Paul, Dolly's brother Danny, and Danny's friends dealt with anything having to do with carpentry and construction. Stevie was the gofer, and I served as lackey. Later, when the arduous task of painting presented itself, he and I got our first promotions to painting crew.

One of Stevie's early jobs had been to take a scraper and pry all the layers of cooked-on rubber gunk from the machinery I had secured and Jimmy had had delivered. As we unpackaged each piece, Stevie would meticulously work his way around and under the machines, freeing them from years' worth of rubber drippings and dirt. By the end of the day, he looked like a giant, grayish Wham-O Superball. During those early days, his lunch was unlimited tacos.

We built a half dozen defined spaces within the factory for pro-duction rooms, plus an office and a warehouse storage area. It took months of hard labor to get the whole inside of the warehouse in decent shape. Even my father-in-law pitched in. Angus McClellan built us a scaffolding so that we could climb the twenty-five-foot walls and reach the vast, domed ceiling.

Stevie and I followed along after the carpentry crew finished and painted the entire inside of the factory. Navajo white was the color of choice. Ten years old at the time, Stevie recalls that the two of us would push the scaffolding five or eight feet and paint for an hour, then we'd move it another five feet and continue painting. We painted the whole inside of the entire factory, around eighteen thousand square feet, in a week.

Cheryl and Janie pitched in, too, painting the lower sections of the walls.

Stevie complained about having to paint that huge factory with just a paintbrush and roller. Hell, I didn't like doing it any more than Stevie did, but what choice did we have? We needed every penny of Serge's investment to buy machines, equipment, and materials to start production. We didn't have spare money to hire workers to do things we could do ourselves.

Luckily, I happened to mention our whole exhausting painting ordeal to my brother Robert on the phone one evening. Puzzled, he asked, "Why don't you just rent a paint sprayer?"

I blinked. "A what?"

This windfall of information was an epiphany. My brother had just taught me one of the most important business lessons: you don't know what you don't know, and if you don't know, ask. Christ on a stick. I'd had no idea such a thing as a paint sprayer existed,

NEVER WASTE AN OPPORTUNITY **97**

but you can believe first thing the next morning, I tracked one down at a local rental place. It was too late to do the inside walls with it, but we banged out the building's entire exterior in a single day with that sprayer.

So far, the Van Doren Rubber Company had been a lot of really hard work, and I was beginning to think it might be a really good idea to bring a partner into the business with me. This project was already super stressful, and we were just getting started. We hadn't even made a dent in acquiring the machinery we would need. I couldn't expect a handful of kids and family volunteers, no matter how generous and capable, to get an entire factory up and running, let alone help me with production once it got going. I had been to-tally unrealistic to think I could do it all myself.

Serge was strictly the money guy. I was the factory expert. He'd left all the practical and logistical stuff to me. Sure, we discussed most everything, but phone calls to Japan were expensive, and I didn't want to bother him with every little detail.

I realized I needed someone here in California to help with the practical aspects, the everyday decisions, and the pure physical effort of setting up the Van Doren Rubber Company. People who'd have a personal stake in the business doing well, so they'd give it their all.

I thought long and hard about the best choice as a partner. I considered my brother Robert. He was a whiz at mechanics and had even worked at Randy's for a while, but by then he'd started his own business making machine parts, and it was doing well. He wouldn't want to give that up. Bernice and Johnny knew nothing about shoes, so they were out of the question.

My brother Jimmy was living in California with his wife. He had moved out here with me to start Randy's West, and he'd been helping me set up the new factory tirelessly. He was also just about the smartest person I knew, an engineer and an expert machinist. What's more, he knew how to make tennis shoes.

So did my good friend Gordon Lee. He was strong, capable, and the most loyal person on the planet. If you gave him a task, he would move heaven and earth to get it done. Having someone that hardworking as a partner would be invaluable, and he and his family were already living in California.

Both Jimmy and Gordy had been part of the original team I'd brought out here from Randy's East, but which one would be best? Then again, did I really have to choose? Why not take on more than one partner? I thought the two of them together would be a perfect, balanced addition to the Van Doren Rubber Company.

I called up Serge and suggested we bring in both Jimmy and Gordy as partners. He thought about it and also concluded it would be a good idea.

We worked out that I would have a 40 percent share of the company because I was doing the bulk of the work. Jimmy and Gordy would each have 10 percent for their contributions, and Serge would have 40 percent for being our investor.

I was excited. Now I felt things could really get rolling, and the factory building was slowly coming together. I'd hired a few engineers and other professionals to do the jobs that needed experts to complete. Angus and Danny had returned home to the Boston area long ago, so Gordy, Jimmy, my two boys, and I took care of everything else.

At last, the whole place looked awesome, inside and out. Well, maybe not awesome, but clean, organized, freshly painted. Now all we needed was the equipment to make the shoes.

While we had some office furniture and a few pieces of used equipment, we still needed to acquire the bulk of the shoe fabrication machines for the factory, including the most critical part—the vulcanizer. Our vulcanizer had to be a really good one or the quality of the finished shoes would be subpar. I was determined that the construction of our shoes would be superior to anything else on the market.

I realized it would take forever to assemble everything we needed for the factory if I had to acquire it one piece at a time. I needed to buy an entire factory, one that was closing down for whatever reason and wanted to divest itself of the whole kit and caboodle.

Pretty much every shoe factory in the country at that time, running or shut down, was on the East Coast. So I flew back home to Massachusetts to see what I could dig up. I had a contact who dealt in used machinery. I gave him a call with my fingers crossed.

Sure enough, Dave knew of a guy in Rhode Island who was selling off used equipment from his father's shoe factory. When he told me what they had on offer, it was too good to be true. In a torrential rainstorm, I hightailed it to destiny. This day is one that will forever stick out in my mind and heart.

The machinery turned out to be exactly the pieces we needed. Exactly. Lasts, dies, patterns, sewing machines, rollers, everything, and the vulcanizer, the coveted vulcanizer was the biggest one available—far more than I had ever expected to find in one place. And it was all the best you could buy, in really good shape.

Apparently, this guy's father had owned a shoe manufacturing plant and had expected the son to take over when he retired, but the son had no interest in it, so the factory was shut down. The dad had held out hope and put all the manufacturing equipment into storage, just in case. I wanted it all. Desperately. I pulled out my brand-new company checkbook and a pen.

"I can write you a check for sixty-five thousand dollars right now," I said with a big smile. I knew it was a low offer, but it was pretty much all we had left.

He frowned, then shook his head. "I've already an offer for three hundred fifty thousand dollars. I just have to get it all down to South America."

My heart sank. That $350,000 was a whole lot more than we had. I couldn't even dicker with him when we were so far apart.

There have only been two times in my life when I have asked for divine intervention. This was one of them. My mother was Catholic, and I was raised going to church, but by that point in my life, I didn't go very often. I couldn't deal with things like confession: you could rob a bank, but if you went ahead and confessed it the next day, it was okay. That didn't wash with me.

Still, as I stood there and the seconds ticked by, I prayed to St. Jude for help. I really wanted this equipment. I needed this equipment.

Just as I finished praying, the seller suddenly turned to me.

"Okay," he said with a grimace. "It's all yours."

I was so astonished I barely remember grabbing his hand and shaking it for all I was worth before he could change his mind and pull it back. The next thing I knew, I found myself outside in the pouring rain standing there like a zombie, wondering how the hell that had happened. The entire conversation had lasted maybe fifteen seconds.

I was absolutely ecstatic. I cannot express in words how overjoyed I was in that moment. How could I have gotten so amazingly, incredibly lucky? Things like this didn't happen. Surely, it was a genuine miracle.

Don't ask me what made up his mind. Maybe it was the old bird-in-the-hand-versus-one-in-the-bush thing. Maybe it was St. Jude—or maybe he couldn't be bothered shipping to South America.

Either way, in my mind it was most definitely another miracle.

From the time we started renovating the building to the time we stocked our shelves with our first inventory of shoes, our start-up process took a whole year. Even with no money available to pay us salaries, for that entire year we'd had to work every day, seven days a week, for as many hours as we could stay awake. It got to the point where Jimmy and Gordy's wives were complaining about never seeing them—which was understandable.

I told the guys, "Well, whatever you feel you need to do, go ahead and do it, but I have to keep working."

Little did I know how often I would say those words in the coming years.

Another thing I said often: we're going to make shoes the right way. Let me tell you what that actually means.

The first step in making a shoe happens in the stitching room, where rolls of canvas fabric are die-cut into the various parts of the upper, a rubber toe is pressed to the inside of the canvas toe, the fabric upper pieces are all sewn together, collars are placed, foam is inserted, and the collars are turned. Then outside and inside heel counters are attached, and the vamp is sewn in.

Work then proceeds to the mill room, where foxing and friction tape, bumpers, and heel tabs are cut from thin strips of rubber, and the sturdy bottom outsoles are molded. My youngest brother, Jimmy, made each and every waffle-cup mold himself by hand after working all day, using his lathe at home. The waffle soles are first molded out of thick sheets of rubber that are heat cured and compressed, then stamped while still warm, using a diamond-patterned mold. That's how we created our iconic waffle-cup sole.

For the soles, we used pure crepe rubber with no filler. Adding filler was the practice among all the other sneaker manufacturers, but doing so weakened the structure, made it less flexible, and allowed the sole to wear out much quicker. After finishing in the mill room, the conveyor then moves the shoes to the fitting room, where the sponge, arches, and insoles are added.

Then everything proceeds to the making, or assembly, room. There, on foot-shaped lasts the uppers and detailing are joined to the waffle soles using latex cement. Three rubber strips called foxing are applied with friction strips over the joint, and the excess rubber is trimmed off. Then the toe and heel are sealed, and the shoes are dipped in latex and dried.

Finally, after the toe bumper goes on, a logo is placed on the heel. In the very beginning the label didn't say Van Doren, but instead consisted of a stylized drawing of a V with wings we called the flying V label. (That first year was the only time we had the flying V heel label on all our shoes. Later we switched some of the styles to a heel label that just said Van. Same thing with the box. Later still, the heel labels and boxes were all switched over to say Van Doren. We experimented to see if it made any difference. It didn't.)

When finished in the making room, the shoes are loaded into the big vulcanizer and cooked in 275-degree heat combined with twenty pounds of air pressure per square inch, plus ideal humidity conditions. After cooling, they go to the packing room where they are cleaned, laced, swathed in tissue, boxed, and crated for shipping.

One byproduct of the vulcanizing process is that the finished rubber soles end up being very sticky. They would adhere to the tissue paper they were being wrapped in before boxing. When we started actual production, this drove me absolutely nuts. I was convinced that during the assembly process, the workers were being sloppy with the latex cement. Since I had worked as a laster, I knew the cement wasn't supposed to touch the sole. Surely that was the reason the paper kept sticking.

After painstakingly ushering a day's worth of shoes through the process myself, I realized I was wrong. The rubber soles were naturally sticky. Those annoyingly sticky soles would turn out to be a huge selling point for skateboarders, so eventually I learned to love the sticky. But that would come later. At the time, all I could think was *Damn, maybe we should wrap them in waxed paper.*

The famous waffle pattern, like many of my really good ideas, was the direct result of improvisation after something went wrong. The first shoes we produced looked good, really good, but fairly quickly we discovered there was an inbuilt flaw in the diamond-patterned soles I'd designed. The soles were cracking across the ball of the foot after only a short time in use. We ended up adding nine vertical lines to the pattern over the ball area to create a denser woven pattern there—and voilà! Our signature feature.

Our bread-and-butter was style no. 44, a classic deck shoe that later became known, aptly, as "the Authentic." Deck shoes were the kind of casual footwear popular all over the country then, but ours was the first to feature an extra-thick waffle sole. Our version of the generic shoe shape called a CVO, which stands for circular vamp oxford, came in both canvas and suede: since any material being vulcanized must be heat resistant, the upper material is typically limited to suede, leather, and cotton with metal hardware. There were five eyelets for the laces.

The rest of our initial selection was equally modest and without pretention. We did this deliberately: no fancy or specialized shoes, just a handful of simple styles. We also offered style no. 19, a women's four-eyelet lace-up; no. 16, a women's two-eyelet CVO; and no. 20, a slip-on. Children's shoes were style no. 15. Style no. 46 was a suede boat shoe with a blue striped outer sole made for better traction on actual boats, and no. 45 was a canvas boat shoe, also with the striped sole.

We'd offer a wider selection of colors once we got going; we'd listen to requests and add popular colors to our inventory when the demand was high enough. But for starters, we offered our four standards in canvas—light blue, navy blue, loden green, and white—and we carried them in sizes for men, women, boys, and girls. The suede shoes came in white, blue, gold, and red. (They didn't have any kind of fabric liner, so if you got them in blue and they got wet, your socks or feet would turn blue, too—a bonus!)

The slogan on our first shoebox was "Canvas Shoes for the Entire Family" and was branded House of Vans. We set the original prices for all our shoes between $2.29 and $4.49.

Bob Cohen, my former boss at Randy's, tried to prevent the Van Doren Rubber Company from succeeding. First, he warned his employees that they would be fired if they had anything to do with us. Then he reached out to every single one of his material suppliers and assured them that if they sold to us, he would never do business with them again.

The old shoe dog who had sold us the bulk of our manufacturing equipment called to tell us Bob had contacted him and urged him to back out of the deal. He had refused, and thank goodness—all things considered, he was the only one who really mattered. His assistance was really critical to us moving forward.

But meanwhile, one by one, down our entire supply chain, other companies flatly refused to work with us.

The first supplier to reject us was the guy we had contracted to make our shoeboxes. He reneged on a deal we had made, and ultimately refused to work with us at all, ever. I took the opportunity to come up with a new type of box.

If I'm being honest, I had always hated standard boxes with their separate lids. When I think back, I can't measure the amount of time I lost in warehouses combing through boxes and boxes and lids upon lids. It's a wonder the ongoing shuffling of cardboard—a routine sticking point, which is a nicer way to say a pain in the ass—hadn't nudged me to design something sooner.

My novel solution was to use a single, flat piece of cardboard, which could be folded with a built-in, fold-down lid. I might have held a grudge against Japan for Pearl Harbor, but the origami I'd seen when I'd first visited my backer Serge there had inspired me.

The box improvisation ended up working in our favor, but I'll be damned if Bob hadn't called all of our West Coast suppliers one by one, and East Coast ones, too, for that matter, to blockade our efforts, sort of like the British during the Boston Tea Party, but he covered both coasts. There wasn't a single material we needed to craft a pair of sneakers that he didn't try to keep us from acquiring.

To his credit, he made this known. A lot of suppliers had empathy, but no one crossed the picket line to help. To this day, when it comes to supply chains, my advice is to control as much as you're able and stay nimble. Never get too comfortable or complacent.

I was still intent on making quality shoes. I made up my mind from the beginning that I was never going to sell shoes to a discounter. I was never going to make shoes just to dump them. Every pair of shoes I made, I wanted to sell in my store. And I decided that when a person came into my store, I had to have their size in stock. And the only way I could do that was to put two of everything in the store and deliver every day. Nobody else delivered every day; they had outlets. I delivered every day. Controlling my supply chain made all the difference in both quality and service.

Finally, we got to the stage where we needed to hire and train the employees who would actually make the shoes and man the warehouse, along with a few supervisors and a handful of administrative positions, such as bookkeeping and custodial.

I had no formal education, but at Randy's, I had learned to distinguish the people who knew what they were talking about from those who didn't. Out of ten people you might find, eight of them didn't really know what they were talking about. Most important, I needed supervisors who were okay with getting their hands dirty. Some people are willing to do that, but most are not. I learned to choose my employees carefully. I never ruled out people based on their gender, race, or other common biases. There were never any invisible barriers or glass ceilings at the Van Doren Rubber Company.

When I started interviewing people for jobs with us, the first thing I would do after someone handed me his or her résumé was toss it in the trash. They would be horrified, of course, and get nervous, but when I proceeded to ask questions and have them tell me about themselves in their own words, they relaxed. How else could I find out who they really were?

My strategy worked like a charm. I was able to get a glimpse of the real person, and applicants ended up in the right job, which wasn't necessarily the one they had applied for. Knowing how to evaluate people that way meant I was better able to hire the right people for the company, ones who had the right skills and attitude and would get along well with everyone. I took pains to do this with every single person we hired. I believe that in both the short and the long run, the company was more successful because of the great people we had working with us.

Not that I was an easy boss. I'll be the first to admit that I was demanding, exacting, and often, well, loud. I blame that on my parents, who rarely bothered with persuasion; when they wanted to get their point across, they just raised their volume. I was never rude or ugly, just loud. Very, very loud.

Being a systems guy, I always valued efficiency, which was key, and I learned how to set expectations. Our employees always knew what I wanted done and how I wanted it done. I was a stickler for those systems. Everything had its proper place, and every procedure had its proper routine, and heaven help anyone who deviated from it.

Take, for example, the trash. We had a rubbish barrel that was supposed to be in a certain place for those who needed to get to it easily. It wandered—not far, just a few feet one way or another. But those few feet made a difference when someone needed to get to it quickly. One day I painted a bright yellow circle on the floor around the base of the barrel and told everyone it needed to stay inside that circle. The next day I saw the barrel was outside of the circle. I kicked it all the way down the hallway, where I left it lying on its side, contents spilling out. That can was never outside the circle again. Point made.

Finally, the day came when all the manufacturing equipment was in place, all the needed employees had been hired and trained, and all the test runs conducted. We managed to get production rolling with no hiccups. When our first pair of sneakers rolled off the conveyor, we all cheered. We'd done it! Our factory was up and running and actually making shoes.

Now we just had to sell them.

# CHAPTER SEVEN

# Listen to Your Customers

B y the time Vans had been in business for fifteen or twenty years, every kid in every school in Southern California had Van shoes, purchased in seventy stores all over the state.

How did we get there?

We didn't change our prices; we didn't do anything. What was the key to our success? The customers themselves, especially the moms who were in charge of all the family shoe purchases. They began to trust us. The next thing we knew, they considered us part of the family—because family does things for family. When we talk about Vans as a family company, we're talking about our core customers, too.

But back in the beginning, as a numbers and production man, I had plenty to learn about dealing directly with the buying public. In the end, my best teachers in the art of retail were the customers themselves.

■ ■ ■

Once we'd come up with our key styles, including style no. 44, the Authentic, we were ready to figure out how to sell them. Not knowing any better, I did it my way. I controlled as much as I could, I kept my options open—and then I let nature take its course.

Our motto was "Quality, Value, and Superior Service."

From the day Vans was born, my idea had always been to sell our shoes right out of the factory. I was convinced once people saw how well made and how reasonably priced they were, they would flock to our factory in droves to buy our shoes, cutting out the middleman. Still, there needed to be somewhere the customers could try on the shoes and pay for them.

To that end, we had carved out a small area at the very front of our factory on East Broadway in Anaheim to put in a tiny showroom, where we could sell our shoes to the public. Customers could walk in right off the street. The factory was actually located in a fairly good part of town, on a moderately busy street, so hopefully people would see us and come in.

The name on our factory sign was Van Doren Rubber Company. Despite it being my own name, I felt it didn't have quite the right ring to it for a retail establishment. The rubber part didn't exactly scream shoe store. Later on, we decided the sign over our first retail store would read "House of Vans."

We had announced that we would open in January. When that didn't happen, we quoted the popular TV hero Maxwell Smart: "Would you believe February?" When February came and went, we said, "Would you believe March?"

We officially opened in March 1966.

We had framed the designated space, put up walls, and painted it to look nice. Navajo white, of course. We had put in shelves, a cash register, a bench for the customers to try shoes on, and we'd acquired the devices needed to measure the customers' feet for the correct sizing. There was nothing fancy about that first store.

When we opened our doors for business, we didn't have any extra pairs stocked. On our shelves, we displayed shoeboxes, empty ones. We had zero inventory. To be clear, those shoeboxes were perfectly organized. Instead of slapping on the usual labels, we used red-striped boxes for children, blue for men's, orange for boys, and green for women. It was a pretty easy system for anyone in both our warehouse and the store to remember. All the shelves were stocked with boxes grouped by color, so customers could go straight to the section they needed once we had actual shoes in them.

That the boxes were colorful and decorative added an inviting warmth to our retail area, but that still left the problem of the lack of inventory for people to buy for the first few weeks while we got production up to speed. We solved it by displaying a single pair of every style of shoe we made. My idea was that, for the first couple of weeks, the customer would give us their order; we'd collect payment, then send the orders into the factory where the shoes would be made. The customer would then pick up their order at the end of the day. We could do that for a few weeks while we built up inventory in the warehouse, starting with the most popular styles, sizes, and colors.

On top of offering a great value, we guaranteed the workmanship of all our shoes. If you bought a pair of Vans and some part of them didn't hold up, or you had another complaint, we'd happily replace the shoes, no questions asked. From our first day in business, our customers have been our number one focus, and we wanted them to believe in our brand. The customer, by choosing our product, trusted that the American-made shoes they had bought were of good quality. We had to prove we really did make great shoes, and we counted on our customers to help tell our story to their friends.

On the wall of our store, we had an eight-foot-long sign that said "Tell a Friend." We knew that if we did a good job, our customers would tell three people, but if we did a bad job, they'd tell seven people. We always strove to do a good job. Our sales motto was, "If you like our shoes, tell a friend; if not, tell us."

Customer satisfaction always came first. Even if someone wandered into one of our stores and didn't buy a thing, or returned a shoe we darn well knew had been worn two summers, we were still happy to see them, because that person was going to tell a bunch of others about how they were treated.

Getting a pair of Vans should be a really terrific and satisfying experience. That's the difference: people wear Vans all day, every day.

On the first day we opened our doors, several honest-to-goodness customers came in to buy our shoes, alerted to the opening by flyers distributed in the neighborhood by Stevie and his friends.

I was thrilled when the very first person to walk into the store brought up a pair of women's no. 19 to the cash register to order. They cost $2.49, our standard price for most women's styles back then. After I proudly rang up the sale, she gave me a five-dollar bill. The bell dinged as the drawer slid open. That was when I realized there was no money in the cash register. Not a single penny.

Wow! I'd totally forgotten to put money in so we could make change. That goes to show how much I knew about retail. What the hell was I going to do now? What else could I do? I handed the money back and told her with a smile that she could pay when she came to pick up the shoes that afternoon.

I did the same for the next customer and the next customer after that. I sold sixteen pairs of shoes that first day, but I didn't take in one thin dime because I couldn't make change. Talk about an epic fail.

The amazing thing was, with the exception of a single customer, every single person came back that evening to pick up their shoes and pay for them. Fifteen out of sixteen? Not bad at all. Honestly, that gave me faith the House of Vans might actually succeed. We just needed to hire someone to run the cash register other than me.

About two weeks later, a woman came into the store while I happened to be working a shift at the register again.

She told me, "I'm from Long Beach. My daughter lives here in Anaheim, but I'm only able to come down to see her every two or three weeks. Here is the money for the shoes I ordered a while back. I'm so sorry it took this long for me to get back to pick them up." Then she handed me $2.49.

She was the one person who hadn't come back that first day we opened. I was bowled over. This was a positive beginning to our enterprise, and that made it feel a lot less risky.

■ ■ ■

The Vans name wasn't remotely recognized as a shoe brand yet, not even locally. The name wasn't bringing in repeat customers, and few people came to our factory store as a random walk-in. Folks could clearly see our "House of Vans" sign, but they didn't know who we were, or what we were selling. Those who did come in, based on the flyers or by word of mouth, often wouldn't come back for months.

Making ends meet was starting to be a major struggle, and it was clear I had a whole lot to learn about the retail business. One experience in particular during the first few months underscored exactly how much I needed to learn, and that my customers would end up being my best teachers.

One day a couple came in with two kids, a little girl around seven years old and a little boy around five. The little girl needed new shoes, so I put on a pair for her to try out. Then the little boy wanted shoes, too. He didn't need them; the ones he was wearing were practically new. The parents didn't say anything, though the mom looked a little uncomfortable when I went ahead and put a pair of shoes on the boy.

The boy wasn't leaving without the shoes, and I realized I'd put mom in an awkward position. I assured her I wasn't going to charge for that pair.

Meanwhile, the father was off looking at the men's shoes. The mom turned and said to him, "Why don't you get a pair of shoes from this nice gentleman, dear?"

The husband wore a khaki shirt and pants with the sturdy black shoes of a blue-collar worker. He definitely didn't seem like a sneaker kind of guy. My hunch was confirmed when the dad replied, "Nah, I don't really need new shoes, honey."

She nudged, "I think you should get a pair of shoes."

He looked at his wife, then glanced down at the floor samples on the shelf. Our only colors at the time were light blue, navy blue, white, and loden green. He said, "Okay, I guess I'll take a pair of these white deck shoes."

The wife shook her head. "They'll get dirty."

The father glanced back over the selection. "Okay, give me the light blue ones."

The wife frowned. "Honey, you don't own anything that's blue to go with them."

The father pulled a face. "Right. The navy ones then."

The wife threw up her hands. "Didn't I just say you don't have anything blue?"

A long-suffering expression slid over the husband's face and he said, "Honey, I like the green best." He turned to me. "Do you have a pair in my size?"

I was thirty-five years old, and until that moment, I had never realized that the mom is really the boss of the family. Mom is almost always the one who decides when, where, how, and everything else about shopping for the family. This changed my entire perspective on our core market.

I had to get more moms. Selling shoes to moms took longer, because our shoes just lasted for a while, and sometimes they wouldn't come back for sixteen weeks or so. We just kept sewing our shoes with moms in mind—that's what we did, for years and years and years.

Another way we accommodated our customers was to innovate.

Back then, men were putting on the same kind of shoes they had been wearing for fifty years or more. There had been some change, but not very much. Women, on the other hand, didn't go very long before they wanted a change in style.

We had a decent range of styles, but I could tell women were getting bored with the limited selection of colors offered in our canvas shoes.

Until we arrived on the scene, most sneakers sold around the world had been white. They weren't originally called tennis shoes for nothing. Any colors offered by manufacturers were usually very conservative, like the standard blue, green, and red. Even black didn't become popular until a decade later. The only black shoes we made for years were our basketball shoes. Randy's had done some prints and different colors, but only as limited special release items, never as standard stock.

Within a few months of opening, we started doing our sneakers in a few different colors, according to the number of requests we got, trying new colors, making more of what sold. Our customers loved the broader selection, which brought us a bunch of new customers.

There was a new line of shoes specifically for women, to help bring them back into our stores more often. We added a trio of new styles: espadrilles, pointed toes, and saddle shoes. It helped a little, but nothing hit big.

Until we made it personal.

One day when I was working in the store, a customer came in carrying a piece of pink fabric. She was looking for a pair of pink tennis shoes that would match the fabric she'd used to make herself a dress. In those days, buying fabric by the yard was still very inexpensive compared to buying ready-made clothing, so lots of women sewed their own clothes.

This customer had been all over Orange County looking for sneakers that would match her dress, but all she'd found were the same old boring colors. We had more colors, so at first, she was very excited, hopeful of finding something in pink. But the only shade of pink we carried clashed with the pink in her fabric. She started to leave, obviously very disappointed.

Watching her, I had a flashback to a couple of years before when I'd met the surfer Duke Kahanamoku at a competition in Huntington Beach, and made him and his surfer pals' sneakers to match their Hawaiian shirts.

Suddenly it hit me. It'd be easy for me to make shoes for this woman that not only matched her swatch but also were made from that very same fabric. I could make them during a scheduled transition between colors on the assembly line, so doing one odd pair wouldn't be a disruption, or even difficult. I could just substitute the fabric and send it down the line. The only requirement would be that the fabric had to be able to absorb water, which was necessary for the vulcanizing process.

"How about I make you a custom pair from that very same fabric?" I said to the woman.

She looked at me wide-eyed. "Really? You can do that?"

"Sure," I said confidently. "No problem."

Then she winced. "How much would you charge me?" she asked.

It would cost us nothing extra to do this other than the employee time involved. "The usual price plus 50 cents," I told her. "That should cover it."

Her jaw dropped. "Okay, yes!" Clearly elated, she pulled a swath of yellow fabric from her purse. "Can you do a pair from this, too?"

"Absolutely."

Learning to be flexible in our approach to both manufacturing and selling grew out of our willingness to innovate in order to meet our customers' needs.

Normally, shoe manufacturers couldn't afford to change colors and styles on a whim. Changing their entire line of shoes once a year was about all they could absorb financially. Vans was different.

Our factory had been set up to be flexible. All our sneaker styles used the same two kinds of rubber soles made with the same vulcanizing procedure, the hardest part of the process. Only the upper fabric part was really different between the styles: lace-ups, slip-ons, basketball shoes, etc. We could change styles or colors every day on the assembly line, or even every hour, if we wanted to. That made us ultra-responsive to changing fashions and able to give people what they wanted right now. That flexibility was one of the big things that would ultimately lift us above the crowd.

I've always hated when a restaurant, or any brick-and-mortar business for that matter, won't make substitutions, or if a company or a school has a "policy." As in "I'd love to help you, but . . ." or "I'd make an exception, but . . ."

If I've learned one thing in my ninety years, it's that people do what they want to. And when they do what's right for them, whether or not there's a policy that directs them otherwise, they'll become unwavering in their loyalty if you accommodate them.

After successfully making the two custom pairs for that first customer, I called a meeting and discussed the idea with my partners. They agreed that offering custom shoes as a service was a terrific idea. The plan was to use the customer's choice from among two or three of our normal shoe styles, but for the uppers we'd use the fabric the customer brought in to us. Eventually, we designed and carried our own fabrics. Each store had sample swatches that customers could choose between, if they didn't have their own.

We immediately saw a huge potential market. Not only would women who sewed their own clothes be delighted to get a pair of exactly matching shoes, but drill teams and cheerleaders, sports teams, private schools, and choirs would all jump on the idea of being able to have shoes that perfectly matched their uniforms or outfits, instead of always relying on boring white, let alone that other brand with the loud, garish stripes on the sides.

In Southern California, every school had cheerleaders, marching bands, and different types of song leaders. To match their school colors, Vans would make lots of shoes in the colors of the schools. Stevie went to a school whose colors were white, gold, and red. Down the street, they were green and white, and farther down the street from that, red and white. Every one of our stores would offer the service, and we started including custom-mades as part of our regular catalog.

To introduce the program, Dolly set about sewing a bunch of outfits and dresses, and I made pairs of matching sneakers with the same fabrics. We carved out a bit of space on one wall of the store and displayed the samples. I hired the kids to distribute flyers in the nearby neighborhoods, just as I'd done when we first opened. I also printed up some postcards, which I sent around to all the local high school and college phys ed departments, letting them know we now offered custom-made shoes for teams.

One ingenious promoter of our custom-mades, one that I wouldn't have anticipated in a million years, was Stevie, then in the fifth grade. I had to laugh one day when he came into the factory carrying a dozen swatches of wild fabrics. On a recent trip to the fabric store with Dolly, he'd seen several bolts of Hawaiian print material that made him googly eyed. (Stevie has always been big on Hawaiian shirts; heck, he still is to this day. He owns hundreds of them.) Naturally, he wanted his own set of Hawaiian customs to match. Since the colorful fabric could be spotted a mile away, his shoes were both a great conversation piece and a true "walking advertisement" for our brand.

Custom-mades as a service was quick to catch on, though I can't say how many sales Stevie's wild shoes actually brought in. But offering that service absolutely helped draw attention to the brand and bring in new customers—people would experience the quality and comfort of our custom shoes and then return to buy our regular sneakers.

The other thing we started doing almost right away, which was totally unprecedented in the shoe business, was to let our customers buy just one shoe at a time. That way if one shoe got ruined, you didn't have to throw out the pair. Or, if a person's left foot was a different size than their right foot, which is often the case, they could now buy two different-size shoes and finally have a pair that fit. We just treated them as normal custom orders. Soon, podiatrists heard about our unique service and started recommending us to their patients. We could make just about any combination of features, one pair at a time, which proved to be a huge benefit for many, many customers.

■ ■ ■

One of the lessons I took to heart most fervently in those early days of retail was the importance of being a style leader—adapting to what our most fashionable customers wanted, instead of imitating what other shoe companies were already doing.

Our customers were never shy about telling us, or simply showing us, what they wanted. We just had to pay attention. I discovered while working at the store that many girls were actually buying boys' shoes, just two sizes smaller. I guess I shouldn't have been surprised; the same thing was happening with blue jeans. In those days, nobody made blue jeans specifically for women, so ladies just bought men's jeans in a smaller size. The women's liberation movement was just on the horizon, and I attributed the trend to young women striving for equality, wanting to be treated the same.

Whatever the reason, we quickly adopted the unisex idea and stopped making both girls and boys shoes. The unisex trend caught on like wildfire. Girls were happy to buy the same styles of shoes as the boys, just in different sizes.

I believe our willingness to listen to customers, to let them make our shoes their own, and to do things differently than the way they'd always been done were all reasons young people started identifying so closely with the Vans brand.

Another selling opportunity inspired by our customers: I had noticed that almost everyone wore white cotton socks with their sneakers, regardless of style. Why not sell white socks in our stores?

We contacted the rep for the Trimfit brand. When the rep came out and spoke with us, I explained my idea to offer only white socks.

He stared at me incredulously for a second, then shook his head. "No," he said. "You can't carry just white socks. It will never fly. You need a bigger selection to choose from."

But I knew what I had seen, so I insisted on just white.

I'm pretty sure the rep just felt sorry for me because I was so new to the business, and he probably figured with time I'd come around to his way of thinking. That may have been the only reason he agreed, against his better judgment, to open a white-socks-only account for Vans.

Could we have done better with a larger selection of sock colors? Who knows? But what I do know is the white socks sold really well. In fact, as time went on, we became that rep's biggest account for white socks in all of the western states.

Did carrying white socks increase our overall sales at Vans' stores? Maybe, maybe not. The truth is, I have no idea. But our customers certainly liked the convenience of having socks available in the stores, so I considered it a win.

If my customers were happy, so was I.

# CHAPTER EIGHT

# Sell What You Believe In

I can't sell a bad idea. If you're going to ask me to sell ice cream that's already melted, I can't do it. Some salesmen are so good, they can sell anything. I don't want that person. I want somebody who can sell right, someone who really believes in the product. In building Vans, I needed people who would live up to our authenticity as a company—there's that word again.

This is the hardest thing to do for any retail operation: how do you get other people to believe in the superiority of your product? First, the people who are working for you have to believe it. If you can convince your employees, then they're going to be able to convince the customer. And when all is said and done, of course, the customer is the one who matters.

■ ■ ■

Eventually I came to realize there was a limit to how many shoes we could sell straight out of the factory. I'd been more than naive to think we could sell our entire production using that one small outlet.

A few months after we opened, we were tossing around ideas at a management meeting. I knew exactly what I wanted to do, but up until then I'd kept my mouth shut for fear of being run out of town on a rail. Finally, I just had to say it.

"Why don't we open another retail store?" I blurted out. "One in a totally different location."

I was met with stunned silence.

We were all aware that no other shoe manufacturer had ever opened a factory store to sell their shoes, let alone an entirely separate retail store dedicated exclusively to selling their own products. At the time, most shoes were sold in separate sections of places like department stores.

A stand-alone shoe store was unprecedented, but was it a crazy idea? By providing the best customer service and products that were available in difficult-to-find sizes and widths, we could turn the tables, open our own branded retail store, and claim all that profit for ourselves.

Admittedly, we were still struggling to get our new operation into the black on our balance sheet. We could have easily ended up bankrupt, as most new businesses do.

That day, everybody around the table looked at each other as they contemplated my idea.

I could see from their expressions that everyone thought I was nuts. But what options did we have? We needed to do something, anything.

Hell, nothing ventured, nothing gained, right?

"Okay. We're in." One by one, they finally agreed. That decided, the conversation turned to how one goes about organizing a retail store. None of us had an actual clue, so the details were left up to me.

This much I knew: we needed a great location. In buying a home, I had used an agent named John Corda. He was a German immigrant and had impressed me as a good guy who knew what he was doing. I called him up, and by the following Monday we found an empty storefront in what we both thought would be a good location for a shoe store. Conveniently, it was in Costa Mesa, near where we lived, and the following day I signed a lease on the space.

Later that night, Paul Jr. and I drew up plans for sixteen shelving units and two benches, based on the size of the store and the standard dimensions of the plywood and studs available at the local lumberyard. The units each had eight shelves that held fourteen shoeboxes per shelf.

The new store was long and quite narrow, the shape of most small Main Street–style storefronts. I decided to add a strip of carpet on the floor to cut down on the echo. Carpeting came in a standard width of twelve feet across, which would fit nicely down the middle between the shoe racks. The store walls would be painted the usual Navajo white, with blue trim. This became our template for every store we opened that year. All stores were deliberately built to look identical and cost $800 to build out and open.

The next day after school was out, I gathered the kids, drove us to the new store, and we divvied up the work. Paul Jr. was in charge of construction, Stevie and I were in charge of painting, and Taffy and Janie and Cheryl took care of the cleaning.

After the interior of the store was sparkling, the shelves and benches built and installed along the two long walls, everything freshly painted, and the cash register installed on the front counter, I decided to put up three wall displays. One had a nautical theme with fishing nets and seashells because many of our customers were boaters who bought our deck shoes. There was also a display with a basketball hoop holding our basketball shoes. A third area would hold a custom-made shoe display similar to the one at the factory store. Dolly had been busy sewing sample outfits at home and ordering custom shoes to match.

I'd never been one to drag my feet, so just one short week after that meeting, our first true retail store opened its doors in Costa Mesa. I put a notice in the *Pennysaver* for the grand opening, advertising that if you bought one pair of Vans, you could buy a second pair for half the price. At the time, BOGO (buy one, get one) was unheard of, but lo and behold the promotion brought people in the door.

■ ■ ■

When we opened our factory-direct location, I had enlisted the help of my older kids and a bunch of their friends to help attract customers. I'd made up a stack of one thousand flyers and paid the kids to distribute them to every house in the surrounding residential areas and leave them on every single windshield in every parking lot in the nearby commercial areas, all during the week before we opened our doors.

Stevie still bemoans what a gargantuan task it was to deliver all those flyers. Because of federal postal regulations, the kids weren't allowed to leave them in people's mailboxes. They had to walk all the way up the driveway to the front door, stick the flyer in the doorframe, and then walk all the way back down the driveway and up again to the next house and so on. They walked miles and miles and more miles. They let out a huge sigh of relief whenever they came to a parking lot, because they could just go from car to car without the added driveway trek.

The same gang was sent out with flyers for the new store in Costa Mesa. The kids did their usual neighborhood blitz, and we also mailed postcards to the area schools. I recruited Stevie to stand on the street out front during the grand opening to distribute flyers to passers-by. Being a real charmer, he excelled at it. Too bad he had to go to school and couldn't be there chatting with people and passing out flyers all week. At least he was available in the evenings.

Overall, our sales slowly increased. The company was still in the red, but we all continued to be optimistic that our brand, along with the personal service offered in our stores, would catch on and that profits would soon follow.

We decided to open even more locations, bringing in more customers and boosting the bottom line another notch.

Again, I went out with John Corda and found what we thought would be good retail locations. The formula we came up with for the placement of a Vans store was to choose a small, free-standing building on a busy street, rather than one that was sandwiched between two other stores. That seemed to work best for us.

Once our first four stores were up and running, they generated enough income to pay all the overhead expenses. Eventually, they also made a profit, but not right away.

We were still dealing with the fact that the name House of Vans alone didn't bring people into the stores to buy shoes. Unless you walked through the door, there was no way of knowing just by our sign that we sold canvas shoes. After opening the first few stores, we dropped the "House of" part of the name and simply painted "Vans Tennis Shoes" at the top of the right-side exposed wall of our buildings. At that time, *sneakers* was an East Coast term. Then we added a mural on the rest of the wall that showed what was inside the store.

Each store's outside wall was unique. For instance, on one store we painted a grand piano with a man sitting at the keyboard wearing high-top basketball shoes. Next to him Mel the artist added, "For All Occasions." He was always as witty as he was creative.

Mel was the one who pointed out to me, during a conversation about a mural for one of our first half-dozen buildings, the importance of opening a business not just on a busy street, but in a location where drivers had a right-hand view of the outside wall. He cited statistics showing that drivers automatically look to their right, not their left. That was where our sign would get the most exposure.

Mel's comment about visibility made a lot of sense to me and also may have explained why our new Lakewood store wasn't doing as well as we had projected. The giant aircraft manufacturer McDonnell Douglas was located in that general area, and we couldn't understand why their hundreds of employees, as well as the local residents, were not coming into our store. After all, we were on a busy street with thousands of cars going by every day. But a driver's view of the outside wall was on the wrong side of the street.

Fortunately, we had one of our best managers, a genuine people person, running that store, and because of her we were eventually able to make a go of that location. But from that time on, we never opened a store with the exposed wall on the left side of the street.

Our Monterey Park store was located in a freestanding building sitting on a little hill by itself. At first there were no outside lights installed to illuminate our sign. The store was open late a few nights a week, but without a lighted sign, few people were coming in. One evening when Danny MacLellan and Stevie were working at the store, Danny decided to try an idea he'd probably picked up from seeing the big klieg lights Hollywood uses to beam up into the sky to attract people to movie openings.

Danny put Stevie in the car and parked it down the hill, pointed up toward the store. He shut off the engine and left the headlights on, telling Stevie to sit in the driver's seat and switch back and forth between high beams and low beams, over and over, flashing onto the "House of Vans" sign. Then he went back up to the store and worked the register as usual.

The flashing lights were working. People started coming into the store, and most were commenting on them.

After an hour or so, a uniformed policeman came stalking into the store, hauling Stevie behind him by the collar. "Does this kid belong to you?" he demanded.

"Um, yes," Danny said.

The policeman said, "Well, he was shining the car high beams on and off the building, making a nuisance of himself. There are laws, you know."

Danny opened his mouth to defend Stevie but must have thought better of it. What if there really was a law against flashing lights on a building? It seemed unlikely, but Vans couldn't afford to pay a hefty fine for something so stupid.

Danny gave Stevie a scowl and said, "Jeez, what were you thinking, you knucklehead?"

Stevie didn't miss a beat. He feigned contrition and said, "Sorry, Uncle Danny. It won't happen again, I swear."

He nodded sagely. The policeman stalked back out of the store, and Stevie got extra tacos for dinner that night for taking the blame.

So much for that marketing idea.

■ ■ ■

Flyers and fun murals continued to do their job, but we really needed to come up with a more consistent way to draw people.

I didn't believe in traditional advertising. Never had for Vans, anyway. We were a local outfit, strictly Los Angeles and Orange counties, so spending money on far-reaching newspaper, magazine, or radio ads did not seem a productive use of our very limited funds. The number of actual sales that kind of advertising might generate would be negligible. To be truly effective, we'd need to spend a huge amount of money we didn't have.

Instead, we needed something to attract customers on the spot, one by one.

We had started to build a store on Topanga Canyon Boulevard out in the San Fernando Valley. Gordy came up with the inspired idea of attracting the attention of passing cars by painting the whole side of the building to look like a colorful circus tent.

What did a circus tent have to do with our shoes?

Well, not much. It had more to do with the moms and kids. Most kids love to go to the circus. Kids naturally love balloons, cotton candy, and a fun environment. We figured kids would spot the circus tent and ask their mom what it was, or the moms would see it and stop to check us out.

Again, we painted the words "Vans Tennis Shoes" in big letters on the circus tent, along with a couple of sneakers. Anyone who saw that wall would know exactly what we were selling. We hoped curiosity, and our growing name recognition, would bring people in the door.

After Topanga, we decided to continue the theme, adding four additional stores with circus tent–painted sides.

That brought our total number of Vans' stores to ten in all, in the first six months of operation. For every added store, our overall profit inched up a tiny bit more.

We kept a tight rein on the budget for each store. I always watched our costs very carefully.

I have a friend who shares my take on "costing." He's a farmer, and he likes to say that on a successful farm, no one eats for free. Everything earns its keep, including the machines. In other words, all the necessary expenses of farming—not just the obvious expenses related to planting crops or raising livestock, but overhead in the form of seeds and rent and fuel and maintenance and insurance—have to contribute to the bottom line as much as they detract from it.

The same can be said of a shoe factory and retail stores. A light bulb doesn't pay for itself, neither does the tissue in the shoe box. The true cost of doing business isn't just the raw material, and that's why costing and knowing everything's real cost is critical.

For the new Vans' retail stores, I'd keep overhead to an absolute minimum. I'd get supply wood, cover it with burlap and some cushions, to make a bench. Vans was coming of age, and rents were getting higher. But I never paid more than $300 per month for a store; in the mall, the rent was $2,000. If I was paying $300, I could hold on long enough to attract repeat customers, which usually took about six months.

Not many of my stores started off making money, but we just kept following our plan.

One thing that helped our bottom line was our policy of replenishing stock on the same day the stores sold the shoes—well, the same night, to be exact. One of the kids, usually Cheryl, would call up each store at close of business and write down everything they'd sold that day on an order form. That same evening, the warehouse would pick and pack the order with replacement stock for the store.

All the day's orders would then be delivered that night. At the same time, we'd pick up any custom orders they'd taken, and those would be made and delivered back to them the next night.

Ours turned out to be a groundbreaking system. Usually retailers had to wait weeks or sometimes months to receive shoes they had ordered. No other manufacturer had standard same-day delivery then. The system helped eliminate the need for backroom storage in our stores, leaving more space for selling. At the same time, our stock was always full and up to date.

Admittedly, selling our product exclusively through our own retail stores was slow going, and sometimes we sold only four pairs of shoes on any given day. But by the end of the first year, we sold a lot of shoes—enough for us to consider our efforts a success.

All things considered, I thought we were doing quite well. I mean, Vans was a well-oiled, if somewhat quirky, machine, and even if we weren't exactly getting rich yet, we weren't losing money, either. Not bad for the first six months in business, right?

I routinely got together with our company accountant to review the financial status of our stores. I was anxious about our retail sales numbers and wanted to keep close tabs on how we were doing.

Marvin Meyer was our accountant as well as a good friend of mine. One day Marvin told me that, in his opinion, we should close down two of our ten stores.

What? I stared at him, bewildered. Close them down? I knew sales were slow, but I'd really thought we were doing okay.

Apparently not.

"What are you talking about?" I demanded, shocked by the prospect of closing two of the stores we had worked so hard to find, fix up, staff with good people, and keep running. The numbers were going in the right direction, weren't they?

Marvin launched into all the reasons he thought we should close down those two sites. Six out of our ten stores were still in the red. These two were our least productive locations, not even close to being profitable. They were dragging down the numbers. Consolidating would boost our bottom line. Blah blah blah.

Well, maybe on paper it might have been a good idea. But not out in the real world—not as I saw it, anyway.

I was already coming up with an alternate plan. I interrupted Marvin and said, "No. We don't have to do that."

"But what about these numbers?" he insisted, waving his ledger sheets.

"Don't worry," I said. "I've got the answer."

Trying to disguise his ample skepticism, Marvin said, "All right, Paul, what is it?"

I grinned. "We need to put in an additional ten stores."

I thought Marvin was going to fall off his chair in a dead faint.

"Look at it this way," I went on to explain. "If we put in ten new stores, and even if they do as badly as our current ten stores are doing right now, the company would still make a profit."

More volume would mean less cost per unit.

Marvin looked doubtful. I said, "You know I'm right. Do the math."

So, he did. After calculating with pencil and paper for several minutes, he looked up, gave me one of those long-suffering accountant sighs, and threw his pencil up in the air. "Okay, fine. You win."

Marvin thought I was going in exactly the wrong direction, but as counterintuitive as the scheme seemed at first, he couldn't argue with my logic, wonky as it was, or with the numbers.

Neither of us pointed out the obvious: there was no guarantee the next ten stores would even do as well as our first ten. Better to ignore that little dark cloud in the sky. It was a risk I was willing to take.

Over the next ten weeks, we rented an additional ten stores. Ours turned into an assembly-line operation. On Monday, I would go out with John Corda to find a suitable storefront, sign the lease on Tuesday and after school, gather the kids to dive in and do our usual tasks of building shelves, painting, and cleaning. Then on Saturday, we would have our grand opening.

In our first nine months in business, we had opened twenty Vans' retail stores. To my satisfaction and immense relief, by the time we had put in the eighteenth store, retail was already breaking even. My crazy idea was actually working.

But as we opened those ten additional Vans' stores in rapid succession, we encountered an unexpected but very real dilemma: finding qualified people to manage them. I was doing my best to keep up with the hiring and training, but our plans threatened to come to a screeching halt each week because I just didn't yet have anyone who could be put in charge of the newest store.

I would be at the new store on the opening weekend, and Dolly could step in and take the weekdays that first week; and we'd usually have someone in place to run the store by the following Saturday and Sunday. But one week the unthinkable finally happened: for the life of us, we could not find someone to manage the latest store. Jimmy and Gordy were going to swap meets every weekend to sell our overstock and replenish the coffers with a small but needed infusion of cash. The person being trained to take over the new store wouldn't be available until the week after.

The only option I could think of was to put my son Stevie, eleven years old at the time, in charge of the store for those two days all on his own. There was simply no one else to help.

Naturally, Stevie was all over it, and super excited to take on the responsibility.

From a young age, Stevie had always wanted to be involved in anything I was doing. Since I had pretty much lived and breathed first Randy's and now Vans, Stevie had grown up living and breathing the same thing, too. It didn't matter where I was or what I was up to, he wanted to be a part of the action. He was always at my side trying to learn and help in any way he could. He never minded getting his hands dirty. In fact, he loved it.

I had every confidence Stevie could handle himself like a champ that weekend on his own, despite his age. Even so, I decided not to tell Dolly until after the fact.

The first customer to enter the store while Stevie was in charge was a middle-aged woman. He approached her and politely asked, "Is there something I can help you with, ma'am?"

Realizing there were no other adults in the store, she was clearly appalled that a retail establishment would put such a young person in charge with no supervision.

But Stevie worked his magic, as I had known he would. The lady talked at length with him, and naturally she received excellent service on the purchase of her style no. 44s. She was so impressed, she felt compelled to send a letter to the Van Doren corporate office, stating, "If this is an example of the younger generation coming up in your company, you have nothing to worry about."

Even so, we clearly needed to find a better way to hire and train great managers to run the stores.

Rescue had come in the form of Dolly's brother, Danny MacLellan.

Danny and his new wife, Louise, took off from their wedding reception in August 1967 and drove straight across the country to come work for us. Danny took over the Costa Mesa store from Dolly and proved to be an amazing salesman from Day One.

Watching Danny work over the next months, I realized he could be a real asset to the Vans' management team. He was just so friendly and likeable and he understood people really well. His natural ability to encourage others to do their very best meant he excelled at training and inspiring people. In other words, he was the perfect person to take charge of our overall sales team.

During our first twenty-five years in business, Danny played a major role in the development of the company by interviewing, hiring, and training a crack team of district managers, a small group of positive and energetic women who did an incredible job of keeping the individual store managers excited and proud to be the public face of Vans.

Thank goodness—in Danny, I had finally found my replacement as head of retail.

Another idea I felt would be a definite win was a promotion we did during one of those first years around the holidays. Christmas was just around the corner, and we knew people didn't generally buy canvas shoes as holiday gifts.

In those days, no retailers I knew of were doing loss leaders— selling a product at a loss just to lead customers to your store or sell them other products. I'm not even sure if it was an actual concept then. Randy's had done promotions by including a toy or two with the shoes for a special price, but they always charged a premium for the package. Back then, it was all about maximizing profits across the board, so selling anything at a loss *on purpose* was unthinkable. And yet most retailers had no problem spending tens of thousands of dollars on advertising, with no way of calculating its true benefit, to bring in customers.

My thought was, why not sell a few desirable toys alongside our shoes for a limited time, just in the weeks before the holidays? I didn't want to package a toy with a specific style, because limiting the selection would likely also limit the sales.

If we had a popular toy available to buy as a separate item in our stores, that should bring folks in the door while they were doing their Christmas shopping. Then hopefully they'd pick up a pair or two of our shoes at the same time, or at least know where to go next time they needed good quality sneakers.

We decided to give it a try. We scraped together a budget from under every couch cushion we could think of and went to the Mattel toy company with our proposal. They agreed to sell us a onetime order of a few selected toys. After looking at the wide variety of their offerings, the biggest draws in our opinion were the Barbie doll, Major Matt Mason action figure, and the Drowsy doll. We swallowed our nervousness and arranged to purchase $15,000 worth of the three toys, which we would distribute to sell throughout our twenty stores. The wholesale cost to us was $2.91 per toy, and that was exactly what we charged our customers. It was the cheapest price in town for the popular dolls and action figure, guaranteed to bring customers flocking to our stores.

We hoped.

When our investor Serge D'Elia heard we were selling toys for exactly the same price we had purchased them for, he was very angry. "What the hell is wrong with you people?" he scolded over the phone when he called to find out if it was true. "You can't buy something for $2.91 and turn around sell it for $2.91! That makes no sense!"

I replied calmly, "Serge, we're in the shoe business, not the toy business. We're using the toys simply to draw people into our stores, so they'll buy our shoes."

My intent wasn't to make money on the toys. The point was that a bargain like that brought customers into the store. It was also convenient for our regular customers to have the opportunity to purchase a Christmas gift or three at the same time they were purchasing shoes. Another win-win.

The promotion worked perfectly. Lots of new customers came into the stores, and our sales did increase noticeably that holiday season. Another positive result was that we sold every last one of the toys, and therefore recouped every cent of the $15,000 we'd spent on them. If we had invested that same amount in newspaper or other advertising, we would never have recovered our initial cash investment, and I'm pretty sure we wouldn't have seen $15,000 worth of additional sales, either. As it was, every sale brought in by the promotion was pure profit.

All in all, I was pleased with the company's progress up until that point. Our profits were increasing, even if they grew at a snail's pace.

The one thing that made me a little sad that holiday season was the news I'd heard through the grapevine about my old friend Bob Cohen.

The previous year, when Bob had seen that our Vans stores were doing okay in the Los Angeles and Orange County areas, he decided to compete with us by going down to San Diego and opening up ten stores of his own that he called the Sneaker Inn. He told everyone he was doing great.

I'd heard through the industry rumor mill that the quality of the shoes he sold was totally random—the level you'd expect to find at swap meets or job lots. The next thing I heard was that Sneaker Inn had closed all its stores. Not only that, but Randy's had also gone out of business.

Though I'd been mightily upset with Bob in those early days when he tried to short-circuit my operation, I was still unhappy to hear this news. Bob and I may not have parted on the best of terms, but I had never wished Bob or his company ill—certainly I never wanted or expected them to fail. I'd worked for Randy's for twenty good years, and I'd poured a lot of my own blood, sweat, and tears into the company.

That Bob and I became enemies when I quit Randy's and started my own venture was a shame. Later on, to our surprise, we managed to become friends again. Before he passed away at age sixty-two,

Bob said to me, "The biggest mistake I ever made was letting you go." Hearing him say those words was bittersweet.

For me, quitting Randy's had probably been the biggest stroke of luck in my life. Opportunity is a strange beast.

■ ■ ■

Listening to our customers, meeting their needs, always being willing to make an exception or customize a special shoe, helped us survive. But even though our numbers were slowly rising as new customers got to know our shoes, we were still just barely hanging on.

To stay in business, we needed to expand our customer base further.

One idea was to get into the wholesale market. We could set up contracts with local store owners who would place regular orders with us to supply their shoe stores or other retail outlets. That was how Randy's and everyone else in the shoe business had always worked.

But I had been trying to avoid going that route. I wanted Vans to do things differently. To sell wholesale, we would need a staff to pound the pavement and set up accounts. Neither Jimmy nor Gordy had been involved in hiring or training sales staff at Randy's, nor had they been salesmen themselves. They were both great at their jobs, but the areas they were currently responsible for at Van Doren Rubber Company were training the factory crew and running production. That had left me in charge of retail sales until my brother-in-law Danny took over. I was no salesman—that had been amply demonstrated. Thankfully, Dolly was great at running the factory store, and we'd found some other good people to help her.

So where would we find new markets, without overextending our already-strained workforce? The Los Angeles County Fair was a golden opportunity.

Held in mid-September, the Los Angeles County Fair is a big annual event that started in 1922. Fair attractions during the sixties and seventies included agricultural, animal, and 4H county fair stuff, plus horticulture and cooking contests. There was a rodeo, horse races, a midway carnival area, loads of fair food, and historical exhibits. At night there would be country or rock concerts. Vendor tents were interspersed between various retail booths.

Typically, the fair lasted sixteen days. Those two-plus weeks allowed us to sell off all our overstock, get styles that weren't selling out of the warehouse, and earn enough to pay off the banknote I took out each year to finance the materials needed for fall production. The timing was perfect, because the back-to-school rush ended around Labor Day, and the banknote was always due the first of October.

That first year, Vans managed to secure one of the best booth locations, and we brought in a truckload of our shoes to sell in our booth. Since our warehouse was located just a short freeway trip from the Fairplex, it was easy to bring in more stock when we ran low. We discounted everything and had a policy that if you bought enough shoes for the boxes to touch the tent's ceiling, you would get the next pair free. This worked out to be about twelve or so boxes. So, a thirteenth pair was free. The largest sizes of all our styles always had lots of surplus, so we sold those sizes at $25 for a whole case. These cases were a huge hit.

Other than the racetrack, the House of Vans' booth ended up being, hands down, the busiest place at the fair. Fairgoers flocked to our booth to snap up the bargains. Our lines of customers got so long that we decided to institute a sort of fast-track reservation system. We gave people a ticket to come back during a certain time slot later in the day. That way, they wouldn't have to waste time standing in line but could go right into the tent when they returned. The system worked great, and our customers really appreciated the efficiency.

Another big draw for our booth was always Stevie. He really came into his own and found his niche at this event. He outdid himself, acting more like an emcee than a shoe salesman. He brought his boom box and blasted music to attract passersby. While the rest of us sold shoes, he amused and entertained everyone in line and lifted the atmosphere. He got everyone talking and chatting with one another.

At the House of Vans, all the promotions we've ever undertaken emulate and celebrate this sort of experience. It didn't matter so much if someone bought something or not; it was all about connecting with our customers.

To this day, Steve's unofficial title at Vans is CEO, Chief Entertainment Officer. Fun is in the company's DNA. We are always trying to figure out new ways to connect with the public and increase our brand visibility.

The best advertising decision we made at the fair was to put every sale we made into one of our large, bright-red handled bags with the name Vans emblazoned across both sides. They were roomy and sturdy, so most people would put all their fair purchases and doodads into our bag. By the end of each day, there were hundreds of people walking around the fair carrying our big red bags, advertising our brand.

After the incredible success of our first LA County Fair, we went back every year. We also started going to some of the smaller county fairs around Southern California. Local fairs became one of our favorite ways to get our name out there and make new Vans fans. Sales were increasing, and the visibility of our brand was rising. People had started coming into our stores because of the name Vans.

All this was well before *branding* became a buzz word in the commercial marketplace. When customers saw our name, I wanted them to register good value, great shoes, and above all, quality service.

If we saw our customers as part of the family, so to speak, they deserved nothing less.

# CHAPTER NINE

# Go Off the Wall

I n the early days, skateboarders were the renegades, the badasses of the sporting world, with their innovative moves, creative vernacular, and even their unusual practice spots. Because designated skate parks hadn't been invented yet, skateboarding gangs would appropriate abandoned or neglected backyard swimming pools. They'd drain the water, leaving a nice, smooth cement bowl for practicing tricks and freestyle moves. "Riding the pool" meant carving paths across the bottom of the cement pool.

Tony Alva, a kid from a Venice, California, neighborhood called Dogtown, was being noticed for his revolutionary stunts and became the first to literally go "off the wall."

It's hard to overstate the influence of the Z-boys, which was short for the famous Zephyr competitive skate crew named after the surf shop run by Jeff Ho, Skip Engblom, and Craig Stecyk, where Tony and his friends used to gather in the 1970s. Fans agree the Zephyr team changed the course of skateboarding when they competed in the Del Mar National Skateboarding Contest in 1975.

Tony and the rest of the Z-boys developed a crowd-pleasing, low-to-the-ground style inspired by surfers that was in marked contrast to the upright skateboarding style that had been so popular in the 1950s and 1960s. Jim Muir, one of the original Z-boys, points out that the "attitudes we created in our approach to surfing translated from the water to the land." Surfers and skaters also shared a culture and a personal look, inspired by both graffiti culture and their individual backgrounds, that set them apart.

Now in his sixties, Tony Alva wound up qualifying as a pro by age sixteen and started his own skateboard and apparel brand that has sustained him all these years later.

To pull off his most daring, now widely imitated aerial move, Tony had to gather speed to work his way up a vertical wall to the rim of the pool. Using momentum to defy gravity, he would grip the front of the board just as he launched himself straight up and off the pool deck into thin air. Then he'd rotate his board and swoop back down the side of the pool.

As the story goes, the first time Tony pulled it off, Skip Engblom exclaimed, "Man, you just went off the wall!"

As an American idiom, "off the wall" had been around for decades. But when it was picked up by other skaters, the phrase caught on as slang, evolving to mean something new and maybe strange or even a little nuts. Say what you will: to me it screamed opportunity, a chance to push things to make the most of every moment. It captured Vans' spirit and became Vans' anthem, mantra, and rallying cry.

Looking back, I see that part of my company's success was that willingness to go "off the wall," from Day One. We were always speeding forward into the unknown, trusting that skill and agility would bring us safely back to earth.

■ ■ ■

Until the skateboarders came along, Vans had no real direction, no specific purpose as a business other than to make the best shoes possible. When skateboarders adopted Vans, ultimately, they gave us an outward culture and an inner purpose.

I'd been introduced to Southern California's "sidewalk surfing" craze back when I had first moved to Orange County. It was impossible not to be aware of the sport's meteoric rise. Competitive skate teams were popping up everywhere. Unsurprisingly, most of them were in our backyard, even skating in our neighbors' pools. Most of the kids in the early skater crews came from single-parent households, from the wrong side of the tracks. They were idiosyncratic, creative, independent—they were seen as the "freaks" of the sport. In so many ways, they were our people.

The Z-boys of Dogtown were, in fact, more than skaters. With their wild-style moves, graffiti-covered boards, and defiant attitude, the Z-boys seemed more like "a street gang than a skate crew," as *SkateBoarder* magazine once put it.

In many ways, it was a natural evolution for Vans to become so closely linked to this brand of youth culture, with its emphasis on the freedom of self-expression. Skateboarders discovered our shoes at a moment in time when the shoe industry was changing, and they helped us find a niche, an identity we maintain to this day.

My daughter Cheryl describes our partnership as "a band of misfits coming together to make something great." But I'll admit, it took me a minute to wake up and smell the Coppertone—without the help of my son Stevie, I wouldn't have recognized the opportunities for synergy that were right in front of me.

Stevie never stops stressing the importance of honoring our roots: "Skaters in the mid seventies adopted us, and I thank them still four decades later, because they gave us meaning."

■ ■ ■

For Vans, the seventies were a groundbreaking decade in more ways than the mere numbers of our stores and the accumulating profits. My own exposure to a wider world began to broaden, as did the way I viewed the business of athletic shoes.

The year 1972 proved to be a turning point for our business, and it also happened to be a defining moment for the world's biggest athletic event, the Olympic Games. That year, the Games were to be held in Munich for the first time in modern Germany's history. My friend and real estate agent, John Corda, a German native, wanted to go back for the occasion. After some thought, my brother Jimmy and I decided to join him. We'd never been to Europe. After the Games, we planned to tour other parts of Germany as well as Italy, France, and England, among others.

As we traveled, I couldn't help noticing that almost no one wore sneakers in Europe when they weren't engaged in sports. Back home, we wore tennis shoes year-round. We lived in them. Worked in them. Played in them.

For a week, the three of us were consumed by glorious human battles of endurance and strength in competition after competition, but our attention always drifted back to shoes. After Mark Spitz won his seventh gold medal and he'd waved to the crowd with a pair of Adidas, there'd been a hubbub over the spontaneous product placement: had he meant to promote a German-made shoe? As it turned out, Spitz had not been paid by Adidas. He wasn't shilling.

During that week I took note of the connection between star athletes and the companies that made specialized shoes engineered for their sport, often Adidas. There were also a fair number of the athletes wearing a new brand of more casual running shoe when they weren't competing but just walking around: Nike's "moon shoes," one of that company's earliest and most iconic.

Turns out that earlier that year, Phil Knight had handed out the shoes to five runners at the 1972 Olympic trials in Eugene, Oregon. I didn't know how many of Nike's twelve styles were being worn competitively, but the Nike Cortez had been released the year before, and the distinctive look of these track shoes had already set them apart.

Our blissful Olympics experience came to an abrupt end, and the Games themselves were forever changed, in the second week when a group of Palestinian terrorists took a group of Israeli athletes and coaches hostage, demanding the release of Arab prisoners held in Israel. Sixty hours later, we learned the extent of the bloodshed and loss. After the whole tragedy had fully played out, twelve people were dead.

Jimmy and I ended up completing our European tour, and meeting friendly, welcoming Europeans boosted our spirits, but the remainder of our journey was a melancholy one.

■ ■ ■

Back in California, I started thinking about what I'd seen at the Games. Vans had never designed shoes to wear in sports competitions like track and field, baseball, or basketball. If anything, Vans were usually on the feet of cheerleaders, drill teams, and sports fans. That was the market segment we'd gone after. I started to wonder: should we expand our ways of thinking?

When I was at Randy's West, I had steered the company to produce sneakers in more colors. Six months before quitting, I had introduced Randy's 720 style, which had, in fact, been targeted to skateboarders. It was akin to a regular Keds-type sneaker, except it featured a cushioned arch, a reinforced steel shank, and a reinforced rubber toe and heel for additional traction. In those early days, skateboard decks lacked grip tape.

The shoe didn't sell, largely because Randy's management had insisted they only be carried in specialty stores. Still, enough wearers found them that the Randy 720 had been adopted as the official sneaker of the National Skateboard Championship and worn by some of the competitors in the 1965 International Skateboard Championships in Anaheim.

Fast-forward a year, when I was starting to design Vans' first collection. I incorporated some of what I had learned building the 720 into our first Van Doren sneakers. I was focused on designing the perfect all-around deck shoe, so naturally I included some of the 720 improvements in our initial offerings, but none of my earliest Vans' designs included all of the 720's refinements.

Now I started to rethink my approach. At the Munich Games I had seen firsthand how fiercely Adidas and Nike competed for sponsorships among big-name athletes. Skateboarding may not have been an Olympic sport yet, but what about skateboarding championships? Might Vans have or create an opportunity to support those?

Skateboarders had been coming into our Santa Monica, Malibu, and Venice Beach stores for years. A few were serious. Tony Alva, then in junior high, had first found Vans because the school he attended was next door to a factory store we'd built in Santa Monica.

Every time he came into the store, he would beg Betty Mitchell, the store manager, to buy irregulars or seconds or one shoe at a time. Skateboarders regularly wore out the toe and heel of one shoe—the back foot, or the shoe that met the street—from dragging it as a brake or turning pivot, while the other shoe—the front foot, or the shoe on the skateboard—got minimal wear. Betty came to ask my permission to sell one shoe at a time, which I gave. Making a single shoe was as simple as it was to make a custom order. Eventually I decided to make that "one shoe" thing a general policy for all the stores, and it turned into a nice draw that won us a surprising number of customers.

Tony and another top skater named Stacy Peralta found out I'd been involved in making the 720 when I was at Randy's—to this day, I don't know how they knew. Every time I ran into one of them at the stores, they would prod me to make an even better skateboarding shoe. Stevie had gotten to know Tony and Stacy and the other skaters better and had urged me to listen to their ideas, but I'd dismissed them because I wasn't a skateboarder.

Now I had a thought: why not go back to the drawing board to finesse a new skate shoe, one that more specifically addressed the needs of skateboarders?

In working occasional stints at all of our retail stores in the late sixties and early seventies, I knew that the Authentic, our style no. 44, had a loyal following among street athletes. They preferred Vans' double-thick sticky sole to other shoes. The general consensus was that Vans' soles let skaters "feel" the board under their feet; the soles also stuck to their boards and helped them steer. The skaters also loved the fact that because it was twice as thick, Vans' soles lasted twice as long; and now, when they finally wore it out, they could come into a Vans' store and purchase one shoe at a time. Wearing one color shoe on the right foot and a different color on the left, or sometimes two entirely different styles, became a badge of honor.

Tony Alva and Stacy Peralta represented the core of the now-legendary Z-boys. When they showed up with navy blue Vans Authentics on their feet as part of their signature uniform at skateboarding competitions, we noticed. But we couldn't have known that the Z-boys would change Vans' entire trajectory as a company.

By the late sixties and early seventies, we had steady custom-made accounts that included Pendleton and Disney, for whom we produced special, exclusive styles, ensuring that their stores were the only places customers could buy those particular styles. It was in this spirit of opportunity and feedback that I finally asked Tony Alva and Stacy Peralta to share their ideas for a skateboarding shoe. If Vans' success with custom-mades had taught me anything, it was that if you consistently deliver what customers want, you'll cross the finish line in the money.

We invited Tony and Stacy down to Orange County to show us their moves and to talk about shoe design. Stevie was enthusiastic about creating a partnership. To gain some street cred for Vans along with some good publicity, he'd already suggested giving free shoes to the top skateboarders , and I'd agreed. Stacy Peralta, Tony Alva, and another star skater, Jay Adams, were the very first skaters to get shoes from a shoe company—as Stacy puts it, "giving scruffy skateboarders free shoes was unheard of in the 1970s." Each Vans store manager was encouraged to choose seven or eight skateboarders and supply them with shoes, and the skateboard companies donated their boards. Vans soon became an important partner and sponsor of the sport.

With the top athletes in the sport next to us telling us exactly what they needed to perform better, and a bunch of other athletes who wanted what these pros had, we were confident that if our collaboration didn't meet with success, nothing would.

Our longtime commitment to the skater community has made such a difference in terms of keeping our brand authentic, even in an era of mass merchandising. Vans is the one and only shoe company in the world that has been involved in skateboarding since the early seventies when modern skateboarding began, and it has remained intimately involved with the sport ever since.

Stacy Peralta puts it this way: "Vans is one of the greatest legacy companies not only in skateboarding, but in the worldwide community of action sports."

Vans' first skateboarding shoe, style no. 95, introduced in 1976 and named the Era, was different from the no. 44 Authentic deck shoe in that it had a padded collar for extra comfort around the ankle and heel. Originally made in Tony's signature two-toned red and blue, we soon offered Eras in different color combinations.

Even our logo began to evolve thanks to the skater influence. At the time, Jimmy's son Mark, my youngest nephew, had been learning how to stencil art in his eighth-grade art class, and he spray-painted a stencil of a turtle on the bottom of his skateboard. Jimmy liked the look and picked up the artwork as the basis of a new logo. We designed a little red label with the silhouette of a skateboard printed on it that resembled Mark's turtle, with the slogan "Off the Wall" written across the board, and put it exclusively on the heel of the Era. All our other shoe styles got the usual Van Doren label on the heel. (At the bottom, we added later, "Made in the USA." We were one of the few, and we were very proud that our shoes were American made.)

The Era was a huge success. Even though we wanted Era to have its own distinctive branding, pretty soon we started using the Era's turtle and tagline as our company's overall signature logo.

■ ■ ■

Somewhere along the line, Stevie had become fully immersed in skateboarder culture. Because most of the young skateboarders didn't have transportation, I let Stevie use one of the company vans to ferry them to the competitions. He would load it up with a big pile of Vans, then pick up the guys from LA, along with their skateboards, and drive them down to the various skateboarding events in Orange County. They became great friends. The skaters would regale Stevie with tales of their greatest exploits, like the times they snuck onto Camp Pendleton Marine Base down in Oceanside by telling the guards at the gate they were visiting a brother in boot camp getting ready to be shipped overseas. They'd be let onto the base and spend the rest of the day skating on the gigantic water pipes the Marines were using to cool nuclear reactors.

Stevie remembers that he started noticing the skateboarders in the mid-1970s, after high school. He started to go to competitions just to watch what was going on. He grew up playing traditional sports like football, basketball, and baseball, so to him, skateboarding was something new and wild. In the early 1970s he bought a boogie board from Jack's Surf Shop—as close to surfing, or skateboarding, as he ever got. But the fascination endured.

When I finally went to the skateboard competitions and saw for myself how many kids were into the sport, and the amazing things they could do on those skinny wooden boards, I was blown away—just as Stevie, Tony, and Stacy had been telling me I would.

As it happened, Tony Alva was also heavily involved in surfing, as were a great many of the skateboarders. When a guy or gal wasn't practicing on one kind of board on a given day, they could no doubt be found on the other. Eric Dressen, another member of the original Z-boys, recalled that when he started skateboarding in 1975, he skated barefoot because he was emulating surfing: "All my favorite skateboarders were barefoot in the magazines." But once he got his first pair of Eras, he wore Vans for his whole career.

I suppose it was just natural that Vans' involvement with the skateboarding community spilled over to the surfing community. To our delight, surfers adopted Vans as their own, just as skateboarders had before them. Because surfing had been a recognized sport since the forties, their teams and contests were already well-established, and getting involved was slightly easier. Stevie started going to a lot of surfing events, making friends and building up an interest and a loyal following in that community. For thirty years, Vans has supported events like the Surfing Triple Crown, the world's premier surfing event. The current sponsored surf team has thirty-three members.

In 2010, Vans also kicked off the Duct Tape Invitational, a joint venture with legendary longboarder Joel Tudor. It's an informal, laid-back beach celebration and longboard surfing contest that showcases the world's most talented progressive riders, focusing on creativity and innovation in surf culture.

In the end, the consistency and longevity of Vans' commitment to these signature sports really paid off.

All those years ago, we found the perfect combination of sports for the brand, and we were thrilled that they embraced our shoes with equal enthusiasm. Thanks largely to the unexpected and unprecedented publicity generated by Tony, Stacy, and the other SoCal skateboarders and surfers, the Vans Era had become the shoe of a generation among cement and surf riders all over the world.

■ ■ ■

By 1977, Vans had been in business just over ten years. The company was doing well. Stevie, newly twenty-four, was an integral part of Vans. After the huge success of the Era shoe, Vans had enough brand recognition in Southern California to keep things running smoothly and turning a nice profit.

We continued to pop up wherever we could, including at fairs and swap meets. Stevie loved to hang out with the Z-boys and took every opportunity he could to be out with them for the day. He would always come home bubbling over with stories of their extraordinary skateboarding and surfing exploits and the unique culture that surrounded them.

These kids from the wrong side of the California tracks had created not just their own way of performing, but also a unique outsider culture that was slowly gaining national and even international recognition.

As a teenager growing up in Washington, DC, future punk star Henry Rollins of Black Flag remembers seeing writer and photographer Craig Stecyk's moody, action-packed photos of the Z-boys in *Skateboarder* and being inspired by their urban guerilla style. Stecyk's work, published in "Dogtown Chronicles," showed kids everywhere that individual expression was key.

The photos showed not just a sport, but a code—a way of living and a genre-defying posture. It was all about being in the moment on the board and adopting a style that defied the norm. Tony Alva sums up the attitude: "Keep it fun. Don't take yourself too seriously. It's better just being spontaneous."

One of the quirkier habits kids had in those days was drawing stuff with permanent markers on the rubber strip around the bottom of their shoes—the friction tape. They drew things such as skulls, unicorns, and checkerboards in different colors, as well as phrases like "I love girls." Since everyone had a signature style, they could more easily spot their own shoes at the pool or on the beach.

Stevie decided to conduct an experiment. He printed up a batch of our friction tape with a black-and-white checked pattern and put it on a few of the Eras to see how they would sell. They sold out instantly, so we started offering them as one of the style options, along with the two-color selections.

Then Stevie got the idea to run a monthly contest. He had strips of paper cut the exact size of a shoe's friction tape and sent the strips out to all of our Vans stores. Kids could come into a store and draw their own designs. Once a month, all the stores would send in the slips, and we'd lay them out to look for ideas to use for our shoes. We would pick out the month's winning design. The winner would get a factory tour, a free day at Disneyland with their family, and a free pair of shoes.

Skateboarding and surfing kids were the driving force behind the success of the Era, all thanks to Stevie's allegiance to the skaters. He was with them come hell or high water. He saw something special in them.

I called them "fly by night people." They did things differently, and we met them where they were.

Stacy Peralta describes Vans' commitment to the skaters beautifully: "There are few companies in the world that can be considered integral to a sport or a culture, and it only happens when that company is there from the very beginning, putting in the hard work and the long hours on the ground. In addition to the support Vans provided, they also developed product from the inside out, and that product is a complete reflection of the sport and of the individuals performing in it."

In magazines, sports shows, and even movies, the Z-boys were consistently photographed wearing our shoes. For competitions, they adopted a uniform of a white polo shirt, blue pants, and Vans. As Tony, Stacy, and Jay Adams won one competition after another and were featured in action photos in popular magazines, like *Skateboarder,* which was widely distributed in outlets like 7-Eleven convenience stores, we started getting almost daily phone calls not just from across the United States, but also from countries all over the globe, asking where they could buy the Vans' Era.

In 1978, Vans opened a second factory with offices just a few blocks away.

Another milestone came when I finally broke down and started advertising—just a little, nothing too crazy. Star skaters like Jerry

Valdez were featured in the 1977 ad launching Vans' "Off the Wall" campaign.

We would run occasional ads exclusively in skateboarding magazines that included an order form, so that people who didn't live locally could send us an order, and we'd ship the shoes out to them. Kids were buying whatever they saw in the skate magazines.

Even more orders came flooding in. Our cutting-edge Era skateboarding shoe was helping enormously with our sales numbers. I was elated. A decade of never-ending hard work was paying off at last.

We were still just a local company, strictly SoCal, with no global ambitions at the time. Even so, our profits started to skyrocket, and we were actually making money. Lots of it. Our modest little company had grown to an annual sales figure of around $15 million.

But by the mid-seventies, we also started to have some stiff competition in the sneaker marketplace, particularly from running shoes, given the increasing popularity of jogging. Stripes, swooshes, and circles were now seen everywhere. I started to feel we needed something that would also mark our shoes visibly, the way those other companies had.

I'd always had a habit of doodling on a pad on my desk while I was thinking. One day I looked down and saw that I had drawn kind of a cool-looking stripe. I liked it, and so did everyone else. We decided to adopt it for our shoe branding and put it on the outer sides of our newest style. Our patternmaker called it the "jazz stripe."

We didn't put the Side Stripe on all our shoe styles, but over time we adapted it for a number of them that still have it to this day. The Side Stripe has become the unmistakable hallmark of the Vans' brand.

The first shoe to get the Side Stripe was Style no. 36, our first skate shoe that incorporated leather panels on the toe and heel for increased durability. Known later as the Old Skool, it came out in 1977.

The Old Skool was the style that Stacy Peralta adopted for his personal look. Given Stacy's visibility wearing his Vans in competitions, he approached Betty Mitchell and asked her if Vans would consider paying him a monthly salary. She thought it over and came back to him with an offer of $300.00 per month.

Stacy recalls: "To the best of my knowledge, I was one of the very first pro skaters to be paid a monthly salary by a shoe company."

He told Stevie that he still has that first $300 check.

In retrospect, one could argue that Stacy Peralta did for Vans and skateboarding what Michael Jordan did for basketball and that other brand. Stacy became a role model for other kids to emulate, and Vans were a signature part of his look.

Around this same time, Stevie came up with the idea of forming Vans' skate team to compete against the other SoCal teams. He figured doing that would really get our shoes out there front and center with our main customer base. He hired our first team manager, Everett Rosecrans, who began building the team. Everett was given a van and a Plexiglass ramp, and he would travel around doing demos and making sure the guys got their shoes. Steve often went to the skate parks to keep tabs on our teams.

Team members over the years have included not just "legends" such as Tony Alva, Ray Barber, John Cardiel, Jeff Grosso, Steve Caballero, and Christian Hosoi, but also "The Boss," Andrew Reynolds, and Kyle Walker, named a "King of the Road" by *Thrasher* magazine. The teams have also gone global, with Chris Pfanner added as part of Vans Europe.

In addition, we started a surf team, and because Everett was into the latest sports craze sweeping SoCal, bicycle motocross, or BMX, he also added a BMX racing team. BMX riders had already adopted the Old Skool because of the padded materials and unique customization options. BMX quickly became our best exposure yet.

Everett was able to work with all the major bike companies, which meant that Vans were being worn in all of the bike ads, not just for one company. The guys on our team were even featured in Hal Needham's 1984 BMX movie called *Rad*, which, well, let's just say it didn't win Sundance. Vans had already been building skate ramps at our factory sites and around the county, so we now also started building a few BMX ramps for kids to practice on.

In the early days, the team members were just given shoes and travel expenses, but after the teams got going, we would also give them US savings bonds as a sort of scholarship.

In 1977, we debuted style no. 98, the Vans' Classic Slip-On. Combining the waffle sole technology and the look of the Era, we created a hybrid that could be worn both casually and as a functional skate shoe. Vans' Slip-Ons were instantly all the rage in SoCal, surpassing all our sales expectations.

Some of the guys from Huntington Beach High School had taken decorating their shoes' friction tape one step further and drawn checkerboards all over the shoe canvas on top. Stevie saw a pair at the beach one day, and the rest, as they say, is history.

In 1981, after much enthusiastic urging by Stevie, Vans started offering the black-and-white checkered pattern as a color option for the no. 98 Classic Slip-On, printed on the entire shoe.

Fans of the checkerboard pattern were soon legion, even overseas. In London around this time, the second wave of Jamaican ska music was rocking the city. The mix of punk rock with Caribbean melodies came to be known as the "two-tone wave" because of its combination of typical "white" and "black" sounds. I was told the Vans' checkerboard pattern came to represent the breaking of racial barriers and intermixing of styles, making it the ideal fashion statement for this particular music subculture.

The checkered Slip-On became synonymous with Vans around the world a short while later, in 1982, when Sean Penn wore his slip-ons in the teen comedy *Fast Times at Ridgemont High.* In an early scene Penn's stoned out surfer even takes one of his shoes from the Vans box and hits himself on the head with it, showing the checkerboards to great effect.

Today the style is more popular than ever with all kinds of influencers. Musician Frank Ocean wore checkerboard slip-ons to the Obama White House in 2016. Everyone from Kanye West to Ryan Reynolds, from Ty Dolla $ign to Justin Bieber, has been photographed in them, as have NBA players like Nick Young and Jordan Clarkson.

■ ■ ■

Our designs evolved to serve both fashion and function. What we started hearing from skateboarders about their most common injuries led us to realize there was an important element missing from our shoes: ankle protection. We had already started making separate ankle guards that could be Velcroed around the ankles, but there was clearly a need for shoes that accomplished the same protection in a better way. In 1978, we released style no. 38, a high-top version of the leather and canvas Old Skool. We called it the Sk8-Hi.

The original Sk8-Hi came in two-color combos of navy-blue leather with light blue canvas, cinnamon-colored leather on rust canvas, and brown leather on beige canvas. But there was so much real estate on a Sk8-Hi that it soon became the favorite choice of style for custom-mades. You can have a really large, beautiful print put on them, an opportunity for design that you don't get on any other shoe. Others opted for a plain color and went DIY, just doodling or painting the shoes themselves.

The style's popularity led to another temporary problem. We had to limit our production of the Sk8-Hi at first because we couldn't get our stitchers to learn fast enough. Making that style took more skill and was much more time-intensive thanks to the additional stitching, variety of materials, padding, and folding involved in making it.

Sk8-Hi was the second Vans' style to carry the Side Stripe, placed above the ankle where skateboarders used and abused their lower extremities the most. The design took skate functionality to the next level, not only shielding bones from skateboards catapulted at them, but also bringing a whole new look to the skate park. During the eighties and nineties, every well-known skater in the world wore either these or the Old Skool. Watch the movie *Bones Brigade*, and you'll see every rider wearing the Vans' Side Stripe.

The Sk8-Hi rounded out the quintet of innovative styles that would, over the next five decades, reach fashion icon status, joining the Authentic, the Era, the Old Skool, and the Slip-On to become Vans' Classics, beloved by millions of fans the world over.

By the end of the seventies, Vans had opened seventy stores in Southern California, and we had begun to sell our shoes through dealers across the entire country, as well as internationally.

■ ■ ■

With the help of Tony and Stacy, and the initial push from the entire skateboarding, surfing, and BMX communities, kids had become part of our core identity. Our origin stories and subsequent evolutions would be indelibly and forever linked.

As Tony Alva observes: "Vans has brought the beach vibe to the street of cities in every part of the world."

We were never a company making shoes for skateboarders, but they bought our shoes. We accommodated them, then we supported them, and still do, after over fifty years in business, providing them with shoes and gear and sponsoring competitive teams—including more girls' teams now—as well as individual skaters.

Even with the global expansion of the brand, Global Brand President Doug Palladini stresses: "Skateboarding is in Vans' blood and always will be. We never want to be anything other than the world's no. 1 skateboarding brand."

These days there are many more girls and women in Vans' advertising, and in the sport of skateboarding itself. In an important development, two years ago the purses for the women's skate competitions were adjusted to equal that of the men's contests. There's no question that pay should always have been equal—but it wasn't. Now things are finally changing.

My daughter Cheryl notes: "Skate is very inclusive in that everybody can do it. But there have been times when skating hasn't been as inclusive, and we're doing a lot across our brand to encourage girls and women to skate."

Vans is evolving as the sport does, by supporting teams like The Skate Witches, a band of girl skaters that also produces a zine. It's all about inclusion, collaboration, and mentorship, building a community and a kind of alternate reality in which girl power is simply the norm. As the girls themselves put it, the great thing about skating is that there's no right or wrong way to do it—and anyone can join.

Another Vans favorite is Gale Webb, a skater whose extreme sports and air shows energize crowds all over the country with her unique mix of skateboarding athleticism and motivational messages. Gale has spent much of her adult life "paying it forward," encouraging kids, especially girls, not to give up on themselves. Vans has worked with Gale for more than four decades and celebrated with her as she was inducted into the Skateboard Hall of Fame in 2019.

Gale remembers the first time she met members of the Van Doren family: "I knew right away that they weren't just about selling shoes. They were real deal people with big hearts. Paul and Steve and now Kristy have always been there for thousands of kids, sponsoring them so they could continue their future in sports, and helping them live their dreams."

Vans has continued to innovate in its outreach. In April 2020, Tony Hawk, an icon in the skater community, joined Vans as a global brand ambassador. One of Tony's protégés, Lizzie Armanto, joins other women skaters like Fabiana Delfino, Breana Geering, and Beatrice Domond, who have enlarged the talent pool of elite skaters in Vans' ranks.

■ ■ ■

The first Vans teams were the genesis of our close collaboration with action sports, and what were many years later dubbed "expressive creators," the artists and out-of-the-box thinkers and designers. The skaters and the surfers and young people in creative fields became an integral part of Vans' identity.

Without them, it's unlikely we'd have been able to reach beyond the sneaker market. Our commitment to these free spirits and their sport came to define Vans globally.

I wouldn't have had it any other way.

**John Bert Van Doren, b. 1882–d. 1957**     **Rena Rita Van Doren, b. 1901–d. 1971**

**The Van Doren childhood home, Braintree, MA, 1949**

**The Van Doren factory workshop near the family home in Braintree, MA**

**The Van Doren siblings in Paul's office, 1982:**
**(L–R) Paul, Robert, Johnny, Jimmy, and Bernice (front)**

**(L–R) Paul and siblings, Robert, Bernice, Johnny, and Jimmy**

**Paul and Dolly when they were engaged, 1949. He was 18 years old**

**Paul as a young manager, working at Randy's East, early 1960s**

Paul's five children: (L–R) Stevie, Taffy, Paul Jr., Janie, and Cheryl (front), the Boston area, 1960

The Van Doren kids: back (L–R) Paul, Taffy, Steve; front (L–R) Cheryl, Janie, Costa Mesa, CA, May 1964

Paul in the early years of Vans, mid-1960s

**Dolly and Paul, 2018, at the graduation of "Kohl"
(Paul's great-grandson), Seminole, OK**

**Paul, Jim, and Gordy, 1965,
putting the first factory together.
They were wearing coveralls**

**Gordy and Serge, 1967,
Old Style 45 Boat Shoe**

Serge and Paul at Paul's 85th birthday party, Las Vegas, 2015

The original Vans management team on the boat *Van Fan*, District Manager's Meeting, 1970s

Paul aboard the *Van Fan*, early 1970s

The first factory at 704 East Broadway, Anaheim, CA, 1966

The original Vans outsole

Unloading the first vulcanizer from the train, 1965

Shoes cooking in the vulcanizer, 1966

An early Vans retail store, Eagle Rock, CA, 1967

The Vans circus tent store, Canoga Park, CA, early 1970s

The original warehouse, Santa Ana, CA, 1970

Vans' second factory location at 2095 N. Bativia, Orange County, covered 14 acres, early 1980s

# The Original Vans Heel Labels

Late 1970s

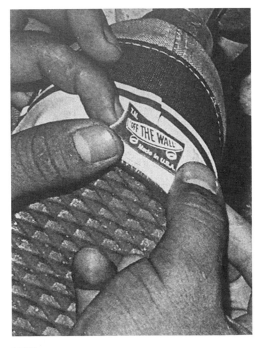

1976

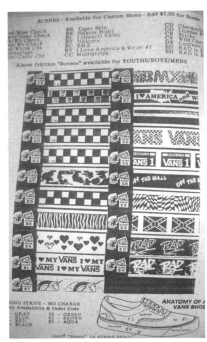

Late 1970s/early 1980s

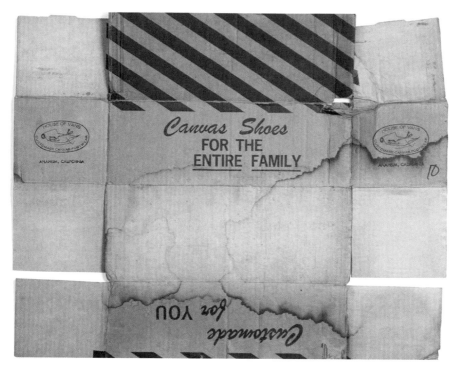

The Vans shoebox was the first to be made from a single sheet of cardboard, 1966

One of the original, iconic Vans boxes, late 1970s

The first heel label and box, 1966

The Tony Alva colorway shoe, 1976,
originally called Style 95, now known as the Era

**Old Skool, released in 1977**

**Sk8-Hi, rereleased in 1978**

**Paul with the checkerboard slip-on and Steve holding the Authentic at Paul's hometown Braintree, MA, store, 2015**

**Paul and Jimmy Van Doren at Picadilly Circus, on the way to the 1972 Olympics, Munich, Germany**

**The original Vans booth at the LA County Fair, 1974**

## Vans Sponsored Athletes

(L–R) Steve Caballero, Jeff Grosso (behind Steve), Steve Van Doren, Eric Dressen, Omar Hassan, Paul, Tony Alva, Christian Hosoi, and Ray Barbee at Steve Van Doren's 50th anniversary celebration at Vans in 2017 for 100 people onboard John Wayne's yacht, *Wild Goose*, Newport Beach, CA

(L–R) Dane and Patrick Gudauskas, Dylan Graves, Steve Van Doren, Paul, Nathan Fletcher, Nathan Florence, Herbie Fletcher, and Scott Sisamis, in front of Joel Tudor's photo, at the US Open of Surfing in Huntington Beach, CA, 2018. Steve was inducted to the Honor Roll of the Huntington Beach Surfing Walk of Fame

Steve Van Doren, Tony Alva, Joel Tudor, Paul and Jeff Grosso at the AMC Cinema in Orange, CA, for the launch of the documentary *The Tony Alva Story*, 2017

Geoff Rowley at a celebration of Vans 50th Anniversary at the House of Vans, London, 2016

Lizzie Armanto in 2018 at Vans European headquarters in Stabio, Switzerland, in front of a photograph of herself as the first woman to complete the Tony Hawk's legendary 360 degree loop, San Diego, CA, 2016

# Vans Sponsored Athletes

Steve Caballero, Dockland, London; the first international stop on the 1996 Warped Tour

Stacy Peralta, the director of *Dogtown and Z-Boys*, at the film's premiere at the Silverscreen Theater, 2002, West Hollywood, CA. Stacy became Vans first paid athlete in 1976

Tony Alva in March 1979, on the small Plexiglas ramp at his house, Malibu, CA

Legendary skateboarder Tony Alva appears for Q and A for his film *The Tony Alva Story* at the 2019 Santa Cruz Film Festival at the Colligan Theater, Santa Cruz, CA

Christian Hosoi puts on a show as he breaks in the just-opened Vans Off the Wall skatepark, Huntington Beach, CA, 2014

# Vans First Advertisements

1967

1976

1977, Jerry Valdez

1977

# Vans First Advertisements

**1970s, Everett Rosecrans and his demo team**

**1978**

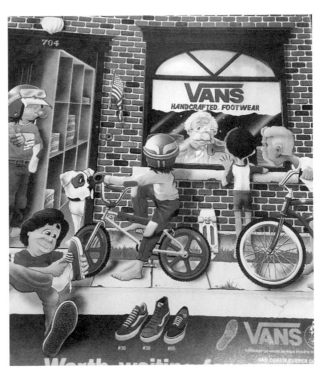

**1978**

# Vans First Advertisements

**Early 1980s, Eddie Fiola**

**1989, Steve Caballero designed the first pro model skate shoe**

# Vans Events

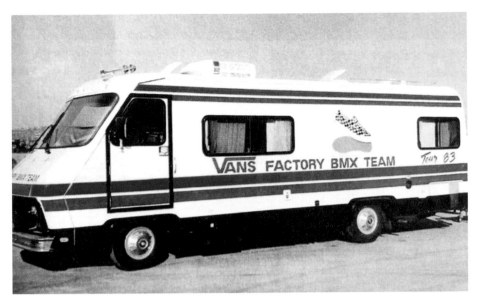

The Vans Factory BMX Team RV, 1980

Vans Park Series Venue during Vans US Open of Surfing at the BMX/Skate Venue, Huntington Beach, CA, 2018

# Vans Events

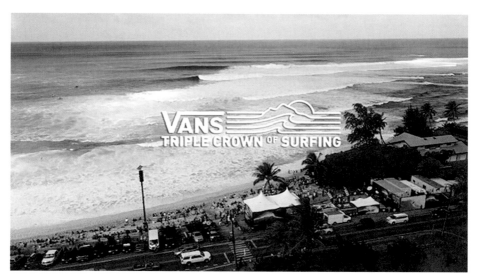

Vans Triple Crown of Surfing, Sunset Beach, North Shore, O'ahu, HI, 2018

Vans US Open of Surfing finals, Huntington Beach, CA, 2019

# Vans Warped Tour

**The Black Eyed Peas, Vans Warped Tour, Randall's Island, New York City, 1999**

**Blink 182 playing with special guest bass guitarist the legendary skateboarder Steve Caballero (middle), during the Vans Warped Tour, O'ahu, HI, 1998**

# Vans Warped Tour

Pennywise playing at the last stop on the 2018 Vans Warped Tour,
West Palm Beach, FL, with Warped Tour founder Kevin Lyman
proudly standing side-stage with his wife, Fran

My Chemical Romance at the 2005
Vans Warped Tour, Randall's Island,
New York City

Katy Perry at the Vans Warped Tour
15th Anniversary Celebration at
Club Nokia, Los Angeles, 2009

# Vans Warped Tour

A Day to Remember during the Vans Warped Tour at Marcus Amphitheatre, 2011, Milwaukee, MI

Robert Trujillo, Lars Ulrich, James Hetfield, and Kirk Hammett of Metallica at House of Vans, 2016, London

**Van Doren racing silks (late 1980s)**

RISE UP

*Boyd Gaming's Delta Jackpot Grd III*

Paul & Andrena Van Doren, Owners
Thomas M. Amoss, Trainer
Gerard Melancon , Jockey  November 23, 2013
Vinton, Louisiana  1-1/16 Miles 1:44.71

Purse $1,000,000
Casiguapo (2nd)
Rankkasprivileges (3rd)
$6.20 $4.00 $2.80

DELTA DOWNS

COADY Photography

**Rise Up wins the million dollar race, 2013**

**Paul at the race track on Opening Day, Del Mar, CA, 2016**

**Paul and Drena, 2000**

**The checkerboard slip-on stars in the film art for *Fast Times at Ridgemont High*, 1982**

**Sean Penn as "Spicoli" with his signature checkerboard slip-ons in *Fast Times at Ridgemont High***

Steve Van Doren with John Wayne and Billy Belcher in the Vans' booth at the Newport In-Water Boat Show, Newport Beach, CA, 1972

Samuel L. Jackson wears custom-made Vans in publicity photos for *Snakes on a Plane*, 2006: hand drawn by Tony Munoz, a Vans' shoe designer for twenty years

Vans collector Weird Al Jankovic with Vans MTV shoes, 1989

**Steve, the current face of Vans, late 1990s**

**Steve and Paul with Robert Vargas and his portrait of Paul, 2018**

**Back (L–R) Kevin Massar, David Tichiaz, Geoff Rowley, Bob Provost, Dirk Jacobs, Ben Sooprayen, and Peter Dericks; front (L–R) Ray Barbee, Christian Hosoi, Steve Van Doren, and Paul at Vans European headquarters, Stabio, Switzerland, 2018**

**Paul with Doug Palladini, Global Brand President of Vans, at the Van Doren Project, Costa Mesa, CA, 2018**

**Paul and his lifelong friend Murph, Brocton, MA, 2016**

**Paul with Terry Roche, acclaimed football coach and longtime friend of Vans, 2019**

**Paul may never catch pigeons, but he feeds them,
Milan Duomo, Italy, 2018**

**Steve, Paul, Cheryl, and Kristy at the first Van Doren Project,
Costa Mesa, CA, 2018**

**Steve Van Doren, Paul Van Doren, and Brian Cook, speaking
at the Van Doren Project, Costa Mesa, CA, 2018**

Sarah Turner, a winner of the
Van Doren Give A Shit Award, 2017

Luis Gallegos, a winner of the Van
Doren Give A Shit Award, 2018

Skateboarder Christian Hosoi, BMXer Dakota Roche, and
the Vans shoe car in action, 2020

# Interpretations of the Original Vans Sole

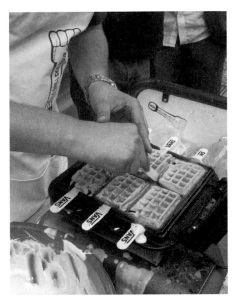

**The famous Vans waffle iron**

**A global advertisement**

**A Vans international showroom**

Paul's children at a family occasion, Fullerton, CA, 2010:
(back) Steve, Cheryl, Janie; (front) Paul Jr. and Taffy

Paul with five Van Doren Vans employees, 2016: (L-R) Kristy, Steve,
Paul, Cheryl, Jenny, and Philip (who left Vans to become a pastor)

Entrance to Vans headquarters, with a statue of Geoff Rowley
for his dedication to skateboarding, 2020, Costa Mesa, CA

# CHAPTER TEN

# Get Out While You Still Have Your Sanity

A nother lesson my father taught me, and without question, this is one to commit to memory: Life is only partly about how you hold and handle your cards. Don't ever be so god-damn sure of anything, because nothing in life is a given.

No matter how good the odds, no matter who's the favorite, no one but no one wins every race. Even when we pay attention, when we hope and pray and prepare and double- and triple-check, things go sideways. People lose their health and hard-earned businesses and the loves of their lives, and no one sees it coming. That's the hardscrabble of life.

Sometimes, you have to know when to fold your cards and call it a draw.

■ ■ ■

Vans had really grown during the seventies. The brand had evolved into more than what it once was and had finally found its niche. For better or worse, the same could have been said of my personal life. I had come into my own as a businessman, and as the years passed and my own kids grew older, our family dynamic began to shift.

The very best thing that occurred during that first decade of Vans was that we truly became a family business. Without exception, family has always been the most important thing in my life. It was one of my great joys that so many members of my family decided to come and work for the Van Doren Rubber Company during those first years. It had been a much-appreciated vote of confidence.

My brother Jimmy was of course one of the original partners in the company. From the start, he had been in charge of much of the production side of the business. My wife Dolly had also worked with us almost from the beginning as a retail store manager and had always pitched in wherever and whenever she was needed.

Dolly's brother Danny had joined us during our first year in business. He was an invaluable help in organizing and training our retail store employees. By 1971, we had opened around fifty Vans' stores throughout Southern California.

My kids joke that it was child abuse, but the Van Doren Rubber Company always had a spot open for them. My kids, their friends, my kids' kids, have had a leg up in getting a foot in the door. The catch was that I demanded 110 percent, and if I didn't get it, I browbeat them until I did. Keep in mind, until they were fifteen, I paid them, at best, in tacos, or whatever a dollar might buy them at the fair. Some might say I was opportunistic.

That's not how I see it.

Not everyone gets a fair shake. Not everyone is given the opportunities they deserve. I'd like to think things like opportunity and rights are inalienable, but that isn't always how it works.

I didn't learn this on my own. My eldest daughter, Taffy, and older son, Paul Jr., taught me. Sometimes opportunity just means that when faced with defeat or loss, a person refuses to say, "Woe is me," but instead looks forward and asks, "What can I accomplish now?"

The way we deal with hardship is our legacy. You can accept defeat, or you can overcome it.

Taffy had worked in one of our stores before getting married and having her first child. She was a dynamite salesperson and the perfect model for our custom-made shoes. She's not as business-savvy as her younger sister Cheryl, but let's just say when she was young, Taffy bent over backward to make customers want to come back. She also helped Dolly in the shop, and often they'd match their outfit patterns to model with their Vans shoes. But it wasn't long after she became a new mother that she and the family received a life-changing blow.

In 1971, at the young age of twenty, Taffy was diagnosed with retinitis pigmentosa, a debilitating, degenerative eye disease, and within a handful of years, she was totally blind. From the very beginning, Taffy was a joyful, gentle person, kind and generous. She was the best oldest sister any kid could have. And she'd turned into this beautiful young woman who gave Dolly and me our first grandbaby.

She wasn't maudlin or bitter, but I was. When she lost her sight, all I could think about was how unfair it was. What sort of opportunities would she have? How would her losing her sight limit her opportunities? I worried about her newborn, a little girl she'd named

Jackie. How would Taffy's blindness limit, even hurt, Jackie's chances at a normal, happy life?

Because of a genetic anomaly, my kid couldn't see her own child or father. This broke my heart. I worried that she would never be happy. I worried that this bright, beautiful kid of mine had been cheated, robbed of the opportunity to have a good life, to provide for her family, and to experience all the goodness in the world.

I'm not saying that if it had been within my power, I wouldn't have taken it back or changed it; what I'm saying is that I was wrong. Taffy's life continued to offer her plenty of opportunities. After she fell in love with Rick and went on to have more beautiful kids, she found work she loved. She was one of the first participants in a study on the bionic eye and somehow, she and her loyal guide dog made it back and forth to St. John's Hospital in Santa Monica, where she worked with the doctors and scientists and served as the project's spokesperson.

Maybe I shouldn't have worried, but then, maybe opportunity means different things to different people, depending on your viewpoint and your circumstances. Each of us has the potential to be successful. A lot of what we accomplish is put upon us: there's what we choose, and what chooses us. Then, too, there are instances when we're not given any choice at all. It was the way my kids responded to their individual challenges, ones that I could never have foreseen, that showed me the real meaning of opportunity and the enormity of their potential.

Taffy never bemoaned her blindness or questioned why. Taffy was, and continues to be, an amazing and accomplished person. She never ceases to make me and the entire Van Doren family extremely proud.

If anything, the way she handled her disability helped Paul Jr. navigate his own vision loss at age twenty-three. Losing his sight was more gradual, but when I think back, I realize that when he began to notice small changes in his peripheral vision, he hadn't wanted to believe that what happened to his sister was happening to him too.

Like his sister, Paul Jr. didn't focus on how blindness might limit his opportunities. He returned to college and finished his degree in accounting. In later years he served at a state-run independent living facility, and for three decades helped people in need, training and placing them in jobs until he eventually became the organization's executive director.

It's easy to be proud of all my kids, but that's such a "dad" thing to say. I've been proudest of them for exceeding any opportunity I could provide. It's in spite of anything I might have planned or hoped for that my life is richer and more meaningful.

Of course, Vans benefitted from their hard work and varied talents.

To this day, Stevie lives and breathes Vans. From the time he could walk, he never passed up a chance to be involved in the Vans' action, whether the job was passing out flyers door-to-door in neighborhoods, charming folks off the street and into our stores, or spending his summers in the warehouse stocking shelves or packing boxes.

It's hard to imagine kids today coming up the way mine did in the family business. Stevie started working in the Vans factory in the summers when he was twelve or thirteen. He wasn't mechanically inclined like his brother Paul, so I put him on one of the assembly lines that made 750 pairs a day. You could work as fast as you wanted, as long as you maintained quality.

He worked the very end of the production line. After the shoe had been lasted, he put the sole on and placed the rubber pieces, foxing, friction, bumper, and heel label around it. Then he rolled down all the parts nice and smooth and put the shoe on a rack before sending it to the vulcanizers to be cooked.

Stevie was a key contributor from the start— he and Paul Jr. had been instrumental in fixing up and painting the original Vans factory, as well as turning each and every newly acquired retail space into a consistently attractive and functional shoe store. Then there was his brief stint as the world's youngest (at age eleven) temporary store manager, and his overwhelming success at the county fair. He continued to be the key factor in our new and growing skateboarding connection.

Stevie worked harder than most of the adults and never expected accolades. When he was young, his biggest reward at the end of the day was five tacos from Pup n Taco. To him, that was the best treat ever. To this day, tacos are his favorite.

Paul Jr. pitched in to pass out flyers and the like, but in the early days his main contribution was his mechanical genius. I definitely could not have opened our retail stores nearly as efficiently without his awesome construction expertise, even as a kid. Paul preferred being on his own, doing carpentry and building things.

From his earliest teen years, Paul Jr. loved working on cars. It had really been a win-win when he took charge of our Vans gas station and garage, which he was in charge of for several years. He did an amazing job keeping our fleet in good running order. A decade later, he joined the Vans accounting department, where he worked until 1992.

Janie also began working part time in one of the Vans retails stores at age fifteen, like Taffy. After high school graduation, Janie went on to join Vans full time and landed in what we now call the IT department. But those were the days of mainframe computers the size of Volkswagens, and they had to be kept in a climate-controlled room and treated like temperamental babies.

In order to run those early computers, you needed to be excellent at math and even better at logic, because you had to learn a whole new language to talk to the machines. Janie did all that and more.

It wasn't unusual for her to get a call in the middle of the night because of a computer problem that needed to be taken care of immediately. That sort of thing didn't faze her a bit. She was also years ahead of the field at that time, and Vans greatly benefitted from her expertise. Not only were we on the cutting edge of sneaker design, we were also on the cutting edge of business technology, thanks partly to Janie.

Our youngest child, Cheryl, has more street smarts than the four other kids combined. But like the others, Cheryl started working at Vans as a teenager in sales. We'd run out of space at the Anaheim factory and opened a warehouse and store in Santa Ana.

She reminds me of myself in many ways. Cheryl has a knack for understanding people and for solving problems. There is never a challenge too tough for her to handle. Not long after she started at the warehouse store, she got a six-dollar tip from a very happy customer. Not knowing that Cheryl was the owner's daughter, the customer made it a point to let management know she was impressed with the excellent service she had received.

After graduating from high school, Cheryl worked as a clerk in the Vans purchasing department, and she was also the mail courier, delivering interoffice mail between the various Vans offices in Anaheim twice a day. She learned so much about purchasing that in 1980 she was promoted to being one of only two people in charge of buying all the raw materials for the entire Vans company.

In 1987, she moved over to human resources to handle employee benefits, employee safety, and the company insurance—a lot of responsibility, but she handled it expertly. She worked her way up to become Vice President of Human Resources in 1999. Cheryl continues to be a very smart and savvy businesswoman, an incredible asset to Vans.

I'm proud to hear her say that what she learned from me was that in order to be good at something, "You need to understand it, you have to work hard, and you need to be part of a team. I've lived with that every day."

How does one acquire the "street smarts" I attribute to her?

"Some just comes from years of knowledge and growth with the brand," Cheryl answers. "And inherently knowing where you've come from to help you get to where you're going, is probably a big part of that."

Cheryl goes on to say: "I've seen and been a part of all the wins and the losses we've had over the years. I've seen firsthand what's worked and what hasn't, and why. You acquire street smarts with experience because you've actually lived something. You haven't just read about it or heard about it. You've been through it."

In other words: you've gotten your hands dirty.

I loved being surrounded by my home family at work, and also by the loyal Vans employees who had become like a family over that first decade together. People who started jobs at Vans didn't leave. To my delight and satisfaction, Vans was developing a real corporate culture of people nurturing and supporting one another, management and employees alike. We treated one another just like family—because that's what we were.

Believe me, I did not miss the irony that it was at this precise moment in 1973 that I made the difficult decision to leave my marriage.

■ ■ ■

I will always love Dolly. I have five kids with her, and I spent twenty-five years married to her. It's painful to lose someone special and to take something important apart, but I just didn't feel there was any possible way for me to change the situation. So, I took the opportunity to change myself.

I guess I always felt that my wife did not appreciate what I did. Sometimes if things weren't going right at Vans, I didn't come home for days. I wasn't running around; I was working. I had made up my mind that when my youngest turned sixteen, I was going to leave.

A random incident pushed me out the door. It wasn't anything momentous. My friend Tom had invited us to an important event he was hosting, something to do with horse racing. Dolly refused to go with me. I tried talking her into it because I knew the event meant a lot to my friend. I knew Dolly's absence would be noted. She still refused.

I'll admit, I saw red. Yes, it was immature, but in that moment, I understood things would never get any better between Dolly and me.

I was delaying the inevitable. At that point, we were pretty much living separate lives, like proverbial ships passing in the night. We didn't like doing any of the same things and we each had our own set of friends. That wasn't a healthy way for either of us to live. We both deserved to be genuinely happy.

I took several deep breaths, packed my belongings, and moved out of my family home. I found a small apartment nearby, and I continued to interact as much as possible with the kids. I didn't want them feeling as though I'd abandoned them completely.

Thankfully, for the most part, the kids took it in stride. They were upset, of course, and for a while, I found it hard to spend much time with them. My daughter Cheryl characterizes it as "a time of absence."

But overall, they accepted my decision. Dolly, however, did not take it well. It was many years before she spoke to me again—not that I blamed her. I felt guilt-ridden for a long time. But in my heart, I knew that leaving had been the right thing to do.

Even after the divorce, Dolly's brother Danny remained a key factor in the success of Vans. At this point in the company's development, we needed to find new ways to grow the business. Well before the advent of Foot Locker retailers, our model had always been to sell athletic shoes directly to our customers. One way to expand was simply to put stores where they hadn't been before.

There is always a chance something will prove to be a waste of your time or money or effort—but recognizing a good opportunity when it comes down the pike is key.

Danny saw an opportunity, and he had a real entrepreneurial spirit. One day he came to me and asked if he could open a dozen Vans retail stores up in the San Francisco area.

I thought, *Well, why not let him give it a try?*

When Danny found a location, Paul Jr. would drive a truck up to San Francisco, bringing up all the usual shelves and the first shipment of shoes. Then Stevie and sometimes Cheryl would fly up on Friday night and help open the store at the weekend.

Over the next two years, Danny ran thirteen stores in the Bay area, but in 1974, the market tightened up. Unfortunately, we ended up having to close those stores. Danny and his wife, Louise, loved living up north. Danny became our first Northern California sales rep, driving all over to various retailers including surf, skate, and BMX shops, like the Oliver Bike Shop, which he did for many years to come. It was the first time we had sold shoes outside of Southern California.

It's hard to exploit an existing advantage while exploring new ones, but that's something we've done consistently.

By 1973, our Vans family was expanding, and so were our markets. Stevie had graduated from high school in the spring and had just started working at Vans full time. That fall, he came and told me he was thinking about getting married to his high school sweetheart, Susan. They'd met when he was a senior and she was a sophomore, and the two of them really had the quintessential boy-meets-girl, wholesome American love story. I really liked Susan, but I was taken aback: I hadn't realized things were so serious between them. They were so darn young.

"Son," I said, "as a husband, you'll be responsible for providing for your wife and kids. You have no clue how to save money or to organize your finances. Every penny you earn you spend on yourself or your friends, and you never have two nickels to rub together."

Stevie just shuffled around on his feet. "Well, I can learn," he insisted.

I thought about it for a minute.

"I'll tell you what," I said. "If you really mean that, this is what we'll do. We'll open up a joint savings account under both our names, which means you can't withdraw any money without my signature. Which you will never get. Every week you'll bring me your paycheck to deposit, and there it will stay until the day you get married."

Stevie blinked, and then his jaw dropped. "B-but," he sputtered, "I have a car payment! How will I pay that?"

At graduation, Stevie had traded in his Mustang and gotten a brand-new bright yellow 1973 Capri.

I shrugged. "If you want to get married bad enough, you'll figure it out."

He wasn't happy. But I'll be damned if he didn't come back the very next day and present his idea to me.

Overnight, he had come up with a novel way to make extra money *and* solve a growing problem at our warehouse: returns and factory seconds.

The thing is, at Vans we always guaranteed our shoes. If there was ever a problem with workmanship, if anything ever went wrong or fell apart, you could just bring back the shoes and get a new pair. For our first several years, the company had donated those flawed shoes to charity—the ones that were just cosmetic—along with any seconds that had been rejected during production. Collectively, we called these the "smellers."

After a while, though, the charities caught on to the fact that they could bring the donated seconds back to a store and get-brand new, first-quality shoes in exchange. Not exactly what we'd had in mind. We'd had to stop donating the smellers, and for several years they'd been piling up in box after box in the warehouse.

"Okay, Dad," he said. "Remember when you first started Vans and we had nowhere to sell our shoes, and nobody had ever heard of us, and we weren't making hardly any money at all?"

"Yeah," I said with a grimace. "Those were the days, eh?"

"Well, do you remember on some of the weekends you used to drive us kids to local swap meets, and we'd sell our shoes there? To get that extra bit of cash to keep the business afloat?"

"Yeah," I said. "I remember."

Those had actually been really fun days. Swap meets were a sunny SoCal institution, and they were always fascinating events, filled with every kind of item you could imagine and some whose function you could never quite discern. The kids and I had a blast hawking shoes at the swap meets. I spent more quality time with my kids there than any other single place. I'd always give each of them a dollar to spend on whatever they wanted, and everyone came home happy, carrying some kind of treasure.

"Well," Stevie said, "how about if on the weekends I take a load of the smellers down to the border and sell them at the big swap meets there for a dollar a pair? It's not like we're getting anything for them now."

Swap meets on the border were wildly popular with Mexican re-tailers. They would come up to buy seconds or overstock of clothes, shoes, appliances, every possible item US sellers wanted to offload. Then they turned around and sold the goods in their little mom-and-pop stores in Mexico. I'd always been aware they were doing a thriving business down there, much more so than the smaller swap meets up in our area, but the border, about a hundred miles south, had always seemed too far of a drive to make it worthwhile.

If Stevie was willing to put in the hours, hell, I was all in.

"Okay," I said. "Provided you share the opportunity with your sisters and brothers and your cousins and let them go in on it with you."

"Sure," he said. "Company would be great."

"You have to split any money you make fifty-fifty with the company." They were still our shoes, after all.

He grumbled a bit at that but agreed.

Sure enough, for the next year and a half, almost every Saturday and Sunday morning, Stevie got up before dawn and made the two-hour drive in a company van loaded with smellers, and every Saturday and Sunday evening he'd come home with a fistful of cash, which we duly split, as agreed. Not one of his siblings or cousins ever wanted to go with him, so he was able to keep half the profits for himself. He was able to make that car payment, and a whole lot more. He also met a lot of those small Mexican retailers, and many of them ended up his good friends.

At the end of a year and a half, our warehouse was empty of all those smellers, and Stevie had paid off the car. He also saved enough money for a down payment on his first house, which he and his new wife bought after they were married in 1976. The kid had done good. If I'm being honest, in my summation, it wasn't Stevie who wasn't ready—I was the one not prepared for him to marry.

It had taken a decade, but things were coming together at Van Doren Rubber Company. In 1976, we began four years of blessings for the Van Dorens: Taffy married Rick, Stevie married Susan, and Janie married, too. Then, between 1977 and 1980, five of my seven grandkids were born: Susan had Kristy, Taffy had Jenny and Debbie, and Janie had Shannon and Jimmy.

As for the carousel that was Vans, by 1981, after fifteen years in business, days went around and around. I could have gone on, giving 100 percent, but—this is hard to admit—I'd become burned out on making sneakers. I was fifty-one and had been working my tail off for more than three decades. I decided it might be the right time for someone else to take over the reins of the Van Doren Rubber Company and usher Vans into the future.

In the early years, metaphorically speaking, it was all me drinking from a fire hydrant. A change of leadership, from me to my brother Jimmy, would infuse new ideas and enthusiasm into the company and its employees.

When I had originally broached the idea of leaving with our founding shareholder, Serge, he wasn't exactly enthusiastic, but he understood and blessed my stepping back from my active role. I suggested we put Jimmy in the top spot in place of me.

Serge agreed Jimmy would be the best choice. Jimmy was one of the four founding partners and had been with the company since Day One. He was super smart, and he knew the shoe business backward and forward.

We spoke with Jimmy and Gordy and laid out my proposal. I would leave, and Jimmy would take over leadership of the company. Gordy agreed right away. He had no desire to be in charge. Jimmy was a little surprised but very pleased and excited we'd chosen him. He said he had lots of great ideas on how to grow the company and promised to do an awesome job.

We had no reason to doubt him. So when he asked the three of us to sign over to him our voting power so he could manage the company however he wanted without having to run every little thing past us with a vote, we didn't hesitate to give it to him.

That one decision turned out to be the biggest mistake I've ever made in my life.

Jimmy also asked for the percentage of shares between the partners to be equalized. Since the beginning of the company, I had been the biggest shareholder with 40 percent, and Serge also had 40 percent, with Jimmy and Gordy holding just 10 percent each. Jimmy wanted all of us to be equal at 25 percent, which meant that Serge and I would have to give up a big chunk of our shares.

I agreed to that, too. I figured at that point it was all academic, anyway. Vans was doing great, and I wasn't worried. There were no plans to sell or to go public, where it would have mattered. It would just be like dividing up shares on a Monopoly board. Or so I thought.

■ ■ ■

For my whole life, I had really had just one dream. Right behind the let me craft the world's best sneaker dream, and the let my kids be healthy dream, and the one that hopes all of us prosper and multiply—right behind what I call essential dreams, was one in which eventually I'd be able to do whatever I wanted financially. For me, this meant being able to go to the races anytime I felt like it.

As a kid, I never wanted to be a fireman or a doctor or even a businessman; I just wanted to go to the races.

So when I retired, for a hundred consecutive days I went to Santa Anita Park. I didn't miss a single day, not one, and it took a solid hundred days for the novelty to wear off. For my new wife, Drena, on the other hand, the excitement hadn't lasted even a month. She had grown tired of being a racetrack junkie almost straightaway.

For the first year after I separated from Dolly, I didn't go on dates or seek out other women. That had never been the reason I left home. Then one day, quite by accident, I met a wonderful woman.

Andrena Aitkenhead was a cocktail waitress at a restaurant I used to frequent with my friend Tom. Drena was my age, but she had a vivacious, youthful spirit. She was fun and adventurous, interested in everything around her, and believed in living life to its very fullest.

I was instantly intrigued, and after a few more meetings, I asked her out. Happily, she said yes. We dated and talked about everything under the sun, and it turned out we had many interests in common. It didn't take long for me to become totally smitten with Drena. Thankfully, she felt the same way. After dating for six years, we got married in 1981.

When we'd been together for about a year, I purchased a forty-two-acre farm in Parkfield, near Paso Robles, California. Paso Robles is a gorgeous little town just north of San Luis Obispo on the Pacific coast. The property didn't have a view of the ocean, but the scenery was breathtaking: rolling hills, wooded dales, and golden fields separated by country roads.

On the farm, I built a home for us, a barn for our horses, and an office. Then I had a fence built around the entire property painted black, much to the disappointment of my neighbors. It was such a pleasure to ride our horses around that beautiful property, breathing in the refreshing, clean air while taking in the expansive view. Drena also turned me on to the fun of going to rodeos.

While living on the farm, Drena and I talked over what we should do with ourselves. Both of us had always been busy people. Sitting idle, however pleasant, wasn't my style or hers. What if we took the woman who loved to ride and the man who loved the track, and tag-teamed a racehorse business? It wasn't until we sat down and talked over the possibilities that we made a conscious decision how to live.

We decided we wanted to take our interest in horses to the next level and get into the racehorse business. Neither of us knew the first thing about raising or training racehorses, but a challenge had never stopped either of us before. We could learn as we went along, right?

We bought Teasable later that year. She was a valuable filly. Her breeding was spot on, top notch. Her sire was Bold Ruler, probably the leading sire in the country at the time. I figured if Teasable couldn't run herself, then she'd make a hell of a broodmare and produce future runners. She had that sort of pedigree.

This was my big shot at getting into racing, so I gladly paid all the bills. If more money ended up going out of the account than coming in, I would replenish the difference. I didn't mind, because by this time I had the means, and this new venture was proving to be so invigorating.

I've learned that life is only fun when it's challenging. The key is to recognize that in any demanding situation there's also opportunity, and you just have to position yourself to best withstand whatever life throws at you.

# CHAPTER ELEVEN

# Shit Happens: Get On with It

f you ask me, one of the biggest problems with many businesses—no matter if they're hot-shot communications companies or blue-collar manufacturers or small mom-and-pops—is always the same. If there are more than twenty employees and they're struggling with bottlenecks, sticking points, or just plain stagnation, it's usually a matter of focus. For me, whenever a situation went sideways and things looked dire, I always called up my one superpower: focus. It's what I do better than almost anything else.

When I focus, I tend to forget about everything else. I am driven to get the job done and just keep doing what I'm doing until it's finished. It stands to reason when someone focuses all their attention on one thing, they do a better job.

The same applies to horseracing. Some horses, especially when they're new to the track, are easily distracted by other horses or the crowds of spectators. When that happens, trainers will affix what are called blinders, which block out a horse's peripheral vision and keep them focused on the task at hand. Quite often a horse will need to wear blinders only once, and from then on they can see their goal clearly.

Frankly, we could all use blinders to help us focus.

What's so great about focus, you ask? Everything. When you learn how to cut distraction, everything gets a hell of a lot easier. Focus leads to success because it's the best way to meaningfully solve problems, and it's how we direct our organization's efforts. An organization's focus rests on its leader's ability to focus. People talk all the time about attention deficit, and I'm not saying people don't struggle with it. But a lack of focus always jams things up, while putting on blinders has the potential to serve a greater good. What I am saying is when leaders limit distraction, they're better able to lead.

■ ■ ■

At first, things went well under Jimmy's leadership. Over the next few years, he set out to expand production, riding the wave of our skateboarding and surfing success, and successfully launched three new styles Stevie had already put into the pipeline before I left: the Old Skool, the Slip-On, and the Sk8-Hi.

Eventually, his focus began to slip. In 1978, Jimmy had opened an additional office and factory, and in 1980 everything other than the original mill room was moved to the new location. In 1981, after I retired, still more new offices and a warehouse were opened.

Stevie had been working full time at Vans since he'd graduated from high school three years earlier, mostly in the warehouse, and he was also responsible for running the booth at the LA County Fair every year. He was really good at that. When Jimmy took over, he promoted Stevie, despite Stevie's young age, to oversee half of the Vans retail stores, including their district managers and employees—around fifty stores at the time.

In my opinion, that was probably the wisest decision Jimmy made in his whole time as head of Vans. Stevie is a people person. Every morning he would hold a short "tell me about your day" meeting with all ten of his district managers, five days a week. That way they could all share their problems and learn from the collective solutions. Everyone benefitted. I thought that was really smart.

When the LA County Fair came around in September, on each day of the fair Stevie would bring out five or six different store managers and have them work with him at the big outdoor House of Vans booth for the whole day. He'd blast sixties music from the boom box, tell stories about Vans and how I'd started it, and they'd all have a great time. Stevie would get to know the managers and see their sales techniques and their personalities, and at the same time, he was instilling in them the Vans culture: work hard but have fun.

Some of our friends and longtime employees enjoyed the fair so much that they would even schedule their vacation days so they could work the fair full time and make extra money. Some would even have their spouses work. My brother Johnny also worked the fair with us, making sub sandwiches while Stevie barbecued. They made a great team.

Stevie was in charge of half of the retail stores, and another guy was in charge of the other half. Stevie was very competitive and always wanted his stores to beat the other stores. He'd have special moonlight sales if his stores were lagging behind. He created something called bargain trucks.

Because the LA County Fair was held only once a year, and we'd quit going to swap meets once the business didn't have to squeeze every nickel, we needed a way to move the warehouse overstock and the colors and styles that weren't selling, what we called dead stock, especially now that we'd increased production so much. Twice a week, the warehouse would fill a bargain truck with a thousand pairs of the dead stock, and one of our workers would drive to two different stores each week. As at the fair, they'd sell the shoes at a big discount, and the store would have a big boost in sales that week.

Stevie also made sure that skateboarding continued to be a top priority for the company. In the early eighties, Vans built skateboard ramps at all three of the factories, so skaters could come over and practice on the ramps without having to break into abandoned pools. We also started sponsoring more skaters, both professionals and amateurs, boys and girls.

By this time, Vans operated seventy stores in California, and the popularity of the shoes was growing all over the country, given wholesale reps were expanding the company's reach and dealers now sold both domestically and internationally. In addition, an increasing number of collaborations with well-known brands like Peanuts and Disney had boosted our visibility further.

In 1982, sales went through the roof with the release of the hit movie *Fast Times at Ridgemont High*, written by Cameron Crowe, based on his book about life at a California high school. In his first

starring role, Sean Penn played Jeff Spicoli, a lovable stoner character and a cool skate and surf dude. He always wore Vans.

If there was ever a character custom-made to wear our shoes,
it was Spicoli. Not only did he skate and surf, but he was also in a
band. He epitomized everything that was cool about Vans. He was
young, fun, and super likeable—an off-the-wall individual who was
always his own man, much to the frustration of his teachers. He did
whatever he wanted, even having pizza delivered to class.

Vans made a serendipitous appearance in the film because Sean
Penn occasionally visited our Santa Monica store to buy shoes.
According to Betty Mitchell, the store manager, he bought a pair of
the checkered Slip-Ons for personal use as soon as they came out.

By the time the movie was released nationwide, Betty had been
promoted to be PR manager for all of Vans. She was always talking
with the Hollywood studios. When she heard about Sean's choice of
shoe for the movie, she took it upon herself to deliver twenty-four
more pairs of the checkered Slip-Ons to Universal Studios in person.

Everyone on set ended up wearing them. The shoe even showed
up, front and center, on one of the most popular *Fast Times* movie
posters. When audiences saw the movie, orders for the checkerboard style exploded.

Stevie, of course, had gone right out and bought the soundtrack,
which also featured the movie art with our checkerboard shoe in the
center of the album cover. This gave Stevie another brilliant idea.
Somehow, he wrangled one thousand pairs of the checkered shoes
from Jimmy. Then he got Betty to call up all the big radio stations
set to debut Jackson Browne's song "Somebody's Baby" from the
movie. The DJs gave away pairs of the shoes while the song was
playing—the first time Vans was really noticed all over the country.

The film made a star of Sean Penn and became a cult classic. It also launched Vans nationwide, bringing our shoes into department stores and independent retailers all over the country. From that time on, the checkered pattern has been a true Vans phenomenon, appearing everywhere from our shoes to the stems of sunglasses. Sales of the checkerboard Slip-Ons have never flagged. In 2011, for example, the actress Kristen Stewart "cemented" the shoes into pop culture history when she wore a pair to her Hollywood Walk of Fame ceremony.

Thanks to the movie, business at Vans was booming. After the release, Vans grew from a $20 million company to a $45 million company.

Jimmy was convinced all this good stuff was happening because of his amazing leadership. His ego swelled like a balloon, and he got greedy. But as the skater kids say, Jimmy didn't quite stomp the landing.

■  ■  ■

When I was a little kid, my mother had taught me a couple of hard lessons about greed, and I never forgot them. If jealousy is a lack of confidence, then greed is an excess of ego, and my mother didn't stand for either. Beyond the more corporal broom beatings of my childhood, the most lasting lessons my mother ever taught me were baked.

One was a cake. The other was an apple pie. As for the cake, back when I was a boy, Mom always made each of us a special cake on our birthday. One year, and keep in mind I was quite young, I told her I wanted to eat my whole birthday cake myself. The thought of eating an entire cake thrilled me.

To this day, I remember how she tilted her head. Mom was stunning: when any of her kids had her favorable attention, it was as if every bit of sunlight in the universe doubled. She smiled such a sweet smile and, with a single eyebrow raised, she said, "Okay, Paul, if that's really what you want."

The following day, there before me on the kitchen counter was a box that held my very own cake. All I could think about was how I had been given permission to eat the whole thing myself. To that end, I threw open the lid with, well, the word *gusto* comes to mind.

My beautiful mother was the best baker and sauce maker I ever knew. So I was wholly crushed to peer in and see one smallish cupcake in the box. Though frosted and chocolate, the cupcake was surely a fraction of what I'd have had if she'd made a regular-size cake.

I deflated in disappointment. Mom patted my head, and with a sympathetic sigh, went to the pantry and brought out another box containing a ginormous birthday cake bigger than my whole head.

"Want to share this one?" she asked, which of course I did.

It might be nice to think I'd learned this lesson—that Mom had baked the insatiable appetite right out of me—but not so long after, I found myself asking Mom if she'd make an apple pie just for me. I pointed out to her that the week prior she'd made one, and when Dad had gone to slice it, mine had been unusually paltry.

It strikes me that I always seem to remember being slighted or snubbed—even the illusion of it—more keenly than I do being rewarded. For me, I remember when someone overlooked or dismissed me more clearly than the times I was chosen or I made my own choice.

I was surprised when Mom agreed to make me my own pie, and even more surprised when she baked two apple pies the following day. She said both were for me. I sat down at the table and ate two entire pies.

I ate an entire lifetime of apple pie in ten, maybe fifteen minutes. If the cake hadn't taught me well to unlearn greed, getting sick on pie sealed the deal on my moral education.

Apparently, Jimmy never learned the same lessons from Mom.

With sales skyrocketing, in 1984 Jimmy boosted production yet again and moved the offices and much of the Vans factory to a new plant on a fourteen-acre parcel of land in Orange, California, raising the number of employees to more than one thousand. He also put in place a slew of licensing agreements, for sunglasses and notebooks, often in the black-and-white checkered pattern.

I had been stubborn about keeping company advertising minimal, but Jimmy went in the opposite direction. He started advertising right and left. Every new style of shoe was introduced with a huge ad campaign. He was spending money as if we had our own mint.

He spent on himself, too. He went out and bought a Maserati.

Far worse, against my firm advice, he also started putting out a fleet of specialty athletic shoes for baseball, football, umpiring, basketball, soccer, wrestling, boxing, skydiving, and even break-dancing shoes. Break-dancing? Seriously? Those weren't even vulcanized, and they were made overseas.

Everything he did was over the top. Vans started offering nine different widths. Jimmy was trying to make Vans into something it was not. We were a company devoted to the indie sports—skating and surfing. Sports such as wrestling and skydiving, and team sports such as football and baseball, were far afield from our core market and mission.

That key factor, focus, was being lost.

I couldn't believe Jimmy was making many of the same mistakes as Randy's, which ultimately caused the company to flounder and fail. I feared the same fate for Vans.

All the profits the company made after *Fast Times* had been long ago depleted, so the added costs for labor, new production, and plant expansion drove Jimmy to borrow money from the bank. Then he borrowed more and more money, snowballing the debt. To make things worse, the US market was hit by a flood of cheap Asian imitations and knockoffs of our popular Vans styles. To compete with the pirates, Jimmy dropped our prices to below our manufacturing costs, hoping to ride it out until US Customs could choke off the illegal sources. That didn't work, which led to even more debt.

Before Jimmy took over the business, the only money Vans had ever borrowed from the bank was the yearly line of credit I'd activate in order to produce the huge volume of shoes for the annual back-to-school rush. That loan had always been paid off by the first of October that same year. I had never allowed Vans to carry a cent of bank debt for any longer than that.

Jimmy was spending way beyond the company's financial means, racking up massive debts with both the bank and our suppliers. Where I had always costed out every single thing and knew down to the penny what each pair of shoes cost, including utilities, rent, and so on, and made my production decisions based on that, Jimmy didn't care what things cost. He just bulldozed ahead.

Jimmy was wasting a ton of money on all the lasts, dyes, and materials for the fancy athletic shoes—and they weren't selling. Vans wasn't known for that kind of shoe. People bought their athletic shoes from the big powerhouses like Adidas and the other brands.

Between 1982 and 1984, my youngest brother managed to lose more than $3.5 million for the company, and to amass a total debt of around $12 million.

I had tried to talk to Jimmy on several occasions over those two years, to let him know I felt he was taking the company in the opposite direction from where I thought it should be going. I kept telling him, "Hey, all these new athletic shoes are costing us a fortune, and we're losing our shirts!"

Jimmy wouldn't listen, because he felt he'd guided Vans through the checkerboard boom and believed we were still flying high. In his mind, we were the hottest thing going. He always brushed aside my concerns and told me to butt out. I'd had my turn, and now he was in charge.

Finally, I had to hold up my hands in surrender. Jimmy was family. I've always put my family first and business second. My relationship with Jimmy was more important to me than the company's profit margin. Though I truly believed pretty much everything he was doing was dead wrong, I bit my tongue and respected his wishes. I stayed out of his hair, kept my mouth shut, and didn't make trouble.

I didn't mind so much because I had other things going on in my life. Drena's and my new business, raising racehorses, was doing well up at the ranch in Paso Robles, and an alfalfa farm with Paul Jr. was also going great. That was where I wanted to be full time, not at Vans trying to fix Jimmy's epic mistakes.

By 1984, Jimmy had put Vans somewhere between the prover-bial rock and hard place. He'd all but abandoned Van's core con-stituents—the surfers, skaters, moms, and kids who'd made us successful. He had gotten greedy and expanded to other markets Vans had no business entering. It was like making jellybeans: most manufacturers do better with fewer than a hundred styles. There are only so many flavors anyone can master. But what made Vans' situation even more precarious is that under Jimmy's leadership and unchecked spending, the company struggled to make ends meet.

In the wake of *Fast Times at Ridgemont High* and the bonanza of the checkerboard Slip-Ons, we'd had a golden ticket. But like 70 percent of lottery winners who go broke in three years, the schmuck who fails to consider what things cost never stands a chance.

Ironically, what sunk Jimmy was a refund check from the IRS for nearly $1.5 million. When it arrived, he was so in debt that when management wasn't exactly sure where the money belonged—to the bank, or Vans—a hasty decision was made to keep it. The bank disagreed. Vehemently. And then they called due one of the com-pany's loan notes of almost $7 million. Vans didn't have it, not by a long shot; and at that point, Vans ran out of options and was forced to declare bankruptcy.

The courts strongly advised us to hire bankruptcy attorneys to deal with the case, so we did. One by one, we were interviewed, which I learned determined whether or not Vans was worth saving or if it should simply be dissolved.

The bank was pushing hard for us to be liquidated and our as-sets sold to repay them. But at my initial meeting with the lead at-torney, he asked, "Paul, who's your competition?"

In the entire twenty-five years I ran the Van Doren Rubber Company, I never made a list of competitors. Not once did I consider which share of the market we might corner. Not once. Not ever. No, what I thought about was vulcanized rubber, and how to do what I enjoyed doing to perfection for my family's business in Southern California.

His question threw me. I couldn't figure out what it had to do with bank loans and debt. A part of me thought that if I said what I really thought, Vans would be toast. I mean, how could I be a partner in a company and not know who our competition was?

On the other hand, I knew the answer, even if I didn't know its importance. I said, "Sir, it's my opinion that we don't have any."

The attorney nodded. "Yeah," he said. "I was kind of thinking the same thing."

As if that was all the consensus the lawyers needed, everyone on the bankruptcy attorney team came to the conclusion that the majority of Vans' problems lay squarely with Jimmy. It turned out Jimmy had kept secrets. He even had a secret office in a different building where he conducted covert business deals.

As a consequence, one of the judge's conditions for our Chapter 11 bankruptcy reorganization called for the removal of Jimmy from the company leadership. The judge then ordered me back to lead Vans out of bankruptcy, as chairman of the board and CEO. I became president of Vans shortly thereafter.

I returned with reluctance. I had my own full life now outside of Vans, with other irons in the fire, not to mention that I lived far away from the company headquarters and did not particularly want to move back to Orange County. I really liked living out on the farm. I had officially been countrified.

But what could I do? Vans was my baby. The employees had become part of my extended family. I knew their names, their kids' and their grandkids' names, and I knew they all depended on their jobs to pay the bills. How could I possibly let them down?

I'd been dubbed "Horizontal Dutch" when I first learned to love Southern California sunbathing, and I certainly earned the name when I learned to love retirement. But now it was time to go back to being Dutch the Clutch.

Obviously, I had to be at Vans headquarters and in the factories to fulfill my obligations and do my job well. Drena and I lived in Paso Robles, way up the coast. Being there in person meant a four-hour drive each way, an eight-hour commute, round-trip, a full day in and of itself. That wouldn't work.

I purchased a home on a golf course in Corona. Drena and I could be in the Corona house during the week and drive up to Paso Robles on the weekends. Corona was less than an hour commute to Vans' headquarters. Unlike Anaheim, Corona was still rural back then, mostly sprawling farms, orchards, ranches, and even the occasional vineyard. A bit later, we bought a small ranch in Corona and moved the horses down there from Paso Robles. I went back to working at Vans every day.

■ ■ ■

The Chapter 11 process blew my mind. Bankruptcy attorneys earn their keep by getting creditors to agree to settle on something other than what is owed. To clear Vans' debts, we would pay 25 cents on the dollar. This was wrong. There wasn't a chance in hell I'd pay a quarter of what we owed. No, Vans would pay 100 percent of its debt.

No two ways about it: if I owe someone $100,000, I damn well better repay $100,000. Otherwise, who would ever do business with us again?

Make no mistake, I knew paying back $12 million wouldn't be easy. That was a whole lot of money. As a company, we would really need to tighten our belts. The only thing that wouldn't suffer, I resolved, would be the quality of the shoes. Other than that, we would wear blinkers to stay the course.

Obviously, we couldn't pay back all $12 million at once, so I went to our creditors and committed to paying 25 percent of our debt each year for four years. It made the most sense, and they agreed. If nothing else, they seemed pleased that I intended to honor Vans' entire debt. Because of this we lost only one of our suppliers.

Now, in going back to the daily grind—and trust me, Jimmy's wasn't a grind operation, but a bloated, fat Elvis of a sinking ship—it wasn't as if I was excited. Keep in mind, I still considered Vans my company, even though in handing him the reins, Jimmy had wanted complete power. Through that restructuring, I hadn't had a say in a few years. To the contrary, any time I might have tried to weigh in or offer Jimmy even the slightest insight or direction, I'd been shot down.

Still, I didn't want this to have happened. Even with Vans as a publicly traded company now, I felt totally akin to the operation to which I had given birth and raised to voting age. And no amount of stock was ever going to distance me from that.

I'm not stupid. I knew the situation with Jimmy would prove tricky. He still owned a quarter of the business and retained his voting rights as a major shareholder. I wasn't his keeper. Even if he wasn't allowed to help run the company, he still had legal papers granting him Gordy's, Serge's, and my voting powers. Technically, he could vote any changes to the company he pleased.

Outwardly, it seemed clear Jimmy resented the verdict that ousted him from leadership. Despite his epic, well-documented failure in running Vans, he made it clear he intended to block us at every turn. It was an all-around untenable state of affairs.

Serge, Gordy, and I asked him to voluntarily return the documents that afforded him our voting powers. To me, it made sense to amend the voting structure. In only four years, Jimmy had driven the company into bankruptcy. The least he could do was to give Serge, Gordy, and me the power to run our own company, but he curtly refused.

His refusal wasn't all that surprising, but it hurt my heart. Didn't he see what he had done? Didn't he see the immense harm he'd inflicted on the company and our employees? These were dire straits, and yet he shrugged off any semblance of blame or responsibility.

To me, Jimmy had always been more important than the company, at least until that moment, but clearly, he didn't reciprocate that sentiment. He refused to play fair. He refused to give us back our votes. Seeing this apathy made me swear then and there that if I ended up with nothing after working my damn ass off, then Jimmy should also end up with nothing. I'm not saying I was right; I am admitting that I was that angry.

The only solace was that even though Jimmy was being exceedingly selfish, and even for a Van Doren, remarkably stubborn, he did, in fact, want to leave Vans. That was a good thing. Now it was a matter of navigating his departure while he controlled the vote and still owned a quarter of the company.

Vans' management decided to take out a loan and buy back his stock, on the condition that he return all the legal documents he held, which he did. Then they sent him packing. To be clear, the company did this, not me. All the same, when Jimmy left Vans, he made it known, loudly and clearly, that without him, we didn't stand a chance.

Was he kidding? I'd been outperforming expectations at every stage of my career.

It's like any skateboarder has ever said: fear is natural. Feel it, and do it anyway. The only difference was, I was fearless. I'd done this before, and I would do it again.

As in skateboarding, it's the concrete, the scrapes, and hitting your shin on metal that leads to improvement—getting better and keeping you sharp.

I shook my head and thought, *Just you watch. You know what? Go ahead and take notes.*

■ ■ ■

In the theory called the Peter Principle, humans tend to rise in a hierarchy till they reach a level of incompetence. Employees do well and are rewarded with promotions. They do that job well and are again promoted. Repeat and repeat until they're no longer performing at a level deserving of a promotion, which leaves them at a level where they're overmatched by the demands of the job. The natural result of the Peter Principle is that too many people holding critical positions in the business and manufacturing worlds are in over their heads.

For years I tried to wrap my head around why some individuals perform worse after being promoted. This happened often enough at Randy's that it was pretty clear to me that something was fundamentally wrong, or at the very least misaligned, in the promotion process. Being promoted implies that a standard has been met; it doesn't guarantee an upward trajectory, only more of the same. In that light, it stands to reason that movie sequels are not better than the original, and that second visits to restaurants are less rewarding than the first.

My brother was a classic example of someone who moves up only to fall down. He made three cardinal mistakes. I would call them rookie mistakes, except that he'd been with Vans the same amount of time as Gordy and Serge and me. First, Jimmy surrounded himself with people who had their noses so far up his derriere, even if they'd questioned him, their voices would have been too muffled to be heard. The problem really came down to ego, and when a company's problem is ego in its leadership, it's screwed.

There is really nothing worse than a brown-nosing suck-up. A team solely comprised of people who agree with one another won't attempt anything provocative. Those who offer nothing but yeses have no heart. Every leader needs people who push and question and wonder, "What if?" Never hire someone whose only answer is "yes." I never promoted people because they liked me. They didn't have to like me or not like me. I put people in charge who could do the things I wanted.

And Jimmy didn't ask for help from people who knew what they were doing.

All too often, when someone makes it to top management or reaches a similar position of power, they fail to hire anyone smarter than themselves for fear of exposing their own incompetence.

I might not have a doctorate or an MBA—hell, I don't even have a high school diploma—but the author of the Peter Principle confirmed what I realized years ago. People are ambitious; they want to grow and be recognized. But power in an organization isn't necessarily based on skill. Different people do different things well, and in that regard Jimmy's rise and fall should serve as a cautionary tale.

The fact is, the most productive worker isn't always the best candidate for manager. Some skills translate to management and some don't. Sometimes the best salespeople make the worst sales managers. The absolute worst thing to do is to lower the bar in order to promote someone who deserves recognition into a higher position. That implies an individual's current contribution doesn't hold value on its own; it should. We give leadership positions more attention than they deserve. Even if employees aren't being groomed for management, they should still be valued; they should still receive benefits; they should still have job security and really good working conditions.

Equality—it's good for business. It also happens to be what I love about skateboarding culture.

The second mistake Jimmy made was one he was destined to make more than once: he ignored the fundamentals.

After Jimmy took the money, we never heard from him again. I wondered if he ever wished he had done things differently. Obviously, we did fine without him. We did better than fine. We dialed in what needed dialing in and we nailed it.

But what haunted me for years is that after he left, he opened his own shoe factory and stores, which he called Awesome. Awesome failed within a year. I can't be certain, of course, but my guess is that as he'd done at Vans, he continued to disregard costs and went bankrupt.

Jimmy just didn't do the math. If you're spending $100 to make a $35 shoe, you're screwed. Whatever it takes to produce that shoe is one thing, but you also can't forget about the light bulbs and electricity and absolutely every single cost that goes into getting your product to a potential customer at a retail store. And since our business model was direct to consumer, well, that's a lot of light bulbs. We were responsible for the overhead in its entirety.

If imitation is the highest form of flattery, then simplicity is the highest form of complexity. Foot Locker had launched in 1975 and was still killing it a decade later, which solidified, to me anyway, that Vans' original retail model was still relevant. Vans needed to keep it simple and focus on what we'd always done better than anyone else.

Third, and most important, Jimmy had moved away from the core. Vans had no business making wrestling shoes or running shoes. What the hell was he thinking with those Reebok-wannabe padded puff losers? We had Reebok for that, and we had a whole slew of shoe dogs designing track shoes. There was no doubt that if we got back to basics, we would be fine. As the skater Steve Caballero has always said, "Don't forget why you started skating in the first place."

■ ■ ■

Paying back debt made us stronger as a company and more tight-knit as a family than ever before. But it also cost us in ways we had not anticipated. Wearing blinders and focusing on repayment meant we were forced to disband our Vans-sponsored skateboarding, surf, and BMX team and let go of the team manager, Everett Rosecrans.

This all but killed Stevie, but we could not afford to support the athletes, not even with free shoes. We needed every spare dime to stay afloat. Unfortunately, that meant we missed out on a number of opportunities that allowed other shoe brands to poach our crucial skate customers. We were helpless to do anything except let our athletes make other deals.

For instance, Stacy Peralta had always been a Vans guy. In his groundbreaking 1987 skate movie, *The Search for Animal Chin*, the members of the legendary Bones Brigade—including Lance Mountain, Mike McGill, and Steve Caballero—all skate in our competitor's shoes. Tony Hawk wore Vans Sk8-Hi's, but only because he had a pair on ice. I doubt those other shoes would even have been in the film if we'd had the budget to send those skaters free pairs of Vans during those turbulent times.

One day during the very darkest times, when we were still very uncertain if we'd even make it through this crisis, Stevie came to me with an idea.

"Remember how back before I got married you made me deposit my paycheck and figure out another way to make my car payment?"

If things hadn't been so dire, I would have smiled. "Yeah. I remember," I said.

"I did it by selling the smellers down at the Mexican border?"

I nodded, starting to get an inkling of where this was going.

"How about if I do the same thing now? Start getting rid of all that dead inventory? It won't be a ton of cash, but every little bit helps, right?"

I could have hugged the boy. In fact, I probably did.

"Do it," I said. Not only would it bring in desperately needed cash, but it would also free up the big storage warehouses for better use.

Stevie went down to the border swap meets and reconnected with the people he'd met back in the mid-seventies, hunting down as many of his old friends as he could. He filled them in on the situation at Vans and told them, "Come up to our warehouse and I'll give you the same kind of great deals I did before."

That started a brisk business with his Mexico connections. Stevie was happy he didn't have to start getting up at 4:00 a.m. again to make that long drive to the swap meets. This time they were driving up to him.

Sometime during those first months, a guy from downtown LA named Shalom Ashkenazi heard we were selling quality shoes at great prices, probably from one of Stevie's contacts down on the border. Known to everyone as Sam, he dealt mainly with wealthy customers from Mexico who flew up to the States to shop for clothes and shoes, then stuffed the merchandise into big suitcases and flew back to Mexico. He also owned businesses in Mexico City and Guadalajara.

Sam contacted Stevie at the Vans office, wanting to buy shoes mainly for his shop in the LA Fashion Mart. The next day he drove down in his Lincoln Continental, and Stevie took him over to the warehouse.

That first day Sam picked out two hundred pairs of shoes, which he and Stevie loaded into his Lincoln. He drove back to LA. The next day he called Stevie and said he wanted four hundred pairs. Stevie was so grateful for the business, he said he'd drive the order up to LA himself. From then on, for the next ten years, Vans delivered shoes directly to Sam, who became one of our very best customers.

In that way, after only two years, Stevie had gotten rid of every last pair of overstock and dead inventory from our warehouses. Vans were so popular with Sam's customers, however, that he wanted to continue getting shoes from us after the dead stock was gone.

Stevie began doing regular business with Sam for his stores in both LA and in Mexico.

Recognizing a great opportunity when he saw it, starting with that one customer, Stevie negotiated with the other Mexican contacts he'd been selling smellers to and set up similar deals. He carved out a real market share for Vans in Mexico, taking sales from zero to one million pairs by the end of the first year of that wholesale business, around $15 million in sales.

He made himself a one-man department devoted exclusively to the Mexican market. He designed the shoes, scheduled them, had them made, sold them, collected the money, and delivered the shoes, all by himself. That way, there was only one salary to put against all those sales on the balance sheet. His efforts were crucial to keeping the factory conveyors going during those lean years.

For several years going forward, Stevie's Mexico exports made up a full third of our business. Our retail store sales made up another third of the business, and national wholesale the final third. He was doing such a good job that in 1986, Stevie was also put in charge of overall retail sales.

Mexico sales continued until 1994, when Mexico had a money crisis, and the peso was devalued so much that people could no longer afford to buy shoes from the United States. When things there recovered a bit, Vans found a regular distributor for Mexico, and we settled into more normal sales methods there. Almost single-handedly, Stevie kept our production humming during the worst time in the company's history.

At a time when major sneaker manufacturers had their production in South Korea or somewhere else in Asia, Vans proudly clung to our tradition of "Made in the USA." I couldn't imagine closing down our American factories and letting our people go, and the upside during this wildly tumultuous time was that it kept our order-to-delivery times at five days as compared with an industry average of nine months.

This alone helped keep orders coming in, but ultimately, we made significant cuts and let many of the factory workforce go. This was rough, really rough, but we told everyone that as soon as we were able, we would rehire them. The employees who kept their jobs agreed to have their pay frozen for three years. I promised to reimburse everyone once we were out of debt.

I knew that if we managed to maintain production, sell shoes, and keep our noses above water enough that we could knock down our debt, we'd make it. To accomplish this, we needed to buy materials from the very suppliers to whom we were indebted. This seemed like a lot to expect, but I figured we might as well ask.

Cheryl, the youngest of my children, worked in the Vans purchasing department, so I instructed her to pick up the phone and call every supplier to ask if they'd agree to sell us the materials we needed if we paid cash on delivery. We'd worked with some of these suppliers since 1966. Save for one, all of our vendors said yes. During those tough times, coming up with the actual cash to pay bills took careful and creative management.

Now, scraping together the cash every month to do this wouldn't be easy, but the one good thing about the arrangement was if their bill was paid in cash, our suppliers always gave us a nice discount. I really liked that discount. Case in point: even after we started making a profit, as long as I was in charge, we continued to pay for our materials cash on delivery in order to take advantage of the discount.

Another cost-saving tactic we came up with involved the shoe-boxes. In the warehouse, we'd found carton after carton filled with label-shaped stickers printed with somewhat primitive drawings of skateboarders, surfers, and BMX bikers. We instructed our retail employees to tell customers if they were willing to let us keep the box from the shoes they'd just bought, we'd give them a six-pack of stickers in exchange. This tactic—which, when you think about it, isn't a big ask—saved us thousands and thousands of dollars.

Another major difficulty we faced was those two huge warehouses that were now filled with shoe styles nobody wanted to buy. All of those bizarre athletic shoes Jimmy had thought were such a good idea were now packed away getting dusty and dated, taking up an immense amount of storage space, and representing millions and millions of dollars in lost revenue both on the making side and the selling side.

In wearing blinders to pay our debtors, everyone stuck to a severe budget. Costs were slashed. There weren't any frills. Hell, sometimes we went without necessities. I remember one day someone alerted me, "Boss, we have no toilet paper."

Given our brutal repayment schedules, there wasn't a damn thing I could do. "Sorry. We have no money. Have everyone bring a roll from home."

And they did, and it was the same with pencils and other such sundries. If these hard times taught me anything, it's that it's okay to let people do for you, even your employees. Turns out, they were more than willing to share the burden. That was a valuable lesson. Asking for employee support during those dire times somehow made for a better, stronger relationship, and their support soon became a critical resource.

Most of Vans' offices and production had already been moved to a new fourteen-acre plant in Orange County, but there hadn't been enough buildings to fit everything, so a handful of scattered locations hadn't yet relocated to that one central place. This included two big warehouses. If we could divest ourselves of all our other properties and bring everything to Orange County, there would be huge monthly savings. To accomplish this, we'd need to put up more buildings on the new property, and for that we'd need a construction loan.

That's the thing about Chapter 11: in Chapter 11, there's no bank on the planet willing to offer loans of any kind. And because no bank on the planet was willing to offer us a loan, the most incredible thing happened: Vans' employees lent us the money we needed. Our management team spearheaded the effort, and a number of workers pitched in. This enabled us to purchase two metal prefab warehouse buildings to put up on our property and sell off the properties we no longer needed.

By the end of the following year, everything had been consolidated to one location. This alone saved us enormous amounts of money and brought in, if not revenue, a good amount of cash to put toward our debt.

Everyone at Vans, from the CEO to the kid sweeping the floors, became a stakeholder in our climb out of the deep hole Jimmy had dropped us in. I started letting the employees know whenever we had a problem or an issue, and they tried to help fix it if they could. All of it made for a more balanced relationship between management and worker and served to foster a mindfully harmonious environment.

When we were able, we paid everyone back with a generous interest. More than anything, the level of worker support reiterated to me what has been an important part of Vans' DNA from Day One.

It's only when the chips are down that anyone shines. Those four years were four years of clutch. We were in the clutch of it. Clutch was all we knew and all we had, and I'd be the first to say that I didn't do it alone: Without a doubt, it was the whole damn team.

More pressure created more opportunities to extend grace and celebrate or extol—I don't actually know the word for it—but to really embrace one another. It's like how some horses are really swell at running in the mud, people even call them mudders as an honor or a compliment. Turns out, everyone at Vans is a mudder; inclement weather didn't slow us down, not one bit.

Think about it. It's pretty damn easy to dance beneath bright moonlight or a sunny sky, but figuring out how to sing or dance or race in the rain takes some effort.

Under Jimmy, the company had lost focus. I was brought back to give the company more solid direction and worked to bring back Vans' core products and values to ensure, once again, that Vans was profitable.

As a condition of Vans' continued existence after the bankruptcy, I had agreed to a plan with the bank. Every six weeks I would go in with a payment check and a business plan. I'd tell them, "This is what we sold, and this is what we are going to sell."

For three years I stuck to the plan and didn't miss a single payment. Thankfully, the crisis was only internal. In the outside world, customer demand for Vans continued to be strong and our sales numbers didn't falter more than a fraction. Gradually, Vans was able to whittle down the amount we owed the bank.

After a couple of years, I had even saved up the amount of seven or eight future payments. I told the bank I wanted to make those payments early to be ahead of the game in case sales ever slowed down. I couldn't believe it when the bank said no. They refused to apply any extra money to the upcoming payments and insisted they would only take the amount off the back end.

We were doing everything the judge and the bank had asked of us and were acting in good faith. The bank was being ridiculously inflexible, clearly unwilling to lift a finger to help us out. They were laser-focused on liquidating the company so they could seize our assets, and nothing we did could change their minds. (So maybe when it's being used by a jackass bully, focus isn't all it's cracked up to be.)

They even went so far as to send people into all our offices and factories and put stickers with an inventory number on every single piece of furniture and equipment in preparation for the liquidation sale. To this day in his office at headquarters, Stevie has stubbornly kept that same old wooden desk with that white sale tag still on it, to remind him of what can so easily happen, and stand guard against ever landing in a similar situation.

The bank's refusal to work with me on those payments was a final straw. We were just coming up to year three in the four-year plan. I'd had more than enough of their bullshit. I asked John Corda to sell my farm near Paso Robles.

The next week I made the company a loan with the proceeds, and we paid off the bank in full. What I really wanted to do was to hire a dump truck, fill it with pennies, and pay the last $50,000 we owed by making a delivery onto the bank's parking lot. Stevie talked me out of it, but then, all that really mattered was being able to support the employees who sustained us and the athletes and artists who inspired us.

It hadn't been fun without the surfers, skateboarders, or BMX riders, so our first order of business was to call up Everett Rosecrans and sign up as many of the athletes who'd previously been on Vans' teams as he could get. Within a year, Vans cruised back into financial solvency.

Earlier I wrote about the importance of enthusiasm, which is one thing. *Ecstaticism* isn't a word but should be. It's something altogether different. It's what distinguishes determination from grim determination. When we survive things like depressions, pandemics, and bankruptcies, what's left to savor is that much sweeter.

We wouldn't look back. At Vans, we would never head that way. No matter what, we would always keep pushing forward.

The gist is this: with success comes reputation, and with hardship comes character. Even when a cost is high or seems too high, it's the downsides that create the most extraordinary upsides. Sometimes, the upside is a fuller sense of culture, and it's something I hope Vans never takes for granted. Vans wouldn't be where it is without its employees; no one is expendable and no one should ever be underappreciated, because when the chips are down, the folks you work with today will be the ones who bring a shovel when the shit hits the fan.

Trust me, the only thing I will ever say with any certainty is that at some point, for all of us, shit happens.

# CHAPTER TWELVE

# Embrace Change

Say what you will about mandating a tradition of excellence. The thing about traditions or conventions and whatever it takes to keep them going or buck them altogether: it's notoriously tricky, if not impossible, to hit the mark every single time. Kind of like handicapping the Derby.

It stands to reason that the only thing you can count on at the Derby, besides the juleps, is that it's famously unpredictable—just like life.

Of course, I like to bet on the Derby anyway, in which case, the only thing better than having a friend with access to a cushy Derby box is having a daughter-in-law with access to a cushy Derby box. Stevie's wife Susan's family hails from Louisville, Kentucky. She has an uncle who loves horse racing as much as I do, and even better, he owned two Derby boxes. One of the boxes was by the finish line, the other was the front box by the sixteenth pole. For years after Stevie and Susan married, on Derby days her uncle would place bets for us, but in 1978, he invited us to attend. I quickly realized that the second-best thing about seeing the Kentucky Derby for the first time is seeing it for the first time with one of my kids.

Stevie and I decided on a betting pool of a couple hundred dollars each. I prefer straight bets because they pay more. Stevie insists that complicated conditional bets are the way to go, because even though they pay less, you almost always have a winner. We ended up putting our money on Affirmed, a second choice at nine-to-five odds, and the horse went on to win the Triple Crown.

That first Derby will always be special, but the 1992 Derby was one for the books and proved how quickly a sure thing can go south, and vice versa. That morning at the betting window, a guy immediately in front of Stevie was taking a really long time to place his bet. Even Stevie, the most easygoing human on the planet, was frustrated. Finally, the guy made his exit, much to Stevie's relief.

He popped up a minute later to tell the teller she'd given him $68 too much in change. He handed her back the money. Now Stevie couldn't help but like this guy, so he asked him what horse he liked for the Run for the Roses.

Without hesitation he said, "Lil E. Tee."

Stevie put $50 on the horse, and damn if Lil E. Tee didn't win. Odds on Lil E. Tee had been against him forty-five to one. What's even more curious is that the eighth-place finish of the odds-on favorite, Arazi, was the worst finish of a betting favorite in Derby history. I'm not trying to make it seem as if horse racing is a stable business, but it just goes to show that even when the odds are against us, we can knock that old leather ball out of the park.

And conversely, even when absolutely everything is coming up roses, even a sure thing, a horse that was supposedly the second coming of Secretariat, can have a bad day. Though pedigree counts, it isn't decisive, and even if a handicapper pairs bloodline with past performance, the horses aren't but three years old. They don't have a hell of a lot of experience.

For every sure thing, there is a surefire flop, and for every surefire flop, there's a surprise winner.

Nothing is permanent. Everything changes. That isn't a bad thing. Talking with Serge and Gordy one day, we tossed around ideas of where Vans might go from that point on. It was the 1980s. Most of the eighties unfolded under President Ronald Reagan. Wall Street and the economy were booming; the whole world was abuzz with affluence and deregulation. But it wasn't all rosy. Mount St. Helens erupted. The AIDS epidemic raged. Gandhi was gunned down, as was John Lennon. Pope John Paul II survived an attempt on his life, but then so did Reagan. Eastern Europe opened up. Bill Gates became the first billionaire in the computer world.

It was the deal decade, with news trumpeting any number of mergers and acquisitions. Philip Morris bought Kraft, R.J. Reynolds bought Nabisco, Standard Oil merged with Gulf Oil, Sony bought Columbia Pictures, General Electric bought RCA (the parent company of NBC), Eastman Kodak bought Sterling Drug.

As much as I loved Vans, I missed my wife and my horses. I missed being Horizontal Clutch. It was time for a brilliant finish. With this in mind, Serge brought in an acquisitions guy, who talked to us about the possibility of selling Vans.

Now, to be clear, Serge didn't want to sell, and I didn't blame him. Aside from sentimentality and ambition, there was the issue of valuation. We had just come out of Chapter 11. What was the company worth? One million dollars? Two million? How could we even have value at all? We had almost gone out of business.

At $2 million, selling wasn't worth it, but the idea grabbed and then held my imagination. If structured correctly, current management could stay in place while responsibility for the whole shifted elsewhere, namely, from me. Two million certainly wouldn't work, but how about a we're really not interested in selling number?

It couldn't hurt to ask, right? I said to Serge, "What if we got a big lump sum, like, say, $75 million?"

Serge blinked, then all but shouted, "In that case, we'd definitely sell!"

I turned to Steve Adelizi, the acquisitions expert, who had been silent as Serge and I went back and forth. "Okay, here's the deal. If we're going to sell, we want three duffel bags with $25 million cash in each bag. Would your people do that?"

Steve lifted a shoulder noncommittally. "Let me see what I can do," he said, but his expression told me my exit strategy—my goal to escape a photo finish—wasn't all that crazy a fantasy. By then, Vans was doing around $50 million a year in California alone. If this came to pass, Serge, Gordy, and I realized we would be insane to turn down the offer.

Steve Adelizi came back to us fairly quickly and said the San Francisco–based venture banking firm McCown De Leeuw & Co. was willing to pay $75 million if we would sell them our shares and ownership of the Van Doren Rubber Company.

Fortune might favor the bold, but my stomach dropped. What would the family think? My kids had grown up with Vans. Would they think I had sold out their inheritance? What about their legacy? Nervously, to test the waters I invited Stevie up to the ranch in Corona, ostensibly to help me with the tennis court, which was kind of dumb since I didn't play tennis. No one in the family did.

Stevie probably suspected something was up, and even though I had wanted to approach selling the company subtly, I blurted out, "What would you say if I told you I was thinking about selling Vans?"

It took him a second to digest what I'd said, then he regrouped and exclaimed, "Great! Go ahead and sell it! What are they offering?"

"Wouldn't you be worried about what might happen to your job?" I asked.

"No." He said what the rest of our family soon echoed. "Heck, Dad, I watched you come within an inch of losing everything you've worked for your whole life. Whatever they're giving you, you deserve it. I'll be fine. Hell, yeah, sell the damn company!"

■  ■  ■

In October 1987, the stock market crash threw a hell of a wrench into Vans' sale. When it became clear that McCown De Leeuw would be unable to complete the transaction, I thought, *Yes, of course, silly me. I'm a fool to have taken it for granted.*

When the sale was postponed until December, I did not hold my breath. When the market fell again and the deal didn't go through until February the following year, I was the very picture of poised.

When it did, there was a slight modification. Ultimately, we'd still be paid $75 million, only they'd give us $62 million up front, and the other $13 million when the company went public. George McCown and David De Leeuw, the two men behind the firm, had a great track record, so we agreed. As a further part of the deal, though Serge made his exit to invest elsewhere, McCown De Leeuw wanted Gordy and me to serve as advisors and vice chairman and chairman of the board for two years. The last condition, minor as it was, officially renamed the Van Doren Rubber Company as Vans, Inc.

Since the acquisition marked an end to my leadership of Vans, for the first time in their lives, Stevie and Cheryl would have to answer to someone other than their dad or uncle.

McCown De Leeuw was onboard to carry on the Van Doren family tradition, a legacy spirited in innovation. Thankfully, they agreed to keep supporting our collaboration with action sports. As if to solidify this, the first thing McCown De Leeuw did after buying the company was to authorize the release of the Caballero, Vans' first signature skateboarding shoe.

Steve Caballero was one of the first guys Everett got back on the Vans team. At first, he wore Vans' All-American hi-top style, but we remembered our success with the Era that Stacy Peralta and Tony Alva had designed, so we asked Steve if he would like to design his own signature shoe. The Caballero style was a padded high-top similar to the Sk8-Hi, complete with dragon scales on the custom label, reminiscent of the dragon graphics he had on his boards.

This was the first in our signature shoe program for which skateboarders designed their own shoes.

At the time the Caballero came out, skateboarding was making a shift from vertical ramps to street skating, and the sport got faster and more technical. While the additional padding was appreciated, a lot of kids found the higher ankle cumbersome and cut their hi-tops to mid-tops to maneuver better.

Steve Caballero came to us and suggested making a mid-top version with a double-reinforced ollie area. Since its introduction in 1992, the Half Cab has gone on to become one of the most popular skate shoes in history, often voted the best skate shoe ever made, still in our line today. There are also just as many skaters out there who feel Vans' Madrid Fly style, released the same year, Vans' first collaboration with a skateboard brand, which paved the way for the 1988 Native American, was the greatest skate shoe ever created. Working with Steve helped us give skaters exactly what they needed to be comfortable and to excel in their sport. Our collaboration with these outstanding athletes has been a real joy for me over decades.

Luckily, Steve Caballero feels the same way, alluding to "the many good things that can come out of years of passion and trust," a belief in the people who helped build and shape Vans to be what it is today. As he puts it, "Creativity can grow when you give it the freedom to breathe."

By 1988, and this really was the last refrain, the final stanza to my encore, things really got rolling. Vans was in full recovery, and we started making an actual profit every month, and doing so consistently. Vans' retail stores, located almost exclusively in Southern California, were pulling in a million dollars a month. Between four thousand and five thousand independent outlets were working with us through our wholesale department.

McCown De Leeuw brought in an expert to take over the retail stores, relieving Stevie, who was still doing his one-man show running the Mexico export division. Until then, other than our sales in Mexico, we'd received only marginal orders from overseas. McCown De Leeuw had international sales experience, so distributors were established in Germany, England, and France, where sales were starting to be significant enough to warrant development. Over the coming decade, more and more countries were added to that list.

Cheryl was promoted to handle employee benefits, employee safety, and company insurance, and Stevie was moved over to

Van's first-ever marketing department, which, at least initially, was directed at private-label shoes, trying to get more manufacturing into the factories. Stevie arranged for Vans to make exclusive shoe styles for Disneyland, Snoopy, Tog Shop, Nordstrom, J.Crew, Hanna Andersson, and in Europe, WP Lavori and Façonnable. These private labels added a couple million dollars a year to sales.

In 1989, the long-awaited raids by US and Mexican customs officials had finally shuttered several sizeable counterfeit operations that had been flooding the market with cheap Vans imitations for ages. Despite losses to counterfeits, Vans' sales topped $70 million in 1990, with international sales accounting for 25 percent of sales, and special orders and private label continuing to play a strong revenue role.

When 1991 rolled around, as McCown De Leeuw had planned all along, Vans was taken public. The initial stock offering on the NASDAQ exchange was just over four million shares, at $14 per share. My feeling was the price per share would go higher fairly quickly. Surely, the stock would rise by at least $2 once it started trading.

As chairman, I continued to preside over board meetings but found that more and more often, no matter the topic, the board rarely decided my way.

Three things I disagreed with most vehemently included McCown De Leeuw's refusal to offer custom-mades. In fact, they stopped doing them altogether. This tradition was just as difficult to see go by the wayside as McCown De Leeuw having Stevie give up going to the LA County Fair. They had tried to run the booth themselves, in a more corporate, structured sort of way, but they just didn't have Stevie's magic touch. More to the point, they didn't have a clue what they were doing, and soon they quit doing the fair altogether. It was too much work for them to bother.

Gordy wasn't even there to help me any longer with the votes at the board meetings, because he'd decided to resign his position as vice chairman and leave Vans a few months after the sale. When the third point I wholly opposed passed by a majority of stakeholders, I did not have a lick of support. By then the tides had turned.

The third bone of contention that final year was about which advertising agency would be selected for the new marketing department. McCown De Leeuw had done the initial interviews and narrowed it down to a short list of three firms. Then members of the board were brought in to listen to the pitches and make the final decision. One firm was the agency that handled MTV, one was Leo Burnett, a large agency from Chicago, and the last one was a smaller local outfit from LA. The first two agencies, impressive as they were, failed to impress me. They didn't seem to have a handle on Vans' DNA. It was only the hometown ad man who got the appeal of our brand.

He compared a pair of Vans to a pair of Levi's jeans. He said, "That's what you are, the Levi of shoes. Vans are like flour and sugar, not fancy, but an everyday staple for millions of people."

I wanted to cheer. This guy knew Vans and he knew our market.

Too bad everyone else on the board hated the pitch except me. Not one other person liked the notion that Vans were a utility product like blue jeans, but if the board had chosen that local company, the result would have been more like the way Vans had always done business in the past. It might also have gotten a lot more customers into our stores. The campaign they ultimately picked was one of these flashy multi-collaborations, which had little to do with our true customer base or Vans' actual image.

When I saw things veering that far off base, I knew I was wasting my time. I decided to step down from the board of directors and end my obligations to the company.

Having struck out so many times at the boardroom that final year, I made only one final demand. I insisted on the right to approve whoever was going to take my place. The most promising candidate was Richard Leeuwenberg. When they handed me his résumé, as was my tradition, I threw it in the wastebasket.

Like everyone else I'd ever done this to, his face just dropped, and the others at the meeting were perplexed. I never care what a résumé has to say about someone. I am more interested in what someone has to say, and I really liked what Richard had to say. Richard Leeuwenberg was hired as president and CEO for the company. In 1991, I stepped down.

For a while, he kept things going and continued to do things the way Vans had always done. The ethos of accountability—a lesson I had learned back at Randy's about being accountable and taking responsibility when you're in charge, whether or not a problem is your fault—was apparently rigorously enforced in what was now a publicly held company. If any little thing goes wrong or even slows down a bit, the president is instantly out of there, fired. Leeuwenberg was a nice guy who lasted four years in the position.

Watching this happen, Stevie announced that he never wanted to be president of the company. Ever. It wasn't that he didn't want to take responsibility; he just didn't like the capricious nature of the position.

The scale of things at Vans was changing. I had once remarked that I ran Vans as if it were a fire hydrant with a kitchen tap attached to it. From twenty years at the Randolph Rubber Company, I knew the dangers of expanding beyond one's means, so I had deliberately kept Vans a small, local Southern California company. Under his control, Richard faced real challenges in scaling up while also retaining our customer base.

Meanwhile, at age sixty-one, I was busy scaling up my life of leisure. Once I resigned my post on the board of directors, I was completely out of the picture at Vans for a very long time. I was once again home before noon, just as I had been the last time I quit.

Drena and I had always loved Kentucky, ever since we'd started going to the Derby. Being in the horse business, we had often thought about buying a piece of property in Kentucky and moving there from California, in order to be at the center of the horse world. With everything going on at Vans, though, it had been impossible for me to leave. Until now. In 1992, we purchased a forty-acre farm on Paris Pike near Lexington, Kentucky, where Drena could build up her stable of racehorses. The routine Drena and I established over the coming years was to spend eight months on our farm in Kentucky and four months in California.

Was it tough for me to walk away from a leadership position at the company I'd founded? There is no denying it.

When I retired, I was presented with a brass-plated shoe that said: "Vans, an American Dream."

There's only so much any of us can do to dissolve our egos. I think everybody wants to be remembered for what they did. Even monks want to be remembered for their sacrifice for better consciousness.

But most of us don't need or even want recognition on a grand scale. We want to be remembered by a select few—our daughters, our sons—and I knew I would always have that.

For all the years I lived away from California, I would still talk to my kids regularly. Our family has always been close, so it was hard being that far away from them. I got in the habit of speaking at least once a week with Stevie and Cheryl. Naturally, we talked about the goings-on at Vans. I was no longer involved in running the company, but I was still interested in the newest developments and what was going on behind the scenes.

I loved getting my steady fix of Vans' news and gossip. It got to be like following a soap opera, with a vivid cast of everyday heroes to cheer for and a few nasty villains to boo at. And it was always full of interesting stratagems and shenanigans.

Even while relegated to the sidelines, I was an avid follower of everything Vans, and I never stopped considering myself part of the Vans family.

By 1992, I didn't like what I was hearing. Yes, revenues from the seventy retail stores and four-thousand-plus wholesale outlets raised the company's net income to $6.5 million. More than a third of Vans' sales came from international exports.

But on the domestic front, Vans was losing ground. Our classic styles such as the Authentic, Old Skool, and Slip-On continued to provide roughly half of the sales, but the world of sport shoe fashion had changed, and the new materials and styles of all the other brands were eroding our market share. They were all producing their shoes in Asia, where labor costs were as low as 14 cents an hour.

I was so happy Vans had kept our manufacturing plants in California. I had always been extremely proud to put a "Made in the

USA" label on every one of our shoes. If it was bad policy to pay our workers less than a decent living wage, why would it be okay to do so in other countries? Right is right and wrong is wrong.

Vans' new owners kept the factories here, but they were running them all wrong. As they desperately looked for ways to increase production, they brought in a handful of young execs I took to calling "the Harvard Grads," who took it as their mission to change everything I had established.

They came up with something called the MAST technique, which stood for make and ship today, an idea that originated in Japan. Using that strategy, they thought they could make a factory more efficient than the ones I had put together.

Vans spent $5 million in 1992 to open a state-of-the-art plant in Vista, California, down in San Diego County, all high-tech, doing things in ways I had known for years wouldn't work. They spent all that money on a factory, and it never, ever made the volumes or ran with the efficiency of the old factory. They screwed up big time.

On top of that, they compounded their troubles by making a classic newbie blunder: all the new factory management worried about was production, not their people. From my first day at Randy's, I had always put people first and profits second. That is the biggest key to success, in my opinion.

Take good care of your people, and they will take good care of you.

Hell, it wouldn't have surprised me if the new owners even brought back those damn stopwatches. For sure, none of the workers were leaving early, because production had gone down the tubes. The make-and-ship-today strategy soon became make-and-ship-never. Sales were slipping badly, from $91 million in 1992 down to $86 million in 1993, to just $80 million in 1994. Actual profits were down from $6.5 million in 1992 to less than $1.5 million just two years later.

The owners' solution? They fired Vans' president.

Walter Schoenfeld agreed to come out of retirement to head Vans for two years. After looking at the competition, he decided he wanted to produce a new line of shoes more in step with the current fashion trends, so he hired new designers and marketing staff. Clearly, he hadn't looked at the sales numbers. It was the OG, or "original gangster," styles that led the numbers. Always.

Vans started importing cold-cure shoes made in Asia, just like all the other brands. As a result, the unique vulcanized shoes Vans was known for nearly ceased production. Over the next couple of years, our amazing vulcanized shoes were reduced from nearly six million pairs a year to only one million. All the rest of the shoes now sold under the Vans name were cold-cure shoes made in South Korea, utilizing a lower temperature process used to make Nikes and others.

Walter Schoenfeld dealt with our fledgling retail stores that had been hit hard by the continued recession equally ruthlessly, closing some and converting others to factory outlets to sell off the dead stock.

For a while, he even tried to enforce a dress code at Vans. Seriously? A dress code?

Schoenfeld implemented a very different business model from the one I had followed. Basically, he changed the whole direction of the company from manufacturing to marketing. Instead of going out and selling what Vans produced, he had Vans produce what was selling out in the marketplace.

In other words, he was chasing trends rather than setting them.

I saw it as a self-fulfilling prophesy. Since Vans was now sourcing the majority of its shoes from overseas, customers started to forget about the classic styles.

However, with all those drastic measures in place, revenues and profits couldn't help but start to rise again. At the end of 1994, Walter Schoenfeld decided it was time to retire again.

A new president was brought in. Sales of the foreign-made "international collection" had taken off and helped boost profits, but overall sales continued to fall, and Vans' stock dropped to a low of slightly more than $3 per share. In an attempt to turn the tide, 450 people were laid off, and factories were shut down for two weeks. The new guy didn't last long.

In May 1995, Walter Schoenfeld came out of retirement again, once more resuming leadership of the company. A couple of months later, in July 1995, Schoenfeld closed the Vans factory in Orange. Shutting down the plant meant the loss of nearly all of its one thousand workers, many of whom had been with the company from its earliest days. The factory in Vista continued limited operations, but most of Vans' manufacturing would now be contracted through a dozen or so factories in South Korea.

I was really glad I lived two thousand miles away or I honestly don't know what I would have done when I heard the news. I was so angry, I felt like punching something or someone. I didn't envy Stevie and Cheryl having to stand by and watch all this happen while biting their tongues. I heard that Stevie had locked himself in his office for several hours because he was so upset when the cuts were announced.

That fall, Walter brought in his son Gary Schoenfeld as Chief Operating Officer, and later president and CEO of the company. Gary had attended UCLA and Stanford, and Stevie thought he was really smart and a good guy.

But the Schoenfeld father-and-son duo just could not push Vans over the line to profitability. The company was doing $300 million in sales but wasn't making any money. When I was running Vans, we had done only $50 million in sales in our best year, but we had chalked up a $16 million profit.

Stevie and Cheryl were doing their best to help turn things around. When McCown De Leeuw had bought the company, Stevie had been tasked with starting Vans' first marketing department. Now he was made the new VP of promotions and events. The job took him out in the field and around the country to various action sports competitions to promote the Vans brand.

The Vans sports teams were going strong, and while the popularity of skateboarding took a bit of a downturn in the eighties, it was starting to come back, as were our skate shoes, largely thanks to the release of the Half Cab style in 1992. The surfing and BMX teams were holding their own, and by then Vans had added snowboarding to its roster of teams.

Soon thereafter, the first Vans snowboarding boot came out and it was a big hit. Sales of the boots skyrocketed, almost single-handedly restoring the company to profitability by 1996 after the disasters of the previous years. The growing popularity of snowboarding in Europe and Japan also gave overseas sales a significant boost, as did Daniel Franck's 1998 Olympic Silver Medal while wearing Vans boots at the Nagano Games, and Danny Kass and Doriane Vidal's wins wearing Vans at the Salt Lake City Olympic Games in 2002.

Meanwhile, back in 1995, Stevie had been telling me about his newest project. He was all excited about a collaboration he was doing with a guy called Kevin Lyman.

We met Kevin at the LA County Fair when he was still a kid. His mom brought him every summer to buy his Vans at our discount tent. Kevin remembers buying back-to-school shoes for something like $10 a pair.

Kevin grew up a big fan of action sports, and during college he orchestrated huge live music festivals, and oversaw the Lollapalooza Tour. Later he combined music festivals with sports demos. Then he got the crazy idea to put on a traveling rock festival, with shows in many more cities and all over the world, with different cutting-edge bands playing at the various stops. He called it the Warped Tour.

Initially, he wanted to call his tour "The Bomb," after the slang term for the coolest thing ever. But the day he was set to announce it, Timothy McVeigh blew up the Alfred P. Murrah Federal Building in Oklahoma City. So instead, Kevin Lyman borrowed the name "Warped" from a magazine where he once worked.

The previous winter, Stevie had gotten an equally crazy idea of putting on an amateur skateboarding contest that traveled around the country and maybe even abroad. Sales of Vans' skateboarding shoes were on the rise and would benefit even more from the exposure. Stevie needed help organizing such an involved tour, so he wrote up a proposal.

The management team at Vans called Kevin Lyman to set up a meeting. It turned out that Kevin had already scheduled a pitch in New York with Calvin Klein to sponsor the Warped Tour when Stevie called. Kevin ditched that meeting and met with Vans instead. Good choice!

It took Stevie and Kevin about fifteen minutes to come up with the idea of combining the two tours. A deal was struck, and the Vans Warped Tour was born.

For Kevin, it all went back to his memories of buying Vans when he was a kid, so proud to have those new shoes. "When I had a chance to meet with them about my music project, I was almost giddy." So began a nearly quarter-century relationship.

Even after he was approached a year later by another shoe company that offered to buy out Vans' sponsorship, Kevin stood firm: "I realized that Vans was my perfect company after witnessing the work ethic of Steve Van Doren. He lived and breathed Vans as I did alternative music, and we had the same thing in mind, bringing the best experience to the public."

He adds, "I sure am happy I didn't jump for the quick buck after that first year."

Who could have known then that the Warped Tour would run for twenty-five years, from 1995 to 2019, and change forever Vans' relationship to the music world, and to youth culture overall? The Warped Tour was so influential that the Rock & Roll Hall of Fame has mounted an exhibit explicitly dedicated to it.

That first summer of 1996, the tour had forty-five stops in the United States alone. The second year they did thirteen stops in Europe in addition to the US portion. In the third year, Australia and New Zealand were added with ten more stops. All in a single summer.

For all twenty-five years, Kevin was in charge of the music side, and Stevie arranged the skateboarding side for just as long. He had special skateboard ramps designed that could easily be broken down every night and transported to the next venue. He gathered a crew of hardcore roadies to do the exhausting work. Eighteen buses and trucks were needed to transport all the gear and the people overnight to the next stop. The tour was a herculean undertaking, with eighty acts a day. Nearly a thousand people traveled with the show.

The schedule for each day's events changed in every city, because during Lollapalooza, Kevin Lyman had seen talented bands play to empty seats because the fans knew what time the main attractions would be taking the stage. Since he noticed that most of the fans arrived as soon as the gates opened, he adjusted the schedule accordingly. Fans could buy a schedule from a kiosk or look at a giant inflatable board that listed the lineup for the day.

The Warped Tour was well known for giving smaller bands big chances to make a name for themselves. The tour provided a launching pad for such diverse talents as blink-182, My Chemical Romance, Katy Perry, Green Day, Ice-T, Bad Religion, and Eminem. Fall Out Boy, will.i.am, and The Black Eyed Peas also performed on the Warped Tour.

A fan favorite was the Battle of the Bands, during which a local band could get a ton of exposure, with their talent judged by professionals from the music industry. Another popular tradition was a show by the barbecue band, which agreed to prepare the post-show barbecue dinner for the other bands and crew in exchange for the chance to perform.

For many of those twenty-five years, Stevie was there, in person. He manned a Vans tent where he sold shoes and shirts to the crowd, just like back in the county fair days. He did thousands of giveaways each day and took charge of the barbecuing at mealtimes. His daughter Kristy went with him on the tour and started running the contests when she was still a teenager.

At each stop, Stevie would lay out tons of Vans shoes and socks to give to band members, and he also arranged to feed them during the day rehearsal. At the Boston suburb stop, his tradition was to make the two-hour drive to downtown Boston and buy 125 lobsters for the rehearsal feast.

By the Warped Tour's tenth anniversary, attendance had hit the 500,000 mark. Each time new stops on the tour were added, Vans' financial contribution increased accordingly. Eventually, Vans ended up owning 70 percent of the tour. Vans' skateboard team members were hired to give demos on the ramps.

Star skater Steve Caballero recalls his time on the tour as "some of my best summers ever, visiting thousands and thousands of kids in city after city, skating the demo vert ramp while listening to my favorite rock bands on stage. Good times and great memories."

Open amateur competitions for skaters were also staged at each stop. At the end of the summer, the winners came to Vans' headquarters for one final contest to determine the overall top skaters in the country, competing for two one-year Vans sponsorships.

In the beginning of the Vans Warped Tour, the skateboard ramps were basic, but as the years went by, the ramps got more complex as the materials became stronger and more lightweight. After fifteen years, though, the pro skaters started getting married and dropping out, and it was tough to find top-notch replacements willing to take on the grueling schedule. The ramps were pared down and made smaller and smaller until, for the last five years, the skateboarding events were discontinued altogether, and the Vans Warped Tour became just about the music.

The last one was held in 2019. The tour was noteworthy for accessible ticket prices. A three-day general admission pass to Coachella, for example, might run $500, or close to $1,000 for a VIP ticket. The Warped Tour, by comparison, cost about $45 for a multiday pass, and there was no hierarchy to the ticketing system.

Even the bigger bands never got special treatment. The whole point was always accessibility: there were no extra fees to meet artists, and fans could visit bands at their tents or run into them in the crowd during another performance. Often band members worked at their own merchandise stands. Fans could get an autograph, a photo, or even musical advice from most of the artists.

When the same crew that made *Dogtown and Z-Boys* (2001) made a film about the tour called *No Room for Rockstars* (2012), they called the Warped Tour "a traveling minstrel show for youth."

Kevin Lyman made outreach a key component of the operation. For example, the Percussion Marketing Council teamed up with the tour to give free drum lessons to concert goers at a Lesson Lab tent. In 2013, the tour collected thirty-three thousand pounds of food for those in need. In 2014, the Vans Warped Tour tried to set a Guinness World Record title for the largest food drive in a twenty-four-hour period at a single location. This give-a-shit attitude also overlapped nicely with Vans' overall philosophy of doing business.

Stevie estimates that eleven million people came to the shows over the years. Commitment has always been at the heart of everything he does on behalf of Vans.

I have no idea how he did it. I get exhausted just thinking about everything involved in putting on those never-ending tours. As his sister Cheryl once observed, "Steve has grassroots marketing in his veins."

The tour was our number-one marketing vehicle for twenty-five years. It got Vans great credibility in the music world and increased our exposure to music fans all over the country, and eventually, the globe.

As Vans Global Brand President Doug Palladini said as the long-running tour was winding down due to declining attendance, "Until we got involved with the Warped Tour, we didn't have a national footprint to talk about who we are. Vans is a brand that really embraces individuality, and Warped Tour is very much the same."

Vans was considered the coolest brand ever, and the counter-cultures of the time embraced us wholeheartedly. I think one would be hard-pressed to find a single American kid who grew up during those years who didn't own at least one pair of Vans. I firmly believe Stevie's Warped Tour helped make it happen, and that was just the beginning.

■ ■ ■

When it comes to Vans, it wasn't that I set out to break a mold; Vans simply didn't fit into any particular box. Generally speaking, no one at Vans was much good at conforming.

If there was a tradition to which we would be yoked, it was that we would always break with tradition. We would never feel indebted to some sacred, unmovable goal or philosophy. What fun is that? Rarely, if ever, does an accomplishment from pure obligation have passion.

When it comes to change, I especially like what the composer Gustav Mahler has been credited as saying: "Tradition is tending the flame, not worshipping the ashes." At Vans, I never wanted us to rest on our laurels; we were always looking for creative ways to become the best version of ourselves.

Ironically, even when you've become the best you can be, you have to recognize that nothing is permanent. Everything changes. That isn't a bad thing.

# CHAPTER THIRTEEN

# Get Back to Core Culture

I used to joke that shoes were a good business. After all, everyone wears shoes. Shoes had to be one of the first things man invented. Some sort of moccasin, I'm guessing, or maybe some cloth or hide wrapped around the foot by rope, with hay for arch support.

It amazes me that fifty-four years later, Vans still makes the shoes we sell in our own stores, the way we did it at the very beginning. My retail dream lives on.

We used to have distributors all over Europe that sold our shoes: we are in the process of taking them back. It's all in the interest of brand integrity. In Israel, we currently have twenty-two Vans stores. In places where Vans used to have distributors and wholesalers, we're putting in our own stores, even in places such as China.

But it took a while for us to get here, and I attribute our longevity to maintaining our connection with our core culture and keeping it strong.

Our skate team member Christian Hosoi articulates it this way: "The key to Vans' success over the years has been the recognition that skateboarding is the core, heart and soul of the brand and its legacy."

For me, making sneakers was always *more* than a business— there's something about making a thing that everybody wears that transcends commerce. The shared experience makes it special, the way a song that everyone loves seems more meaningful. Vans isn't just a pair of sneakers; it's also a good story, one we call our own. There's poetry and style to it. I like that.

■ ■ ■

More than anyone else on the planet, myself included, Stevie embodies the spirit, the voice, and the face of Vans' culture—the expression of its DNA.

In 1993, he'd held a skateboarding event at a big SoCal shopping mall together with Hard Rock Café and *Transworld Skateboarding* magazine. The following year they added two other cities to the competition and decided to call it the Vans Triple Crown of Skateboarding.

The year after that, Vans purchased the Triple Crown of Surfing, which had been going on in Hawaii since 1983. The marketing department quickly latched on to the Triple Crown concept, and Vans launched Triple Crown competitions in skateboarding, snowboarding, wakeboarding, surfing, BMX, supercross, and moto-cross and signed a worldwide television package with NBC.

Huge audiences were watching both in person and on TV, all of which rocketed Vans into national visibility. Naturally, the television networks recognized this golden opportunity to reach a young audience, and soon a bevy of action sports competitions, such as the X Games, flooded the airwaves.

When Stevie learned the networks were dumping Vans' sponsorship in favor of a big competitor's infinitely deeper pockets, he was pretty angry. So ticked off, in fact, that when the first X Games opened, he and my granddaughter Kristy motored up to the venue in an RV packed with every piece of Vans swag he could find. He went guerilla marketing big time on the X Games, as only Stevie could.

His crew loaded up backpacks and spread out, handing out Vans hats, shirts, stickers, and Frisbees to everyone in town who was working the games. Every guard, parking lot attendant, ticket taker, and fan in the stands watching were all wearing something from Vans. They figured they would probably all be arrested. To their delight, the cops and security guards only asked if they could have some Vans swag, too. They told me even the ESPN cameras were sporting Vans stickers!

Stevie considered it a moral victory.

With the Triple Crowns, Vans wasn't really interested in matching the size and extent of those big media productions. After having their fun at the X Games, Vans turned around and went in the opposite direction, doing things the authentic, old school Vans way, with smaller, more intimate events that were more fun for the athletes, more entertaining to watch as a fan, and more accurately reflective of Vans' DNA.

Vans sponsored a huge indoor skate park in Orange, California, that quickly proved profitable, inspiring the company to open a series of similar parks in New Jersey, Virginia, Texas, and Colorado. All those efforts helped sales climb to $118 million in 1996, with earnings finally reaching $4 million. Vans' stock rebounded to $11 per share.

The company finally seemed to be back on track. One of Vans' most hyped and valued streetwear collaborations started that same year, 1996, with a fledgling New York City skate shop called Supreme putting out a series of cobranded Old Skools. Vans also took a tentative step toward diversification and introduced its first line of young men's apparel. That was followed by a line of shoes designed for a slightly wider range of outdoor sports than our usual skateboarding fare.

The product expansion made me a bit nervous, reminding me too much of the failures with diversification at both Randy's and at Vans under Jimmy. Clothing had never been part of our core business.

This time I was proven wrong. Sales of the clothing line were negligible at first, but received a major boost in 1999, when Vans joined forces with Pacific Sunwear to form VanPac, with the goal of becoming the dominant name in skateboarding apparel in the United States. That joint venture was overwhelmingly successful. Apparel and accessories are now about 20 percent of global revenue.

One sad reason for the associated financial boost was Vans' shift from American-made to overseas manufacturing. The factories in Asia were simply able to produce shoes and clothing much more cheaply and quickly than in the United States, which unfortunately made domestic downsizing inevitable. I saw the writing on the wall, and I didn't like it.

Sure enough, in 1998 Walter Schoenfeld shut down the last of the Vans California factories, fired two thousand employees, and shipped the entire manufacturing side of the business over to Korea's cold-cure factories, along with others in Spain and Mexico.

I was totally heartsick at this development, helpless to do anything but watch in horror as they systematically undermined everything I had ever believed in and everything I felt Vans had always stood for.

Stevie and Cheryl didn't agree with what they were doing either and made it no secret. Customers kept asking them, "Why can't we get the old styles anymore? What happened to the waffle soles?"

Neither Cheryl nor Stevie was in charge of product development. No one listened to them.

We all felt the company had gone astray. Vans no longer made the best shoes possible, but the cheapest shoes possible. Because the company was buying all their shoes from overseas factories, some of the Vans styles were exactly the same cold-cure styles as every other shoe brand was selling; you literally couldn't tell them apart. The only difference on some of the shoes was the stripe, the circle, or the swoosh. There was no way to tell a pair of Vans from a cheap bargain brand. Because, oh, yeah, we were now a cheap bargain brand, too.

Stevie got fed up that no one in charge was listening to his protests, so he put together a visual statement that management couldn't ignore. Before a staff meeting, he bought a hundred different shoes from a variety of brands and lined them all up on shelves on the conference room wall.

When the staff meeting convened, he stood up and told the emotional story of how, only a decade earlier, poor leadership had led Vans into bankruptcy with making bad decisions and not continuing to do what Vans had always done so well, and not giving customers what they had come to expect of their Vans.

"Vans went off the rails trying to beat the athletic shoe brands at their own game. We didn't stick to the core of what Vans was and what the customers wanted," he said, then pointed a finger in their direction. "Just like you people are doing."

When they started to object, he cut them off and indicated the wall of shoes he had assembled. "I defy anyone here to stand up and point out to me which of these are the Vans."

Nobody could. Not one person. The people running the company could not even tell their own shoes from those of their competitors.

"That's not the Vans way!" Stevie declared hotly. "This is not who we are!"

Thank goodness Stevie was there to represent our core values.

Finally, they did listen, by doing a collaboration with the hard-rock band Motörhead, the first music-based shoe, reinforcing Vans' growing place in the alternative music world established by the Warped Tour.

They also launched a new skate line named for world-class athletes, starting with the new British superstar skateboarder Geoff Rowley. Shunning trendy air-pocket-laden foot beds, lace loops, and the abundance of plastic prevalent at the time, Rowley's signature skateboarding shoe was inspired by my classic Vans design and sported our OG vulcanized sole. At the time, vulcanized shoes had nearly vanished from the marketplace.

Geoff Rowley explains that he was influenced by the design and bright-colored brand detailing we'd adapted in the 1970s. He wanted the primary colors back on the shoes.

As he puts it: "The idea was to get all the brand DNA in one model and bring back the old Side Stripe and the vulcanized detailing, with a more modern, more comfortable shoe built for the demands of skating at that time."

His design also featured more supportive insoles than the originals, and rubber underlays on the pattern that made the shoes more durable.

You know what happened? They sold a lot of shoes. The style caught on immediately with skaters, and to my satisfaction, it also rekindled an interest in vulcanized shoes as a whole. People were saying, "Yes! That's what I remember and loved about Vans!"

Management finally started really listening to Stevie, and slowly, very slowly, they refocused Vans' overall shoe design. Around the year 2000, Vans again began doing vulcanized soles in a big way—which changed the whole momentum. The ball started rolling, and Vans finally got its mojo back. Designer Steve Miller was moved to work on classics and vulcanized shoes began once again to succeed. Vans' unique blend of business and culture even led *Forbes* magazine to call it one of "America's Best Small Companies for 2000."

Not a bad way to start a new millennium.

Vans' various collections were now being sold through a large network of independent retail stores including skate, surf, and snow shops, specialty athletic and lifestyle retailers, and Vans' own 137 stores and factory outlets, as well as selling to 80 countries through our international distributors, sales agents, and subsidiaries in the UK, Mexico, Brazil, Uruguay, Argentina, and Canada.

In 2001, Vans assisted with the film production of *Dogtown and Z-Boys*, Stacy Peralta's classic documentary on the Zephyr team and the early days of skateboarding. No way did Stevie want to miss out on this new opportunity, as Vans had with Stacy's earlier film, *The Search for Animal Chin*.

Vans happily invested $80,000 in the production. Our shoes were featured heavily in the film, and once again the company became part of cinematic history. Narrated by Sean Penn, another major player in the Vans story, the documentary took both the Audience Award and the Best Director Award at the Sundance Film Festival.

The new century seemed to have genuinely breathed new life into the culture of Vans. After many years of languishing in style obscurity, our shoes once again began to make inroads into popular fashion. A guy by the name of Rian Pozzebon joined the company in 2002. He had grown up skating in nearby San Gabriel Valley, California, watching legends like Jeff Grosso and Ben Schroeder surf the streets in their old-style Vans.

Stevie told me that in Rian Pozzebon's job interview, he asked if he and his design partner Jon Warren could "mess with all the classic stuff." The shoes Vans made at that time were puffy, ugly, and in no way resembled the OG Vans we had designed back in the day. Pozzebon and Warren wanted to bring back a bit of the history of skateboarding, so they put together a retro line called Skate Originals.

They designed the line using the closest specifications of the original USA-made shoes, bringing back the Half Cab in its old shape with the old woven label on the side. Contrasted to the puffy, high-tech look of the current styles, the retro line fizzled at first, but Pozzebon stayed the course. It took a few years, but in the end our customers rediscovered the authentic Vans styles they had always loved.

In 2002, the Vault collection was launched, specifically to reinvigorate my classics—Authentics, Old Skools, Sk8-Hi's, Slip-Ons, and Eras—our brand's DNA, styles that had largely been gathering dust for the past decade. Steve Miller was put in charge of making this happen. The idea was to catch the attention of influencers and boutiques by putting out a very limited production that would set the bar for the Vans Classics line as well as create products that were innovative and unique, allowing Vans to break into the high-fashion scene. It forged innovative collaborations with design giants like Marc Jacobs, Karl Lagerfeld, and more recently, even the Museum of Modern Art.

The MoMA collaboration was particularly exciting, with Vans' fans and MoMA members able to buy shoes, shirts, and hats embellished with elements of such iconic works of art as Jackson Pollack's drip paintings, Edvard Munch's *The Scream*, Faith Ringgold's patchwork, adding new colors to the classic checkerboard, and from the Russian avant-garde, Lyubov Popova and Wassily Kandinsky's colorful abstract lines and shapes. There is even one inspired by Salvador Dalí's classic *The Persistence of Memory*, where the Vans team literally reoriented the construction of the shoe to echo his surrealistic ethos.

Interestingly, the museum's business development director began the two-year collaboration process by touring the galleries and looking down at the feet of art viewers—many in Vans! In turn, Vans was inspired not just by MoMA's commitment to creativity overall, but specifically to its education program, aimed at bringing art appreciation to new generations. It was a unique and timely pairing, allowing the museum to make art accessible to a wider global audience, and for Vans to ramp up its ongoing commitment to inclusivity and creative expression.

As Avon Helford, from Vans' color and trend team, put it as he held up a pair of Vans featuring splatters in the Jackson Pollock mode, "Shoes can tell a story of the creation of an artwork: the stain becomes part of the piece."

I believe all this has genuinely energized the company, steering it back to my original intent: making the best shoe possible and keeping a spirit of innovation in the mix at all times, while also preserving the classic styles.

The four main pillars that define Vans today are art, music, action sports, and street culture—all about individual spirit and creativity. It all started with Tony Alva, Stacy Peralta, and those first skaters, and that same spirit of individuality continues, amplified in the Vault line.

When the Van Doren Rubber Company was first sold in 1988, we were just emerging from a rocky period in Vans' history. Under Jimmy the company had lost focus, and I was brought back to give the company more solid direction. I worked hard to bring back the core products and values to ensure, once again, that Vans was profitable enough to attract the sale to McCown De Leeuw. In a way, that same thing was happening in 2003. The McCown De Leeuw leadership had lost focus for more than a decade, and although sales had increased from $50 million in 1989 to $320 million by 2004, the company still wasn't making money.

But because they had begun to refocus on quality and design, by 2003 things started to turn around. The profits weren't there yet, but the potential was being felt in spades.

By this time, Drena and I had sold all our California properties and divided our time between Kentucky and Florida. Our lives revolved around going to the track and watching our horses in action. From 1997 to 2014, almost every time one of our horses ran, we were there watching in person. We loved the life.

■ ■ ■

One week in April 2004, Stevie called from China, where he was on his first trip to Hong Kong, visiting Vans' overseas factories. He told me he was pretty blown away by the size and scale of the factories over there, gigantic structures with thousands of employees. He had more important developments to tell me about. That morning, Stevie had gotten a phone call from the head of Vans with an astounding bit of news. A North Carolina–based fashion conglomerate called VF Corporation had just bought Vans for $400 million.

Stevie was floored, and so was I. Founded in 1899, VF was an apparel giant. They also owned The North Face, Nautica, Wrangler, and Lee, just to name a few of their brands. What was going to happen to Vans in a huge company like that?

When the sale was announced to the public, some pundit was quoted in the *Los Angeles Times* as saying VF was buying "a tired brand that still had a strong niche position." I resented that characterization. Vans was not a tired brand!

It was the leadership that hadn't understood what Vans was about and had tried to mold their product to be the same as every other brand out there. Vans had retained a strong niche position solely because of our core culture and our roots. Our loyal fans stuck with us, because they knew what Vans could be, not necessarily what Vans was at that moment.

Would the company have to start over again at ground zero with VF?

I was pleased when VF did not go outside the company to find a new president. They appointed Steve Murray, who had been working at Vans since 1998 serving as chief marketing officer and senior vice president of the international division. With the exception of the new president, the entire rest of the executive team remained intact. I took that as a very good sign.

Murray instantly won me over by bringing back custom-mades. Called Vans' Customs, they could be special-ordered right on the Vans website. You could design your own shoes by applying hundreds of color and pattern combinations to the Classic Slip-On and Old Skool styles. I wanted to cheer! The new owners had clearly embraced what I'd recognized from the very beginning of the Van Doren Rubber Company: if you give customers what they want, they will come back over and over again.

To give customers what they want, you have to know what they want. To that end, VF launched a Global Consumer Insights Assessment, a comprehensive survey of twenty-six thousand customers in twelve countries to determine who and what constituted our core market. Imagine that!

They asked customers what they liked about Vans, how they viewed themselves in terms of subculture, and how our shoes fit into their lives. The marketing team actually went into people's homes and even into their closets to see what they wore for both clothing and shoes and asked them what they do in life.

They found out that these people pride themselves on being in-dividuals. They rarely play team sports, favoring individual pastimes such as surfing, skateboarding, or motocross. They like art, music, action sports, and street culture.

Instead of trying to market to all people, Vans would target the ones we called "expressive creators." The term originated with this survey.

Since then, the concept has become the keystone of Vans' de-sign strategy and fashion culture. Where other big brands stand for athletic performance, Vans stands for creative expression—the "off the wall" spirit.

With a focused mandate, the new leadership of Vans set out to engage directly with its core market segments, and as their cultures changed, Vans' styles could evolve alongside them. Vans' deep roots would be preserved and honored. The shift made a difference in terms of scope. I was impressed. For the first time since 1984, I felt nothing but optimism for the future.

VF turned out to be a good steward. I felt that Vans, along with every other company in their portfolio, got the appropriate amount of attention and marketing dollars, along with the opportunity to ex-plore our heritage, be authentic to our origins, and grow as a brand. VF seemed keenly aware of what it takes for a brand to be success-ful: authenticity. VF truly respects Vans' company history and under-stands how a company's origin story can strengthen the brand. VF values the contribution our past achievements could make to Vans' future success.

One example was Duke Kahanamoku, the famous surfer I'd met on the beach and made those custom shoes for in 1964. In recent years during the US Open of Surfing, which took place right next to the Duke's restaurant, Stevie had arranged for Vans to make all the shirts and matching shoes for the restaurant wait staff, based on the shoes I'd made for Duke all those years ago.

In Duke's honor, in 2007 Vans also decided to reissue the very first authentic Hawaiian-print surfer shoe I had made for him. It came in three colors and was an instant hit. We donated the royalties to Duke's charitable foundation, as we did with so many of our special customs.

Around that same time, the retro checkerboard Slip-On started to become cool with the New York hipster crowd. Once they embraced it, the style once again gained in popularity across the board, which helped a new generation rediscover the whole Vans Classics line.

Even if our sweet spot for customers is young people fourteen to twenty-five, lots of other people used to be fourteen to twenty-five, and to them Vans is still relevant. They still feel cool wearing our shoes—which is an honor.

If Vans advertised to fifty-year-olds, it might turn off teenagers. Today the company gears its marketing primarily to young people, but also to older people who still want to feel young: they can still ride a bike, surf, or skateboard. They still listen to music; they still want to feel inspired. Vans is one of the few brands that crosses generations because people know where we come from.

Global Brand President Doug Palladini describes Vans' universal appeal this way: "We have fans who are newborns, fans who are senior citizens, and every age in between. It's all good, because as we say, 'Off the Wall' is a state of mind. It has nothing to do with a chronological age. It's more about how you approach life, no matter what stage of life you're in."

From our roots in Southern California, the brand has grown not just across the United States, but also in Europe, all over Asia, and in South America.

Palladini stresses that Vans is an accessible brand to people around the world, not just because of the focus on action sports, but also because of the company's "center point, creative self-expression. Action sports is just one manifestation of that creativity."

To support creative culture, Vans runs a Custom Culture contest in schools across the United States. In 2010, for example, 326 schools across the country participated in a high school shoe customization contest that culminated in four schools traveling to Vans' home turf for a weekend of activities. The winning school, in New Mexico that year, received a $10,000 grant toward the school's art programs.

And in 2014, Vans partnered with the Berklee College of Music in Boston to award the Vans Berklee *Off the Wall* Scholarship, a four-year award covering tuition and room and board.

At the other end of the spectrum, the high-end Vault line and collaborations gained traction among the haute couture and fashion-conscious influencers. Walking down any busy street, you were sure to see at least one person—from self-aware fashionistas to regular jeans and T-shirt guys—wearing Vans.

Hollywood Boulevard was no exception, or should I say Rodeo Drive?

Stevie had heard through the grapevine that Samuel L. Jackson was a Vans fan. When word circulated that he was making a movie that involved snakes on a plane, Stevie asked the art department to design a snake-themed pair of Vans, then had them sent to Jackson at the film studio. The next thing we knew, Samuel L. Jackson was seen wearing those Vans everywhere: on *Late Night with David Letterman*, on *The Tonight Show with Jay Leno*, and on the front page of *USA Today*.

As Vans experienced renewed popularity, VF expanded Vans' retail operations, putting in more than seven hundred stores world-wide. From 2008 to 2013, Vans increased revenues from $750 million to nearly $2 billion. Holy shit!

Vans had quickly become the star performer in VF's portfolio. The reason? Partly because of the great leadership of Steve Murray, Kevin Bailey, and later Doug Palladini. All three terrific presidents allowed Vans to stay authentic and true to itself. They may have tweaked and evolved the shoes and had fun with design, but they never strayed far from the basic styles Vans made when I started the company. The tech might be new, but the design cues were always classic Vans.

What I like best is, in addition to all the new technology, Vans remains anchored in the real world. The company has always been dedicated to giving back to the groups that helped nurture us along the way. The Triple Crowns, the recently suspended Warped Tour, and the Duct Tape Invitational are all great examples, along with the new venues called the House of Vans London and Chicago, which are showcases where local skaters, musicians, artists, and filmmakers can perform.

As far as the shoes themselves, the new owners hit the perfect balance between keeping the basic silhouettes largely unchanged while also constantly offering new versions, palettes, editions, and customizable options. In terms of price, Vans are accessible to all, yet still desired as something unique. That is no small feat.

VF has found the sweet spot for Vans' core clientele. It's a hard balance, but they've been doing it by tweaking designs and by listening to our customers. In one example, surfers expressed having a hard time climbing up cliffs to get their gear after they finish in the water. Voilà the Ultra Range, a lightweight walking shoe with an all-terrain grip, breathability, and the Side Stripe.

There are also new Vans with insoles you can remove, and shoes with different kinds of outsoles with more grip for climbers of all kinds. The designers are also using new canvases and recycled materials. You have to keep it current while also honoring the classics that don't go out of style.

When we sold the company to McCown De Leeuw, they expanded Vans' marketplace considerably. They started selling our shoes throughout the United States, and even globally. What they lacked was focus on the product. They made a ton of shoes, and sold quite a lot of them, but those shoes looked like every other sneaker out there. Vans lost its uniqueness as well as its profitability. McCown De Leeuw had replaced the kitchen tap, but only with a garden hose.

When VF bought Vans, they understood what they had, a vast untapped pool of amazing potential. Increasing Vans' physical footprint beyond Southern California was a major goal for VF right out of the gate. Unlike me or McCown De Leeuw, VF had the means to expand it right at their fingertips. They already had long-established sales offices overseas, as well as a seasoned wholesale network. Vans evolved into a true action sports powerhouse, with nearly $4 billion in yearly sales.

In 2009, Kevin Bailey, who had worked at Vans from 2002 to 2007, returned as president. I've heard Kevin call himself the world's oldest teenager. He was a terrific president, partly because he had been immersed in Vans' culture for years. He told me he wanted it to continue to feel like a family-run operation, which I appreciated. Kevin also felt it was important to make sure the culture of the brand was ingrained in all Vans' employees.

Vans no longer conducts surveys or focus groups to stay connected to customers in the age of digital outreach. For example, at this writing the company has eighteen million Instagram fans and twelve million US Vans Family loyalty members. Vans keeps listening to loyal customers and including them in the products the company makes and the stories it tells. It's less about collecting fans and more about having real and sincere connections that run deep with each and every one of them.

One person who helped Kevin stay in close touch with our customer base and continues to do so today is the Vans VP of retail sales, Cristy Johnson, a gem. When you go into any Vans store, you always see smiling faces. The employees are knowledgeable and they don't look at customers as if they're a pain in the neck. That's all because of Cristy, who has done an incredible job running more than six hundred stores.

I first met Cristy when I was visiting my granddaughter Kristy at Vans' headquarters. Cristy grew up in SoCal and she loves her Vans. She'd heard stories about me from Kristy, Stevie, and Cheryl, about how I started Vans and was the driving force behind the company's motto of "Quality, Value, and Superior Service." Cristy has taken that philosophy to heart and made it a major part of the service strategy at her stores.

She always chose great people, surrounding herself with talent. Cristy makes it her business to get to know people, and, like me, she believes in the best of humanity and in being kind to all who enter the doors of a Vans store. Cristy sets the standard, which trickles down to the rest of the store managers and their salespeople.

Today, Vans is in a unique position as part of a major conglomerate with global reach and ambition that is also true to its roots and core customers. What I always saw as authenticity in the way I did business now anchors the brand.

I can think of no better legacy.

# CHAPTER FOURTEEN

# Surf the Waves

We don't always get to choose all of the stories that happen in our lives. And it's not anyone else's job to make anyone's life easier. The only thing anyone can count on is controlling who we are and how we behave.

We control our integrity, and when someone has genuine integrity, their character is immoveable and wholly intractable. Strength of character shows in everything you do, especially when hard times hit. I like to put it this way: it doesn't matter if I'm behind the barrel or if I just got my ass handed to me. If I have to tell you what I stand for, I'm not doing something right.

■ ■ ■

When Drena and I were raising and racing horses, our biggest win was when our two-year-old Thoroughbred Rise Up took first place and the $1 million purse in the 2013 Delta Jackpot at Delta Downs.

A six-length victory earned Rise Up a shot at entering the 2014 Kentucky Derby.

Twenty horses run the big race on Derby Day. Four more are selected as "also eligible," in case any of the twenty starters are scratched. In order to qualify, Rise Up would have had to win another big race and earn at least ten more points, but one more point and Rise Up would have made the "also eligible" quartet.

Unfortunately, Rise Up missed out on qualifying by one point. Normally, not achieving that would have been a huge disappointment. In truth, by the time the Derby was run, it no longer mattered.

Twenty years earlier, Drena had undergone a quadruple bypass surgery, and the doctors had found a spot on her lung. They hadn't wanted to take any chances, so they'd removed it, along with two-thirds of one lung. Ever since, she'd been fine. It looked like she'd beaten it.

In November 2013, doctors found another spot. She'd started chemo. The day Rise Up was racing at Delta Downs, she was feeling very weak, but she insisted she wanted to attend the race. We had to walk very slowly, but she made it to the box. She was so happy to be there, her smile lit up everything around her. I couldn't take my eyes off her, she looked so at peace.

When Rise Up won the race and claimed the $1 million purse, her triumphant horse was paraded into the winner's circle with the jockey wearing the burgundy and white silks of our stables. Drena positively glowed, beaming with pride and accomplishment.

She had lost forty pounds. She may have been weak, but the treatments, awful as they were, seemed to be working—until the day they weren't. Suddenly, she couldn't move her arms or legs. In the emergency room, they told us she had developed an infection. Antibiotics didn't do any good.

Days later, when she asked to go home, her doctor advised against it, then acquiesced, saying it wouldn't make any difference.

I stared at him until it hit me: she wasn't going to make it.

Two days later she died, and our love story of thirty-four years had an ending I had not anticipated.

I was in shock—utterly devastated.

Over the years, I've known sadness. My father dying in 1958 was especially tough, but then I had two sons, a daughter, and Dolly to lean on. If I'm being honest, the only thing that helped me navigate his death was my second daughter Janie's birth, and then Cheryl's, which followed not too long after. If the day of my father's funeral was one of the darkest of my life, at least I had another twenty years with Mom, so I felt less cheated.

Burying Drena left me rudderless in a black hole of despair.

Writing this now fails to convey that, in her absence, everything was wrong, nothing mattered, and my grief was filled with fear. The dread of it masked everything that had ever brought me joy.

You hear people coach one another on how life goes on, that we are somehow duty bound to do so, and that everything has a purpose. That's a crock of shit. The hole Drena's absence left in my life is just a big, gaping hungry abyss, and I will miss her forever.

I decided to return to California for a few weeks. Stevie insisted I fly to Hawaii for Vans' Triple Crown of Surfing with him, Cheryl, and Cheryl's husband, Larry. It was the twenty-fifth year Vans would be hosting the contest, and since Hawaii is where I had married Drena, it seemed like a decent idea.

Our first leg was in Sunset Beach, Oahu, where I tagged along to special events, like Vans' sponsored luncheons, barbecues, and skateboarding demos. We visited all five Vans stores on the island. The kids immersed me in the enthusiasm, energy, and spirit of Vans, but it was only in my retelling stories about the early days that I felt, as cliché as it sounds, fire in my belly. More than any other single factor, my reminiscing with stories about my life returned me to my senses and ignited a familiar spark. In business, as in surfing, you get back on your board or your game if you're knocked down, or off. I would argue that surfing is more difficult to master, in that no wave is ever the same: the "field," watery as it is, is constantly changing. Elements of wind and tide and swells might be predictive, but so, too, might your surfboard. Bigger boards are typically easier to use.

On days that the surf was up, Stevie took us to a four-story spectator tower where announcers and judges sat. Since no one can predict when conditions will be optimal to compete, event coordinators create "holding windows" over the span of a week or two when a contest might take place.

In monitoring things, every morning is blanketed with "will they or won't they," a fairly apt metaphor for how I felt then, except that I didn't really care one way or another. For months I didn't care about anything because I felt nothing; and yet I found myself clinging to stories, the narrative of my life—the whole of it, the tidbits, the toil, the crazy exuberance.

While Stevie and Cheryl worked, heat after heat, Larry and I sat and watched the surfers. I would describe Larry as unflappable. He isn't the type for small talk. His company is good company. Add to this the repetition of the waves, as is typical in Hawaii—the waves' brutality and relentlessness, their grandness, some as big as thirty feet, sweeping in and out. I felt a measure of relief or release, or whatever it is that allows a man enough grace to accept that there are things we can't control and cannot change.

The Banzai Pipeline, a surf reef break off Ehukai Beach Park on Oahu's North Shore, is a flat-top cavernous reef that forces water up and over itself into four different waves to create perfect barrels. Back in the early sixties, when surfers discovered it, there was a construction project on a nearby underground pipeline, which is how it got its name. The water there is pretty, and so is the beach, one of the prettiest I have ever seen. Its water is symmetrical, almost too perfect, as if a kid had drawn a beachscape with white foam cotton atop blue curlicue waves.

Here, on the final leg of the competition, in 2015 I decided to relocate home to Southern California, where my kids would watch out for me and where I knew I belonged.

■ ■ ■

Back in Kentucky, I owned thirty-three Thoroughbreds. Over the following weeks, I spent a lot of time with my farm manager talking things over, going through various scenarios. Counting our various partnerships, our horses had won more than one hundred races and earned almost $4.5 million in purses. I would really miss the excitement, but breeding and training horses had been Drena's passion, not mine. What I loved was going to the races and owning racehorses. I enjoyed farm life, but it wasn't ever my passion. I decided to sell most of the horses. Once all but two were sold, I put the farm on the market and sold that, too.

Stevie's good friend Joe Ciaglia, famous for designing skate parks, offered me an opportunity to buy 10 percent of two of his horses. I'd never done that before. I had always owned our horses outright, but I took him up on the offer. A year or two later, Stevie bought 10 percent of another horse as a surprise for me. Joe named the horse Vantastic, and in his very first race, Vantastic came in second. The next time out, he won.

Stevie, Cheryl, and my granddaughter Kristy continued to coax me to be a guest speaker at employee events. Soon after Cheryl marked her fortieth anniversary, Vans celebrated its fiftieth birthday. There were a dozen House of Vans parties, where skating and music and art joined forces, and a special fiftieth-anniversary edition of the Authentic, featuring the phrase "Off the Wall Family," was distributed to all nine thousand employees.

When Stevie called to see if I was keen on a road trip to Las Vegas in Vans' forty-two-foot RV with Tony Alva and Christian Hosoi, I thought I might be in the way. I had known Tony since the late 1960s, of course, when he helped us design the Era. In the end, I figured it would be really nice to catch up with him and to get to know Christian, who has been a member of the Vans team since 2005 but to whom I had never been introduced.

As Christian articulates it, "When we travel, we take the Van Doren spirit to the masses. The Vans RV tours are always done in an organic way, authentic and sincere in their intentions.

"It's always about showing up and being present—telling people in person that we appreciate them. No matter how big the demo, event, or competition, we show up with the same attitude—that we are all family."

On our way out to Las Vegas, we stopped by our Vans Outlet stores in Barstow, California. Then at Zappos in Vegas, one of Vans' biggest online distributors, Stevie barbecued, and we gave out Vans' promotional material to more than seven hundred Zappos employees. I told a few stories to the crowd; and since I had held up so well, Stevie invited me to tag along on a Vans trip he had planned to Europe.

This time it would be for nine days, not eight hours, and Steve Caballero would join us. I've known Steve, a world-class skateboarder and all-around great human, as long as I've known Tony Alva. Steve, Tony, and Christian were all named in *Skateboarding Magazine*'s top ten list of most influential skaters of all time, so having their company is a little like being with royalty.

As many changes as I've seen in Los Angeles and Orange County since the 1960s and 1970s, every single skateboarder I know from back in the day hasn't changed, not one damn bit, at least in terms of character. But these guys sure have mellowed out. Back in the day, skateboarders were wild. Even at their wildest, though, they were really good people. I was excited to travel with them.

On the European trip, our first stop was Malta, where 250 of Vans' European retail store managers gathered for their annual meeting. I found myself reminiscing more and more about founding Vans, and the times when it felt like a puppet master was in control of things. Like the time I'd prayed to St. Jude that I could buy all the equipment I needed at a fraction of the price, and too, when Jimmy had put Vans in a really bad place, a precarious position of uncertainty when Vans might have otherwise gone kaput.

As soon as Stevie handed me a mic, off I went.

The next stop on our trip was Milan, Italy. During those four days, we visited three different stores where managers had arranged parties to greet us. One of our stores in Milan has a warehouse with a factory below and a big, wooden skate bowl above that looks like Noah's ark, with wooden ribs underneath. They call it the bastard bowl. Geoff Rowley, Lizzie Armanto, Christian Hosoi, and Ray Barbee were with us.

In another store in Milan, in an upstairs room with benches and chairs, people could come and have things painted on their shoes by an in-house artist: flowers, bugs, whatever they liked. For no extra money, they could make their own custom shoes, unlike anyone else's. I thought it was a terrific idea, even better than making a pair of custom shoes. This store let the customers design their own on the spot.

More than eight hundred people showed up to watch the demos, and when we visited Vans' flagship store, more than eight hundred people turned out there too. I ended up signing autographs for three solid hours. Our last stop was at VF headquarters in Stabio, Switzerland. VF had arranged a town hall gathering for people who worked in the Vans office there. Again, we spoke, answered questions, showed videos, and signed autographs for more than two hundred people.

With each inscription I thought about how Vans had become the biggest small company the world had ever known. The shoes I spent my life making walked people to the ocean, to their dreams, their marriage proposals, down the aisle, to their jobs, and their family gatherings.

■ ■ ■

In the summer of 2017, Vans flew in 220 employees to the Costa Mesa headquarters from Europe, Asia, and South America in addition to other parts of the United States and Canada. They worked for Vans worldwide in the finance, operations, retail sales, wholesale, administration, and legal departments. People from all over the world met colleagues they dealt with every day, from accountants to warehouse workers to district managers and clothing designers.

The Van Doren Project, as it was called, was a huge success. It all started when my son Stevie went to Steve Rendle, the president and CEO of VF. VF had been asking the leaders of each wholesale region to meet in their respective countries, rather than coming to California. Traditionally, they'd come in from all over: Europe, South America, and Asia.

Steve pointed out that California is Vans' "secret sauce." It's a Southern California by-the-beach company. If you shut down a collaborative gathering there, you really lose something vital.

After Steve got the go-ahead to organize a gathering back in Costa Mesa, Doug Palladini came up with the name the Van Doren Project. One of the Vans artists created a logo with a figure of a globe, showing Stevie flying around it.

Four or five days during the 2017 Van Doren Project coincided with the Vans US Open of Surfing, which was exciting for participants who organized in ten groups of twenty, rotating to different departments like strategy, product, apparel, and marketing. At the end of each day we presented panels, such as one that featured athletes sponsored by Vans, with a skating demo thrown into the mix.

We even had the participants do an art project. Four groups of about fifty-five people got together to create a panel we put together into one big mural. Each segment was judged by a group of our skaters: Tony Alva, Christian Hosoi, and Steve Caballero.

There were concerts, group lunches and dinners, even movies on the beach with popcorn and gelato served. The final day featured a big party with a DJ and break dancers.

The company plans to make the Van Doren Project an annual event. Doug Palladini describes it as "a global cultural immersion for our people to feel, absorb, experience the brand. Because we have tens of thousands of employees representing our brand in almost one hundred countries, this kind of immersion will remain critical to our purpose, and to the ongoing commitment to being a people company that makes footwear and apparel. People first, no matter what."

One day during the gathering, I joined Cheryl, Kristy, and Stevie to talk about the beginning of the company. Then we took questions from the audience.

During my talk, I was asked, "If you could sum up your advice on how to find the right track and succeed in life, what would it be?"

I have never really gone in for deep philosophical thoughts or contemplation of my own mortality. I just got on with life and dealt with whatever was thrown my way. After Drena passed, though, I couldn't help but think about my place in the world and about how I would frame my legacy. I had actually been thinking about that very question.

My answer? "Shit happens."

Shit happens—it really does. Letting yourself get stuck in it doesn't do any good. Acknowledge it and then move on. Don't let it weigh you down—just cope. Tackling things in a positive way will help you succeed more often than not.

Shit happens: these two words fully acknowledge the difficulties in life, but you can put them firmly in the rearview mirror, without letting them mess with your head or your path in life.

■ ■ ■

When I look around now, I marvel at the profile our shoes have developed. I chuckle at the fact that one of the Kardashians started wearing a pair of black Old Skools, still the most popular shoes in the Vans vault.

Picking one pair of Vans over another remains a highly personal choice, it seems. A few years back, a guy from Pennywise, a well-known punk band, went to Stevie and told him he couldn't wear his Old Skools anymore, because everybody was wearing them. He went back to wearing his Eras instead.

Then Steve heard about a pitcher from the Cincinnati Reds who took a pair of Sk8-Hi's, skate shoes, and had a cobbler put spikes on the bottom. He was pitching in the major leagues with a pair of spiked Vans.

The company doesn't pay people to do these things; they happen organically. Our customers, famous or not, just like the shoes. And I am proud that the price points we've kept over the years have enabled a wide range of people to join the Vans tribe.

From my perspective, our longstanding loyalty to both the athletes we support and to our customers is the key to our longevity. We've supported some of our athletes for decades. People see the loyalty, the commitment, and they want to be part of it.

But when I look at my legacy at Vans today, I am proudest of the values the brand still holds. As my daughter Cheryl describes these values, "Integrity, authenticity, and focus on people. Everything we do is about interacting with people and consumers."

One of the things that best exemplifies these values is an award Stevie dreamed up a few years ago: the Van Doren Give A Shit Award. You don't get it for baking brownies; it's for those who go above and beyond.

One of the earliest award presentations was something of a surprise. Vans was hosting the VF board of directors, and, after lunch, Steve had brought them out to the big ramp, a half-pipe forty-two feet wide and thirteen feet tall, where they could watch the skaters.

When the meeting resumed, Steve asked a young staffer named Luis Gallegos to come up; Luis had no idea what was going on. Still a college student at the time, Luis was a part-time team member who had started in the warehouse and gradually assumed more responsibilities, especially for events, which led to his helping out on the Warped Tour.

With Luis standing next to him—looking rather bewildered—Stevie told a story about something that had happened while they were setting up for the first day of the tour. Stevie and the team were hurrying to get together three thousand pairs of shoes, socks, laundry bags, and drinks. Everybody on the tour came by and got a couple pairs of shoes. We never told people on the Vans Warped Tour they had to wear Vans shoes. But every year, they came to get their gear and felt good about it.

Stevie relayed how Luis saw a young person in a wheelchair—he was a roadie or a tour manager—struggling a little as everybody else was getting their sizes. The Vans swag was all spread out, with shoes of different sizes in well-organized piles, but not particularly accessible to someone in a wheelchair. Luis went over to the guy in the chair and worked with him for about twenty minutes, taking his braces off so he could try on the shoes.

Luis has a disability himself, one he was born with. He explained to the man in the chair that he had struggled many times in his own life. As Luis remembers the encounter, "I wanted to help someone who needed that extra help, as I have."

"You know what?" Stevie told the audience at the board of directors meeting. "The next day at the Vans Warped Tour, I saw the man in the wheelchair with his new Vans on, smiling."

Luis, by then a member of what's called the Vans Family Team, expressed surprise at being recognized for a simple act. But it's people like him who deserve the award—people who go above and beyond, reaching out to help even when it's not in their job description. It's part of what it means to join the "family."

Stevie was also inspired by a guy named Jim McIngvale, who owns furniture stores in Houston, Texas. When Hurricane Sandy hit in 2016, Jim drove around in his truck and picked up people who were left homeless in the flooding. He had 250 people sleeping on his mattresses and sofas.

Stevie loaded up two trucks and a motor home and headed down to Houston. He called Jim, nicknamed Mattress Mack, and said, "I'm heading your way. I got shoes."

He said, "I got people."

In Mack's store, Steve handed out fifteen hundred pairs of shoes. He wound up staying for several more days and gave out six thousand more pairs. From there, he and Mack struck up a friendship. So when Mack called right before Christmas and asked if he could buy fourteen thousand pairs of shoes, Stevie found a way to make it happen. First, he tried to crunch the numbers to give Mack the shoes at cost. Then Stevie heard back from Doug Palladini. He said give him the shoes.

Mack also bought $87,000 worth of gift cards to give to his employees, and to people in Houston who needed them.

Jim McIngvale was invited to the Vans annual sales meeting and presented with the Van Doren Give A Shit Award, a skateboard autographed by Vans' staff.

In 2017, the award went to Sarah Turner, a senior manager in the Vans creative services department. Sarah raises money for an organization called Boards for Bros, which gives skateboards to kids in underserved communities and sponsors skating events to help kids and adults bond through boarding.

Sarah's original impetus was to initiate a team building event with her coworkers. After meeting Ryan Vanderweel, the head of Boards for Bros California, she asked her Vans creative team colleagues to help build fifty skateboards. But to pull it off, she needed funds.

At each meeting where Sarah and Ryan spoke with Vans team members in different departments, Sarah ended with the exhortation, "We are Vans. We are the Van Doren family. Giving back is what we do best. So let's DO IT!"

She and her creative team set up skateboard donation bins in the front lobby of Vans headquarters, where employees, friends, and family donated more than one thousand skateboard decks, parts, and tools, as well as $1,000 to buy extra parts. For the first skateboard build event in June 2017, eighty volunteers from all over the company built more than 250 skateboards in a day.

At skate events with nonprofits like A.skate, Boys & Girls Clubs, Girls Inc., Skate Kids, KidWorks, Next Up Foundation, and others,

Sarah and the crew from Boards for Bros distributed the boards as well as Vans shirts, hats, and sometimes shoes to kids all over LA and Orange counties.

Three years later, Vans and Vans employees had enabled Boards for Bros to build more than three thousand skateboards for underprivileged kids. And in 2019, they worked with a physical education teacher in the Los Angeles Unified School District to start a skate program at a junior high school—the first time a California school district allowed skateboarding as part of a school curriculum.

In September of that year, seventy Vans team members, Boards for Bros, and Skate Kids volunteers taught students how to build skateboards, and then for an entire school day how to skate in each physical education class. By the end of the day, more than 250 kids had learned how to skate. Later, Boards for Bros donated 120 skateboards to the school to start a skate program.

Teachers wrote to say that this was the happiest they had ever seen their students; the volunteers were equally enthusiastic about their day in school.

Vans has also enabled Boards for Bros to spread the love of skateboarding to other countries. Sarah, Stevie, and other members of the Vans family have given Boards for Bros skateboards to kids all over the world. I can't imagine a Vans team member more deserving of the Van Doren Give A Shit Award than Sarah Turner. And I am so proud to hear her describe the way she asked for support from her colleagues: "We are the Van Doren family."

This is my legacy, too, one that goes beyond shoes: many team members at the company today honor the family tradition of giving back. It's also key to maintaining Vans' unique identity within a big corporation.

There's also the Vans Sole Award, given once a year to people at the company who've been nominated for teamwork, creativity, leadership, or showing the Van Doren spirit.

Recognizing people for what they contribute is at the core of all good business practice.

Yes, shit happens, but we can all recognize that we need one another. I said it at the outset of this book, and I'll say it again: no one gets anywhere alone. And in the final analysis, what you make will never be as important as how, and with whom, you make it.

Vans is a people company that makes shoes—not the other way around.

# Dress in Overalls

I've heard it said that opportunities don't happen—we create them. In that regard, I agree with Thomas Edison, who said, "Opportunity is missed by most people because it is dressed in overalls and looks like work."

I've certainly worked hard for my opportunities. And there was a time when I felt thankful to Bob Cohen for the opportunities he gave me, but the thing is, he didn't give them to me, not really. I proved myself time and time again, regardless of compensation or reward. I found solutions to problems that management didn't know existed. Everything that I accomplished at Randy's, I pulled off without management's support.

But it's also true that sometimes opportunities are presented to us, and they look a lot like luck. I was lucky to find a partner in Serge, tough as nails, who best exemplifies the truest sense of what I would call the "spirit of opportunity." I will always consider it fate that he phoned the factory the afternoon I walked out, and fortune that he pressed the secretary to give him my phone number.

To me, the spirit of opportunity is half free fall and half safety net. I was given free rein to hire my own people, build my factory from the ground up, and run things as I saw fit—without a pigeon or power struggle in sight—and I also had an investor who shared my confidence that I could build a small sneaker factory in Southern California that was worthy of his $250,000 investment. That was a hell of an opportunity.

Still, whether an opportunity is made or given, at the end of the day you have to be in a position to make the most of it. Really, it's simply a set of exploitable circumstances that makes it possible to do anything, and no one does anything alone. Without a doubt, I had the support of my family. Without Dolly's support, I wouldn't have had a chance. Early in our marriage, she gave me more than enough latitude to embrace opportunities whenever they presented themselves. I never could have gotten Vans off the ground without the help of my children, my extended family, and my loyal friends. And it never would have thrived and grown into what it is today without first-class corporate partners. For anyone in business or starting a business, being supported by family and friends—your community, whatever it looks like—is critical, now more than ever.

As I finish writing this manuscript, the world is crippled by a pandemic, and we are only at the beginning of the economic fallout that's come with it. No doubt the world is harder for entrepreneurs everywhere. But given the right circumstances, I have to believe it's still worth the effort and the risk.

Even in the most unusual circumstances, I believe that anything's possible. Case in point: the 2020 Kentucky Derby, run for the first time in August instead of May, without any spectators in the stands, was won by a horse named—of all things—Authentic. I take that as a good omen. And as trainer Bob Baffert praised jockey John Velazquez afterward to CNN, "He rode the most incredible race, but he had the horse to do it with." Baffert and I would agree: having the right partner is everything.

I told you at the start that I was never really a gambler, but a guy who calculated the odds. So let me leave you with this parting thought: when you have good people with you, the odds are with you, too. And the longer I live, the more I see the truth of it.

**Paul Van Doren**

Painting by Robert Vargas

# Acknowledgments

love the fact that whenever I share my Vans story, other people want to share their own story—and they always have one. At every event I've been to over the past decade, someone has told me about their experience with Vans. A ton of folks remember buying Vans with their parents; others talk about coming to the store with their friends, kids, and even grandkids. I get a big kick out of it. To me, it's proof that Vans isn't just mine or about any other Van Doren's story. They're a shared experience.

But as much as I love telling my story, writing this book has challenged me. I will openly admit that the way I remember something won't necessarily be how someone else remembers it. People change, priorities change, and the way we see things changes. And because Vans isn't my story alone, I asked Steve and Cheryl and others to help tell it.

So many friends, family, and business partners contributed their time and attention to this project. I wouldn't have had a story to tell without the Van Doren family: my parents Bert and Rita, my siblings

Johnny, Robert, Bernice, and Jimmy. My children Taffy, Paul, Stevie, Janie, Cheryl, and their mother, Dolly. My in-laws Dan and Louise MacLellan. My sons- and daughters-in-law Rick Blake, Mary Van Doren, Susan Van Doren, Larry Studt; and my grandchildren Jackie Blake, Jenny Battiest, Kristy Van Doren Batson, Debbie Hoffman, Shannon Jordan, Jimmy Harland Jr., and Philip Van Doren. And of course, my story isn't complete without the love of my life, Drena.

Then there are all those who became family along the way: my old friend Victor "Murph" Damiano, and partners Serge d'Elia, Jimmy Van Doren, and Gordon Lee. Thank you all for being part of the journey.

It takes a team to put a book across, and I want to give special thanks to the many Vans family members who helped both shape this story and bring it to the page. Sincere appreciation goes to Doug Palladini, the dynamic head of Vans Global Brands, for his support and contributions. Thanks also to past Vans Presidents Kevin Bailey and Stephen Murray. I was lucky to have help from Steve Weiss, Kia Wimmer, Michael Villec, Katie Bell, Libby Stockstill, Delbert Pickney, Simon d'Elia, Jared Abe, Graham Nash, Peter Derricks, Bob Provost, Jenna Lyter, and so many other dedicated Vans employees.

I thank photographer Alex Baret, artist Robert Vargas, and everyone else who provided their photographs.

Our loyal athletes also chimed in. Many thanks to Geoff Rowley, Gale Webb, Tony Alva, Christian Hosoi, Steve Caballero, and Stacy Peralta.

I owe a debt of gratitude to Richard and Jack Joseph of Vertel Publishing for initiating this project and seeing it all the way through. Richard spent many hours helping me clarify and craft these stories.

Last but absolutely not least, I owe another debt of gratitude to the editorial and production team: Patricia Mulcahy and Amanda Murray gathered reams of material and fashioned it into a coherent narrative. Their professionalism and attention to detail came through at every stage of the process. Thanks also to Louise MacLellan, Nina Bruhns, and Ellie Davis for their early contributions, and to Christine Marra for getting us over the finish line.

So many others contributed to this project—I regret there isn't space here to acknowledge everyone who deserves my thanks.

# Photo Credits

Page 1: *Top left*, John Bert Van Doren; *top right*, Rena Vita Van Doren; and *bottom*, the Van Doren childhood home. Photos courtesy of the Van Doren family.

Page 2: *Top*, the Van Doren factory workshop; and *bottom*, the Van Doren siblings. Photos courtesy of the Van Doren family.

Page 3: *Top*, Paul and his siblings; *bottom left*, Paul and Dolly, engaged; and *bottom left*, Paul as a young manager. Photos courtesy of the Van Doren family.

Page 4: *Top*, Paul's five children; *bottom left*, the Van Doren kids, 1964; and *bottom right*, Paul, 1960s. Photos courtesy of the Van Doren family.

Page 5: *Top*, Dolly and Paul. Photo courtesy of the Van Doren family. *Bottom left*, Paul, Jim, and Gordy; and *bottom right*, Gordy and Serge. Photos courtesy of the Lee family.

Page 6: *Top*, Serge and Paul; *bottom left*, original Vans management team; and *bottom right*, Paul aboard the *Van Fan*. Photos courtesy of the Van Doren family.

Page 7: *Top left*, first factory; and *top right*, original Vans outsole. Photos courtesy of the Van Doren family. *Mid-left*, unloading first Vulcanizer. Photo courtesy of the Lee family. *Mid-right*, shoes cooking in Vulcanizer; and *bottom*, early retail store. Photos courtesy of the Van Doren family.

Page 8: *Top*, Vans circus tent store; *middle*, original warehouse; and *bottom*, second factory. Photos courtesy of the Van Doren family.

Page 9: *Top*, Late 1970s; *bottom left*, 1976; and *bottom right*, Late 1970s/early 1980s. Photos courtesy of the Van Doren family.

Page 10: *Top*, iconic Vans boxes; *bottom,* Vans shoe box. Photos courtesy of Henry Davies, a Vans Collector.

Page 11: *Top*, first heel label and box; and *bottom*, Tony Alva signature shoe. Photos courtesy of the Van Doren family.

Page 12: *Top left*, Old Skool; and *top right*, Sk8-Hi. Photos courtesy of the VF Corporation. *Bottom*, Paul with checkered slip-on and Steve with Authentic. Photo courtesy of Alex Baret.

Page 13: *Top*, Paul and Jimmy at Picadilly Circus; and *bottom*, original Vans Booth at LA County Fair. Photos courtesy of the Van Doren family.

Page 14: *Top*, 50th anniversary celebration; *mid-left*, US Open of Surfing; *mid-right*, Steve, Tony Alva, and group at AMC Cinema; *bottom left*, Geoff Rowley at the Vans 50th celebration; and *bottom right*, Lizzie Armanto in Stabio, Switzerland. Photos courtesy of Alex Baret.

Page 15: *Top left*, Stacy Peralta. Photo by Gregg DeGuire / WireImage. *Top right,* Steve Caballero, Docklands. Photo © PYMCA / Universal Images Group via Getty Images. *Mid-right*, Tony Alva, March 1979. Photo courtesy of Jim Goodrich. *Bottom left*, Tony Alva at Santa Cruz Film Festival. Photo by Arun Nevader / Getty Images. *Bottom right*, Christopher Hosoi. Photo by Mindy Schauer / Digital First Media/Orange County Register via Getty Images.

Page 16: *Top*, 1967, House of Vans; *mid-left*, 1976, Vans News; *bottom left*, **1977**, Off the Wall!; and *right* 1977, number one skateboard shoes. Photos courtesy of the Van Doren family.

Page 17: *Top left*, Everett Rosecrans and demo team; *top right*, Hi-Powered Hi-tops; and *bottom*, bike advertisement. Photos courtesy of the Van Doren family.

Page 18: *Top*, "For Kicking Bootie & Blazing"; and *bottom*, "Legends." Photos courtesy of the Van Doren family.

Page 19: *Top*, Vans Factory BMX Team Van. Photo courtesy of the Van Doren family. *Bottom*, Vans US Open of Surfing. Photo courtesy of Alex Baret.

Page 20: *Top*, Vans Triple Crown of Surfing; and *bottom*, US Open of Surfing finals. Photos courtesy of Alex Baret.

Page 21: *Top*, Black Eyes Peas. Photo by Scott Gries / Getty Images. *Bottom*, Blink 182. Photo © Lisa Johnson.

Page 22: *Top*, Pennywise. Photo © Lisa Johnson. *Bottom left*, My Chemical Romance. Photo © Jamie McCarthy / WireImage. *Bottom right*, Katy Perry. Photo © Paul Hebert / Icon SMI / Corbis / con Sportswire via Getty Images.

Page 23: *Top*, A Day to Remember. Photo © Daniel Boczarski / Redferns. *Bottom,* Metallica. Photo by Jeff Yeager / Metallica / Getty Images.

Page 24: *Top left*, Van Doren racing silks; *top right*, Rise Up wins; and *bottom left*, Paul Van Doren. Photos courtesy of the Van Doren family. *Bottom right*, Paul and Drena. Photo courtesy of Linda Finch.

Page 25: *Top, Fast Times at Ridgemont High;* and *bottom,* Sean Penn as "Spicoli." Photos © Universal / PictureLux / The Hollywood Archive / Alamy Stock Photo.

Page 26: *Top*, Steve, John Wayne, and Billy Belcher. Photo courtesy of the Van Doren family. *Bottom left*, Samuel L. Jackson. Photo © Todd Plitt / Getty Images. *Bottom right*, Weird Al Jankovic. Photo courtesy of the Van Doren family.

Page 27: *Top left*, Steve Van Doren. Photo courtesy of Christy Stephens. *Top right*, Steve and Paul with Robert Vargas; and *bottom*, the group at Vans European head-quarters. Photos courtesy of Alex Baret.

Page 28: *Top*, Paul with Doug Palladini. Photo courtesy of Alex Baret. *Bottom left*, Paul and Murph; and *bottom right*, Paul with Terry Roach. Photos courtesy of the Van Doren family.

Page 29: *Top*, Paul in Milan, Italy; *middle*, Steve, Paul, Cheryl, and Kristy; and *bottom*, Steve and Paul with Brian Cook. Photos courtesy of Alex Baret.

Page 30: *Top left*, Sarah Turner and Give A Shit Award. Photo courtesy of Sarah Turner. *Top right*, Luis Gallegos and Give A Shit Award. Photo courtesy of Luis Gallegos. *Bottom*, Christan Hosai, Dakota Roche, and the Vans Shoe Car. Photo courtesy of the Vans archives.

Page 31: *Top left*, the famous Vans waffle iron. Photo courtesy of the Vans archives. *Top right*, a global advertisement; and *bottom*, a Vans international showroom. Photos courtesy of Alex Baret.

Page 32: *Top*, Paul and siblings; and *middle*, Paul with Vans employees. Photos courtesy of the Van Doren family. *Bottom*, entrance to Vans headquarters. Photo by Steve Cukrov / Alamy Stock Photo.